Lionel Jobert and the
American Civil War

Lionel Jobert and the American Civil War
An Atlantic Identity in the Making

STEPHEN D. BOSWORTH

Cover art: Caricature of Lionel Jobert d'Epineuil (drawn in 1860); from the author's collection.

Published by State University of New York Press, Albany

© 2021 State University of New York

All rights reserved

Printed in the United States of America

No part of this book may be used or reproduced in any manner whatsoever without written permission. No part of this book may be stored in a retrieval system or transmitted in any form or by any means including electronic, electrostatic, magnetic tape, mechanical, photocopying, recording, or otherwise without the prior permission in writing of the publisher.

For information, contact State University of New York Press, Albany, NY
www.sunypress.edu

Library of Congress Cataloging-in-Publication Data

Name: Bosworth, Stephen D., author.
Title: Lionel Jobert and the American civil war : an Atlantic identity in the making / Stephen D. Bosworth, author.
Description: Albany : State University of New York Press, [2021] | Includes bibliographical references and index.
Identifiers: ISBN 9781438485096 (hardcover : alk. paper) | ISBN 9781438485102 (pbk. : alk. paper) | ISBN 9781438485119 (ebook)
Further information is available at the Library of Congress.

10 9 8 7 6 5 4 3 2 1

Contents

Illustrations	vii
Acknowledgments	ix
Introduction	xi
Abbreviations	xv
Chapter 1 The Allure of Aristocracy	1
Chapter 2 Opportunity and Indiscretion: Commander of the Haitian Naval School	15
Chapter 3 Atlantic Sisyphus	35
Chapter 4 A Second Ascent: The Rise of d'Epineuil's Zouaves	51
Chapter 5 A Second Descent: Shattered Hope Amid Civil War	73
Chapter 6 Paternity and Performance in Philadelphia	89
Chapter 7 The Count and Countess d'Epineuil	111
Conclusion	135
Appendix	137

Notes	141
Bibliography	173
Index	185

Illustrations

Figures

2.1 Caricature of Lionel Jobert, printed by A. Beillet, 35 Quai de la Tournelle, Paris.   20

3.1 William P. Bosworth, private, Co. H, Fifty-Third New York Volunteers in Zouave uniform.   41

3.2 Recruiting poster for Colonel d'Epineuil's regiment.   42

5.1 Sketch by Lt. Col. Thomas Bell of "Madam" d'Epineuil (Mrs. Theodosia Lloyd), 1861.   78

7.1 Watercolor miniature of Count d'Epineuil, ca. 1872.   116

7.2 Georgiana Somerset, Countess d'Epineuil, ca. 1872.   117

7.3 Count d'Epineuil. Photograph taken in Port Said, Egypt ca. 1875.   120

Tables

2.1 Maiden voyage of the Haitian warship *Geffrard*, September–December 1860.   25

7.1 Surname variation for Frederick John De Pineuil (1868–1960).   133

A.1 United States patents witnessed by Lionel J. d'Epineuil's firm.   139

Acknowledgments

William P. Bosworth, my great-great-grandfather, served as a private in the Fifty-Third New York Volunteer Regiment during the Civil War. Pursing genealogy as a hobby, I have gathered many facts about William from censuses, city directories, newspapers, and his military pension file. My family also has photographs of him as a newlywed, as a young soldier, and as an elderly civilian. However, there is no evidence that William recorded his war experience in any way, and no oral tradition of his service survives. A bit of investigation into the history of William's regiment did present us with his mercurial commanding officer, Lionel Jobert d'Epineuil. Casually seeking to learn more about Jobert, my brother and I began searching the internet in 2011. That endeavor increasingly revealed Jobert to be a complex individual whose exploits continually surprised us. It became clear that no one knew anything substantial about Jobert beyond his connection to the Civil War, and what had been written about him often was in error. Lionel Jobert's story entertained us, and I think others will enjoy it as well.

I gratefully acknowledge the constructive remarks of the anonymous readers engaged by SUNY Press who encouraged me to hone this work to its present state. Many thanks are due to the archival staff at the repositories listed in the bibliography. The Chanter family and Marilyn Wright graciously allowed me to consult and use papers in their private collections. I would be remiss if I did not also express appreciation for websites that provide free access to a large number of digitized newspapers, including the Library of Congress's Chronicling America at http://chroniclingamerica.loc.gov, the archives of the Department of Calvados in France at https://archives.calvados.fr/, and Thomas M. Tryniski's Old Fulton New York Post Cards at http://www.fultonhistory.com, the latter collection being particularly strong on newspapers from the state of New York. Finally, my brother Michael

H. Bosworth composed chapter 2 and provided much assistance with internet research and translations of French language sources for the book overall.

Introduction

Contemporary historians have focused their attention concerning human activity on and around the Atlantic Ocean to the point of describing it as a "world"—a distinct region that, while not isolated from the rest of the globe, formed in the mid-fifteenth century as Europeans and enslaved Africans increasingly traversed the Atlantic and began to inhabit the Americas. Analysts of this large expanse have developed an overarching view of the Atlantic as a cohesive entity that for about 400 years had the unifying features of being under European colonial dominance and sustained by captive labor. Toward the middle of the 1800s, these characteristics had faded as people in the Americas created nations out of once-dominant empires, the slave trade ebbed, and steam navigation facilitated a global commerce that more fully integrated the Atlantic with the rest of the planet.[1]

In such studies, the nation-state cedes center stage as the unit of analysis in what David Armitage has called circum-Atlantic history: "the history of the Atlantic as a particular zone of exchange and interchange, circulation and transmission . . . It is the history of the people who crossed the Atlantic, who lived on its shores and who participated in the communities it made possible."[2] Viewing the Atlantic afresh also has "freed historians to rediscover biography, prosopography, and narratives of individual lives, as the macro-turn has made possible a micro-turn."[3] Moreover, historians continue to probe the conceptual limits of Atlantic history. Author Don Doyle, for instance, pushes the temporal boundary of the mid-nineteenth century, identifying the issues of slavery, republicanism (popular governments), and national sovereignty as threads that ran through the 1860s in an essay revealingly titled "The Atlantic *World* and the Crisis of the 1860s [emphasis added]."[4] Indeed, "regardless of its scope or focus," several scholars today embrace unconstrained research on any facet of the Atlantic past, appreciating the richness of such a "dog's breakfast."[5]

Lionel Jobert (1829–1881) personified what interests scholars today. He was a citizen of France, but a denizen of the Atlantic region. Being born to a French father and an English mother attenuated his sense of national identity, while providing him with the advantage of navigating comfortably between French- and English-speaking populations on both sides of the ocean. Jobert went to sea at age seventeen, spending the large majority of the rest of his life away from his native France. He called at the Atlantic Coasts of South America and Africa; lived for a time in the Caribbean; spent a decade in the United States; and ultimately settled in England. He was not a major historical figure, yet Lionel Jobert made decisions and acted based on his understanding of the transnational dynamics—political and technological—of the Atlantic. He used unstable governmental conditions in Haiti and the United States to pursue his private interests. His life spanned the shift from sailing vessels to steam navigation with the Atlantic being both a barrier and a conduit throughout. The ocean was Lionel's occupational arena; it provided escape routes to distance him from his troubles; and its great size worked to inhibit—but not always prohibit—the transoceanic transmission of information about him. Hence, part of what Lionel Jobert's odyssey shows us is that throughout the Atlantic one could enjoy a wide latitude of action—appropriate and otherwise—that the political realities and the technology of the era afforded, yet within constraints those same factors imposed.

Authors intrigued by Jobert have considered him only in his role as colonel of the first organization of the Fifty-Third New York Volunteer Regiment, also known as the d'Epineuil Zouaves, during the American Civil War. Invariably, their books present him as one of many figures related to a different emphasis: the Battle of Roanoke Island; the history of ethnic regiments; the flamboyant uniforms of Zouave soldiers.[6] Broadening the focus on Jobert from the eastern seaboard of the United States in the early 1860s to the Atlantic basin in the half century spanning approximately from 1830 to 1880 allows us to view the Civil War from the vantage point of the flow of events that comprised the life of a foreign participant, a perspective that supports another contention: that Jobert's identity is best seen as an *Atlantic* individual for whom big picture ideas such as republicanism and sovereignty meant little. For Jobert, his own advancement mattered more than the outcome of the American conflict; the war was a means to an end he pursued his entire life, and that end was an elevated social standing.

This book relates the remarkable exploits of a man driven by ambition—and unhindered by scruples—to attain position and prestige. It provides the reason for Lionel Jobert's arrival in the United States shortly before the start of the Civil War, details his command of the Fifty-Third, and shows how he used his war experience in years afterward. The Civil War constituted one in a series of opportunities for advancement that Jobert seized and then let slip away, lending a Sisyphean quality to the narrative of his life. The Greek mythological character Sisyphus outwitted the gods for his own benefit, reveling in his ability to be master of his fate—for a time. His ultimate punishment consisted of repeatedly pushing a boulder to the peak of a hill only to have it roll back down; in short, to toil endlessly without achieving success. The ancient Greeks knew the potential pitfalls of ambition; they would have discerned them in Lionel Jobert. Thus Jobert's story is universal, but at the same time its unexpected twists make it uniquely his own and one colorful tile in the vast mosaic that makes up the history of the nineteenth-century Atlantic.

Abbreviations

ADC	Archives Départmentales du Calvados
ADSM	Archives Départmentales de Seine-Maritime, Rouen
BM	The British Mail
EMHC	Eugene Maximilien Haitian Collection, New York Public Library
FdC	Feuille de Commerce (Port-au-Prince, Haiti)
MAEN	Ministère des Affaires Étrangères, Nantes
NARA I	National Archives, Washington, DC
NARA II	National Archives, College Park, MD
NYSA	New York State Archives

Chapter 1

The Allure of Aristocracy

"Je me rejouis bien sincerement de la naissance de votre petit Garçon," wrote Marianna de Lamartine to her cousin Frances Jobert on December 8, 1829.[1] The two Englishwomen, both in their thirties, came from a prominent family. Marianna and Frances were granddaughters of William Birch, a London lawyer, and Sally Holwell, daughter of John Zephaniah Holwell (1711–1798), a survivor and memoirist of the infamous Black Hole of Calcutta. Both women married established Frenchmen: Marianna married the aristocrat, writer, and statesman Alphonse de Lamartine, and Frances wed Louis Edme Jobert, grandson of the Count d'Epineuil. Writing from Lamartine's native Mâcon, France, Marianna's letter conveyed the news of her mother-in-law's death and alluded to Lamartine's nomination to membership in the prestigious Académie Française. Yet in the opening sentence, after a reference to Alphonse's mother, Marianna expressed her joy at the birth of her cousin's first boy, Edme Lionel Holwell Jobert, born seven weeks earlier on October 20, in Caen, France.[2] The child's family connections augured well for his future—a future that revolved around the Atlantic.

The Jobert clan's roots in Caen went no deeper than Lionel's paternal grandfather, Edme Pierre Jobert. He was born in the Parisian parish of St. Gervais in 1767, the son of a wine merchant and his wife, Catherine Claude Baroche. Pierre's father, also named Edme Pierre, was a man of some distinction in the region of Burgundy. He represented the department of Tonnerre in the provincial assembly of L'Isle de France in 1787 before departments were reorganized during the French Revolution. The Burgundy hamlet of Epineuil, known for its wine production, lay just north of the town of Tonnerre, and the prestige-minded Monsieur Jobert had purchased the title of Count d'Epineuil when his namesake son was still a youth. However, Edme Jobert—wine merchant, property owner, and *Seigneur d'Epineuil*—mismanaged his estate in pursuit of a life of luxury. His firstborn son, Edme Pierre, left behind the memory of family failure and moved northwest to the coastal department of Calvados in the region of Normandy, working as a purveyor of military supplies. In the city of Caen, his wife Marie Louise Olympie Turpin bore two sons: Louis Edme Jobert and Edme Charles Ambroise Jobert, born in 1795 and 1797, respectively.[3]

Louis Jobert did not use his grandfather's title of Count d'Epineuil among his fellow citizens in Caen, who knew him simply as St. Edme Jobert, businessman, civic leader, and lifetime resident. As a young man searching for his niche in life, St. Edme tried selling fire insurance, and even invented a shale pencil with superior qualities to that of existing leads. Then late in 1821, urged by Alexis Haudry, chief engineer of the port of Le Havre, located some ninety-eight kilometers (sixty miles) northeast of Caen—or half that distance as the crow flies—St. Edme Jobert began his career as a quarry master, extracting and shipping local Calvados stone. Less than two years later, St. Edme and his brother Charles teamed with Jacques Breard from March 1823 to April 1824, buying out their associate Breard at the end of the yearlong partnership. The Jobert brothers thenceforth built up their business in the ensuing years. Surveying seventy-four shipping entries in a local newspaper from 1825 to 1829 reveals that stone, predictably, was the company's main export, and plaster and boards the most common import. The firm did business mostly with the interior city of Rouen and at several ports along the northern coast of France. Jobert Frères had become a thriving concern, despite a rumor in 1828 that they sought to abandon their quarry. The brothers squelched that speculation, informing the public that "[n]ever have we had more zeal and more activity, and it is not at the point when we have just renewed all our markets and when we receive positive proof of public confidence that we would abandon an establishment we pride ourselves of having created." Indeed, in addition to extracting stone in the department of Calvados, Jobert Frères also began operating a quarry in Sainte Honorine la Guillaume in the department of Orne, immediately south of Calvados. The granite supplied by Jobert Frères became such items as pedestals, pillars, sidewalks, steps, and troughs. Last (and perhaps least), they made pencils. Their enterprise opened new markets beyond French borders in Belgium, and eventually across the English Channel in England.[4]

During the early years of the business, St. Edme and his English bride Frances Birch had married in the British embassy in Paris in October 1826, and returned to Caen to start their family on Rue de la Fontaine in the heart of the city. Daughter Clémence entered the world in 1827, followed by Lionel in 1829, and another son, Edme Pierre Ambroise Jobert, early in 1832. The children grew up knowing their father not only as a quarry master, but also as a firefighter. In November 1830, St. Edme served as a first lieutenant in the local National Guard fire company. Soon rising to second captain, Jobert distinguished himself as a firefighter to such a degree that in 1837 the government awarded him a silver medal "for acts of courage and devotion." St. Edme became the fire company's commanding captain in November 1840 after a decade of service. When the Duke of Nemours, son of King Louis Philippe, reviewed the National Guard in Caen in the summer of 1843, it was Jobert who introduced the duke to a young orphaned boy whose father had died the previous year while fighting a blaze in Caen, and who the company of firefighters had adopted. That same summer also brought the highlight of Captain Jobert's firefighting career: he became a chevalier in the Royal Order of the Legion of Honor.[5]

St. Edme's wife matched her husband's energy and ambition in her own way. Intelligent and cultivated, Frances surely served as the source of son Lionel's English language proficiency. She undertook the daunting translation into English of cousin-in-law Alphonse de Lamartine's lengthy and celebrated poem *Jocelyn*; her opus appeared the year after the French language publication of the 1836 original. Frances would receive criticism for her approach to the translation that she characterized as "a translation of a novel species, but which I recommend to my countrymen, as being peculiarly adapted, from its very great *literality* to give an idea of the beautiful poem of M. de Lamartine, of which it is a very *faithful* copy." With evident relish, *Fraser's Magazine* used the fourth installment of the serial offering "Our Club at Paris" to ridicule mercilessly Madame Jobert's effort at a literal rendering of *Jocelyn* as, among other things, "arrant nonsense."[6] If her talents were not appreciated by some, Frances did not lack for friends in Caen. Among them was the chief engineer of Calvados, Jacques Pierre Guillaume Pattu, with whom St. Edme and Frances became well acquainted. After Monsieur Pattu died in 1839, Frances penned a detailed memorial that only one of his inner circle of friends could have written. "Modest, gentle and affable in his personal relationships," wrote Madame Jobert in French, "Mr. Pattu was in intimate society more secure and more enjoyable. His great literary and scientific education gave his conversation a special charm to his few friends, who he was able to keep through the difficult phases of our political upheaval."[7]

Thus, Lionel Jobert spent his youth in a prosperous household headed by accomplished parents. His native city of Caen had a population of just over 44,000 inhabitants in 1841, comparable in size to Cincinnati, Ohio in 1840, yet far smaller than New York City's nearly 313,000 people in that same year and the more than 935,000 Parisians in 1841.[8] Bisected by the Orne River and surrounded by farmland, the city's built environment boasted centuries-old structures, including the castle erected and occupied in the eleventh century by the Norman Duke William, later known as the Conqueror; the men's and women's abbeys, also built by William (whose remains lie in the men's abbey); the Saint Pierre church; and on the opposite east side of the Orne, the Saint Michel church of Vaucelles. The busy trade conducted on the Orne and Caen's proximity to the sea—approximately fifteen kilometers from *la Manche*, or the English Channel—likely figured in the selection of a maritime career for both Lionel and his brother Pierre.

But the desire to train as a seaman may not have been Lionel's. In July 1844, when Lionel was fourteen years old, his parents sent him to the port city of Brest on the Atlantic Coast, where France had been operating a school for seafaring instruction since the 1830s. In Brest, Lionel began his preparation as a *mousse*, or ship's boy, the entry-level maritime position. However, on February 1, 1845, after six and a half months of training, school officials sent him back to his parents' home in Caen, now on Rue Guilbert. Lionel's mousse record gave "did not appear at the office" as the reason for his dismissal; apparently, he had not followed orders.[9] Why he did not do as he was directed one can only guess, but Lionel may have been resisting a choice that his parents had made for him. The immediate result was that the Jobert home once again rang with the clatter of three teenagers: seventeen-year-old daughter Clémence, thirteen-year-old Pierre, and the returned Lionel, age fifteen.

St. Edme Jobert bore his paternal responsibility into the next—and his most trying—year, 1846. On March 21, laborers were busy working in one of the Jobert brothers' quarries in Allemagne (now Fleury-sur-Orne), a commune adjacent to Caen. The workers had left unsecured wooden rollers on the rim of the quarry overhead. One of the rollers fell down into the quarry, striking a worker in the head and killing him. Already shaken by this tragedy, in May the company lost a legal decision stemming from an earlier contract to construct and maintain sidewalks in Paris. Jobert Frères had eyed the capital's market as the company expanded in the 1830s. In 1837, a group of associates received legal permission to form the *Compagnie des Berlines de Caen* in order to operate a transportation network that would carry passengers and merchandise between Caen and Paris. St. Edme Jobert served on the Berlines company board in Caen, while brother Charles served on the board in Paris. The Jobert brothers also established their own office in the French capital, and in 1841 reached an agreement with that city to build sidewalks using Normandy stone. The following year, likely for cost effectiveness and to avoid exhausting their quarries in Calvados, Jobert Frères secured authorization from the prefect of the Nièvre department to extract stone from Clamecy, well to the southeast of Paris; the French minister of public works also approved the plan. However, Monsieur Lemoyne, the owner of the land in Clamecy from where the stone was to be extracted, took Jobert Brothers to court, arguing the company had no right to take stone from his private property without his consent. The court ruled in favor of Lemoyne in 1843, annulled the authorizations unduly granted by the Nièvre prefect and the minister of public works (the latter defending his decision, unsuccessfully, to the court), and ordered Jobert Frères to pay costs. In May 1846, in order to avoid potential additional expenditures, Jobert Brothers challenged the authority of the Seine prefecture council to assign costs at their discretion, but the Joberts lost that challenge.[10]

The lone bright spot of 1846 for St. Edme Jobert came in midsummer when he was reelected to the Caen municipal council. But that celebration was short-lived, as less than two weeks later the most devastating event of the year befell Monsieur Jobert. Frances, St. Edme's wife of nearly twenty years, died on August 20 at age fifty-two, two months before son Lionel's seventeenth birthday. The elder Jobert now found himself juggling workplace headaches, his town council responsibilities, and providing for his three teenage children on his own. It was in this context that in March 1847, Lionel Jobert felt obliged to sign up as a novice seaman, a position that would last the better part of four years and take him around the world.[11]

Lionel thus embarked on a circumnavigation of the globe, learning the craft of seamanship and expanding his horizons while maturing from age seventeen to twenty-one, the transition from adolescence to young manhood. The newly constructed sailing corvette *La Bayonnaise* served as the vessel that carried Lionel on this voyage. Commissioned for the French Navy, the warship *La Bayonnaise* bore twenty-eight cannons of thirty caliber, and carried a crew of 240 men. Among Captain Edmond Jurien de la Gravière's principal responsibilities was to transport Alexandre Forth-Rouen to his new position as French charge d'affaires in distant China. The long journey began on April 24, 1847, when *La Bayonnaise* set sail from Cherbourg, a port on Normandy's Cotentin Peninsula that juts out into the English Channel. The ship reached Falmouth in Cornwall, England four days later, staying another four days in that British port. After a sojourn in Lisbon lasting the better part of three weeks, *La Bayonnaise* sailed down the Atlantic coast of North Africa to Santa Cruz de Tenerife in the Canary Islands. From Santa Cruz on June 14, the corvette began its twenty-three-day Atlantic crossing, reaching Bahia, Brazil on July 7. The voyage resumed sixteen days later, leaving South America and navigating the South Atlantic to Simon's Town, a port near Cape Town, resting there for two and a half weeks before rounding Africa's Cape of Good Hope and venturing across the Indian Ocean.[12]

Lionel Jobert's education abroad was just beginning. Six months and one week removed from his native Normandy, *La Bayonnaise* reached Timor in the Indonesian archipelago. Captain Jurien de la Gravière's description of the island, equal parts travel account and botany lesson, conveys the lure of an exotic realm far from Caen.

> A magical spectacle is offered to the sight. The banyan figs, jackfruit with digitated leaves, the cassia with pink clusters and monstrous pods, lining the edge of the forest and mixing various shades, the odd cut of their dark mass of foliage and uniform cut of the lataniers or the cycas [species of palm tree]. The yellow-crested cockatoos inhabit the dense shelter of the tamarind and at the tops gigantic canaries; pigeons frolic amid the wild nutmeg; the lories, of carmine and azure plumage, gently lull themselves on the long petioles of the palm trees, while around emerging bunches flit numerous swarms of bee-eaters and sunbirds, living jewels that insert their beaks bent to the bottom of the tubular corolla to seek insects and the nectar of flowers.

Ambon, the next island port of call where *La Bayonnaise* spent eight days in November, provided another lesson. "On all the points where our corvette was previously stopped," the captain noted, "in Lisbon, in Tenerife, in Bahia, the Cape of Good Hope, our foreign quality was enough to ensure an eager and sympathetic reception. In Ambon, it was not as strangers, it was as compatriots that one greeted us."[13] Lionel Jobert would make effective use of his distinction as a foreigner in the future.

La Bayonnaise finally reached Macau in China just after the new year dawned, on January 4, 1848. Macau's Portuguese governor invited the impressive warship into the port's inner harbor on one of its visits early that year, but the vessel could not enter because, laden as it was with its weighty cannons, it could not pass the bar into the harbor, and the captain thought it imprudent for a warship to remove its guns to lighten the craft even for a short while. Nevertheless, during the next two years, the well-armed *La Bayonnaise* made multiple stops in the harbors at Macau, Hong Kong, and Manila; it called at Singapore and Guam;[14] and everywhere it went in Asian waters the ship advertised French power and global reach. Even for a novice seaman like Lionel Jobert, the various encounters over the course of the long voyage must have reinforced in his mind the widely held continental sense of superiority over the inhabitants of the non-European world.

The Pacific crossing of *La Bayonnaise* began with its departure from Macau for the last time on May 4, 1850. The ship paused in Honolulu for a few days at midyear, leaving Hawaii on July 4 en route to French Polynesia, where it stayed for the first three weeks of August. From there, Captain Jurien de la Gravière set a course for Rio de Janeiro, where he arrived in mid-October. On December 6, 1850, after more than forty-four months away from France, *La Bayonnaise* returned to Cherbourg where the odyssey had begun in the spring of 1847.[15] Now a young man of twenty-one, Lionel Jobert stood five feet, eight-and-a-half inches tall (1.74 meters), with brown hair, brown eyes, and a large mouth. While Lionel grew into adulthood aboard *La Bayonnaise*, life for his family in Caen likewise progressed. Clémence, Lionel's older sister, married in November 1847 at age twenty to Edmond Breuil, a twenty-seven-year-old native of Amiens with a law degree to his credit and a career as a diplomat in front of him. Breuil received the post of second secretary of the French Legation in London the following April, where he and Clémence resided for most of the next three years. Pierre Jobert followed in his older brother Lionel's footsteps, becoming a novice seaman in December of 1848, one month short of his seventeenth birthday. At six feet, two inches (1.88 meters), the chestnut-haired, brown-eyed Pierre already stood half a foot taller than Lionel. Aboard the commercial vessel *Myosotis*, Pierre arrived in New York City in early March 1849, returning to Havre in mid-May. Later that same year, Pierre gained further practical experience on the *Myosotis*, this time sailing to Martinique in the Caribbean.[16]

France had changed, too. While Lionel Jobert and *La Bayonnaise* were halfway around the world in Hong Kong at the end of February 1848, France's King Louis Philippe bowed to mounting discord and abdicated the throne. None other than French Foreign Minister Alphonse de Lamartine declared the advent of the Second Republic. As Lamartine strove to fashion a new political regime for France, life continued apace for his cousin-in-law St.

Edme Jobert. In the wake of the demise of Louis Philippe's July Monarchy, Jobert Frères ceased payments they owed related to their Parisian sidewalks legal case, and ultimately liquidated the company. St. Edme, however, operated his own quarry business in Calvados, still employing fifty workers there in 1850 and another 150 workers in the neighboring department of La Manche. Monsieur Jobert continued to be a presence in community affairs in Caen as well. He was reelected to the municipal council's Committee on Public Works in May 1847, and the next year he earned reelection as first captain of the second battalion of the local National Guard firefighting company. In addition, both St. Edme and Charles Jobert numbered among the members of the local masonic lodge. Indeed, one can see the masonic influence in the former's signature—three dots arranged in a triangle to represent the period after "St"—as early as 1826 on his marriage record.[17]

The Jobert brothers also became theatrical impresarios. Both men had achieved local recognition in 1827 for their artistic energies that they channeled into managing the Caen entertainment hall (*salle de spectacle*) twenty years later.[18] Nationally known performers such as actress Anaïs Fargueil and singer Sophie Méquillet graced the Caen stage during the Joberts' association with the local theater. Benefit performances were de rigueur, and these two ladies complied with the etiquette of the day. From the May 5, 1847 performance, for instance, the poor were the beneficiaries: "Before the last act of *Grâce de Dieu*, Mademoiselle Fargueil, accompanied by Mr. Jobert, municipal councilman, made, in all parts of the room, a collection that was quite abundant. Everybody paid his tribute. Some people even deposited gold coins in the alms collection." Two years later, during the March 31, 1849 performance, Sophie Méquillet made the same gesture: "Mlle. Méquillet, accompanied by Mr. Jobert, venerable member of the Scottish lodge, made a collection for the poor."[19] For St. Edme Jobert, the camaraderie with the theater talent filled the void left by his departed wife, and he gave of himself to them. On behalf of young Mlle. Méquillet, Jobert penned a glowing letter of reference: "Sophie was divinely inspired to make use of her talent to achieve the sustenance of her family. Disdainful of the vain presumptions of the world concerning the ladies of the theater." A thank-you note from Mlle. Fargueil to M. Jobert, on her departure from Caen in October 1847, conveyed respect and affection in a style lost today: "You will accept, my dear Mr. Jobert, my farewells and the most sincere vows that I will always retain for you the remembrance of your kindness."[20]

The theater, in time, also would become an emotional refuge for Lionel Jobert, but after his return to Cherbourg in December 1850, he had only a brief period to reconnect with family before he set out again for another lengthy stint away from France. The Breuils in 1849 had christened a daughter, Marie, making St. Edme a grandfather and Lionel an uncle. In mid-January 1851, Lionel arrived in London, one week before his young niece, his sister, and her husband departed for the latter's new post as French consul second class in Danzig, then part of Prussia.[21] Lionel did not see his brother Pierre, for Pierre had left Havre as a mate aboard the civilian trader *Zélie* in September 1850, bound for Trinidad. The ship called at Trinidad in mid-October and then sailed on to Martinique, arriving on November 1. Pierre checked in to a local hospital at St. Pierre a week later. The *Zélie* left Martinique and took on cotton at Mobile, Alabama before returning to Havre at the end of January 1851, without Pierre Jobert. Four days later, on February 4, 1851, Lionel, accompanied by his father, officially registered in Caen as a *matelot*, or mate. Lionel left Havre on the commercial vessel *Mont Béarn* on March 2, destined for St. Thomas in the Caribbean. Perhaps St. Edme Jobert had received word of his youngest son's hospitalization and urged Lionel to sign on for a Caribbean-bound ship in order to check on Pierre, and perhaps Lionel was able to see his brother. What is certain is that Pierre Jobert, age nineteen, died in St. Pierre, Martinique on July 19, 1851, the cause of death unrecorded.[22] Pierre's death dealt St. Edme Jobert another severe blow. Six years earlier, St. Edme, his wife Frances, and their three children filled his Caen household. Now, in the summer of 1851, he was alone.

Lionel's father turned to political engagement and a new relationship to help assuage his grief. In the same month that Pierre expired, the French Chamber of Deputies defeated a proposed constitutional amendment to allow Louis Napoleon to continue for a second term as the nation's president. As French citizens debated the direction the country should take, St. Edme and Charles Jobert signed their names to a ringing statement of pro-Republican ideals published in a Caen newspaper revealingly titled *Le Suffrage Universal*. Louis Napoleon, a proponent of universal manhood suffrage, took matters into his own hands on December 2, 1851 by staging a coup d'etat and violently repressing dissidents. One year later, he became Napoleon III of the Second French Empire. Louis Napoleon's heavy-handed actions alienated many of his compatriots, including noted author Victor Hugo, who left France for exile in Belgium shortly after the December 1851 coup. In February 1852, in order to get a letter to his wife, Hugo relied on the kindness of a volunteer courier—St. Edme Jobert. Offering his assistance to a well-known political exile constituted more an act of compassion than a political statement on the part of St. Edme, who did not overtly challenge the continued rule of Louis Napoleon. Indeed, St. Edme's new passion was entirely apolitical. Not two months after his encounter with the celebrated Victor Hugo, St. Edme Jobert, age fifty-six, married again, this time to twenty-year-old Emilie Ernestine Floreska Mathieu.[23]

When his father got married in April 1852, Lionel Jobert was nearing the end of his voyage as a mate aboard the *Mont Béarn*. Lionel disembarked from that Marseille-bound ship at Rio de Janeiro and joined the Havre-bound *Ville de Rio*, serving as a lieutenant with the requisite boost in pay from a third-class mate's fifty francs up to eighty francs per month. The *Ville de Rio* returned to Havre at the end of spring. Lionel then received permission to make the short trip to London as a temporary second captain on the *Médicis* at the end of July where, for an undisclosed reason, he introduced himself at the residence of the French consul. Lionel returned to Caen two weeks later, now on leave from maritime service. In October, Lionel Jobert turned twenty-three years of age. He had spent nearly all of the last five and a half years at sea, and found himself at a crossroads. Clémence had her own family in Danzig, doubtless fulfilling the role of a diplomat's wife as she had done in London with frequent social gatherings among the well-placed and influential. St. Edme had a new wife, content to once again have companionship in the comforting surroundings of his native Caen where he had spent his life. What ought Lionel to do with his future? Should he be married to the sea? Should he pursue some other occupation while he was still young? He must have mulled over such questions in his year away from seafaring. With his mother and brother deceased, his sister living abroad with her family, his father focused on his new bride, and all his work experience having been at sea, there was little reason for Lionel to remain in Caen. His decision: at the end of November 1853 he formally declared his return to the maritime profession.[24]

But his plans were quickly scuttled. While in Cherbourg in mid-February 1854, the local health council declared Lionel unfit for service. Given that there is no extant record of what ailed him, or if his affliction was related to his recently concluded leave from maritime service, one can only speculate as to what the health council had found. One can say, however, that Lionel's convalescence coincided fairly neatly with French participation in the Crimean War. At the end of March 1854, both France and Great Britain declared war on Russia in a conflict sparked by bickering between Catholic and Orthodox Christians over access to holy sites in the Muslim-controlled Ottoman Empire, but that equally involved a geopolitical power struggle among the warring parties. France's war effort lasted two years; Lionel sat it out. The beginning of the end came when the yearlong siege of the Black Sea port city of Sevastopol finally ended with a Russian defeat in September 1855. By February 1856, hostilities had ceased. In that same month, Lionel got clearance for his remobilization from the health council at Cherbourg, having secured permission in January to take a course in hydrography at Dunkirk in preparation for taking the examination to earn the maritime rank of *capitaine au long cours*, or master mariner.[25]

Had Lionel read the tea leaves, correctly sensing a pending military involvement by the French, and feigned illness a month before France declared war? What, if anything, is to be made of Lionel recovering his health in the same month as the armistice of February 1856? Did St. Edme, having lost one son, urge his remaining son to try to avoid military service? Based on the evidence in this case, it would do the Joberts a disservice to conclude anything other than Lionel's temporary infirmity was coincidental to the duration of the Crimean War. On May 20, 1856, he indeed took and passed the examination for becoming a capitaine au long cours and was elevated to that status one month later.[26] Now a master mariner, Lionel would have to match the energy of his father if he sought to enjoy the standard of living to which he had been accustomed as a youth. St. Edme Jobert set an impressive example. In 1856, his and Emilie's household included their two-year-old daughter Ernestine, a domestic servant, a chambermaid, and Emilie's parents, who both were younger than St. Edme. The Joberts gave Lionel another half-sister, Henriette, in October 1856. In his sixties, St. Edme stayed active with his business affairs. He owned one house in Caen and another on the Normandy coast in Beuzeval (now Houlgate). He possessed horses, a carriage, and watercraft—the sloops *Protégé de Dieu* and *La Risle*.[27] St. Edme Jobert was a success.

Lionel's first turn as captain came in January 1857. He landed a job at the helm of the *Arche d'Alliance*, a brig built in 1851 in Dunkirk. Drawing a captain's salary of 150 francs per month, Lionel had to pilot the ship and its cargo of diverse merchandise from Dunkirk across the Atlantic to Martinique. The crew consisted of ten men: Captain Jobert; twenty-six-year-old Second Captain Jacques Mercier, who was one year younger than Lionel; a boatswain, Pierre Congoeur, the oldest crew member at age fifty; six mates; and a ship's boy. Newly minted Captain Jobert managed to complete the ocean voyage, arriving in St. Pierre on February 25. With his position had come other responsibilities. One mate, sixteen years the captain's senior, received a ten-day suspension of pay for drunkenness and indiscipline. Dealing with the deaths of crewmen was not uncommon on such voyages, and Lionel handled that obligation as well. While in Martinique, two mates, both in their twenties, died within three weeks of each other. Second Captain Jacques Mercier preceded them in death, expiring on March 7. These deaths had to remind Lionel of his brother's passing in St. Pierre less than six years earlier. Another issue for Captain Jobert was the desertion of the fourteen-year-old ship's boy. To replace him, Lionel took on a sixteen-year-old youth from Martinique named Louis. The boy had been born to enslaved parents—"Big" Jean and Manette—and gained freedom by France's abolition of slavery decree in 1848. The next year he received his new identity—Louis Galiby—in the presence of local officials. In mid-May 1857, a few days after Galiby joined the *Arche d'Alliance*, the ship departed Martinique bound for Havre, where it arrived on July 2.[28]

The experience of commanding the *Arche d'Alliance* gave Lionel his first full opportunity to exercise authority, and in charge of the vessel he had successfully navigated two Atlantic crossings. Power and position fed his vanity. When called on to witness the death record of Jacques Mercier, Lionel Jobert added "d'E"—d'Epineuil—to his signature.[29] That choice revealed that Lionel embraced the idea of being from a noble lineage; that his self-perception and the identity he projected to others contained the notion of a distinction above the average individual; and suggested that he shared the same aspiration to status pursued by his great-grandfather, the first Jobert to be Count d'Epineuil. But that goal cost money. Two days before Christmas 1857, Lionel set out on his next foray across the Atlantic, this time as second captain aboard the South America–bound ship *Le Frédéric* under the captaincy of Havre native Isidore Venard. The *Frédéric* reached port at Montevideo on February 12, 1858, staying two weeks before sailing to nearby Buenos Aires. The ship shuttled more cargo across the Río de la Plata back to Montevideo on March 22. After spending the month of April in Uruguay, the *Frédéric* prepared to return to France. Monsieur Maillefer, French charge d'affaires in Montevideo, jotted on the ship's record that Second Captain Jobert owed Captain Venard 143.20 francs.[30] Notations of money owed and pay advanced commonly appear on ships' records. For Lionel Jobert, however, this considerable debt was a harbinger of things to come.

The *Frédéric* returned to Havre on July 8, 1858. In the fall, Lionel signed on again as second in command of the *Frédéric* under Captain Venard, departing Havre on October 3, for Port-au-Prince, Haiti.[31] To regard the receding French coastline while feeling the motion of the *Frédéric* was to contemplate the past while sensing the pull of the present. Lionel

Jobert in many ways had become what his father was not. St. Edme Jobert, the son of French parents, grew up in the era of the "Citizen Emperor" Napoleon Bonaparte and achieved financial success without employing his family's noble title. Married at age thirty, St. Edme became a family man, a community leader, and a fixture in Caen. By contrast, Lionel's mother was English, adding a bicultural component to his identity that his father did not share. Lionel fancied the status connoted by the surname d'Epineuil; he had not married; and his chosen career had made Caen a more temporary than permanent home. Seventeen days out of port on the *Frédéric*, Lionel Jobert marked the beginning of his thirtieth year. Was the life of a ship captain worthy of his ambition?

Chapter 2

Opportunity and Indiscretion

Commander of the Haitian Naval School

Lionel Jobert arrived at Port-au-Prince, Haiti, aboard the *Frédéric* on November 28, 1858.¹ He found a nation on the brink of revolution. Less than a month later, the rebel General Fabré Geffrard seized power from the self-styled emperor of the country, Faustin Soulouque. On the latter's formal abdication in January 1859, Geffrard proceeded to have himself appointed as president of the Republic of Haiti. Jobert capitalized on the fitful political climate to secure a position in the employ of the Haitian government, yet his hubris would lead to a dramatic fall from the lofty heights he had attained.

Jobert watched the momentous events in Haiti firsthand while the ship's crew set about the unloading of its cargo and the processing of diverse consignments for the return journey to Havre. In mid-February 1859, days before the *Frédéric* was due to depart Port-au-Prince for France, Jobert indicated his desire to disembark from the ship and end his service on board. This step was approved by Captain Venard effective February 17, and noted by the French Consul-General Alexandre Mellinet, who also arranged with the captain to settle Jobert's outstanding wages and clear his accounts. Someone or something had exerted enough attraction for Jobert to be willing to take the major gamble of seeking his fortune in the Haitian republic rather than continuing as a capitaine au long cours in the service of the French merchant marine.²

During the first two months of his rule, President Geffrard had moved quickly to introduce a number of reforms related to the social, political, and economic life of the country. These included the creation of a Naval School (*École Navale Militaire*) that aimed to train officers for a nascent coastal patrol force. The decision to establish the school was taken by Geffrard's Department of War and the Navy on February 15, 1859 and announced via a published advisory dated February 22. Those interested in applying as cadet candidates were to present themselves to the newly appointed director of the school, who was none other than Mr. Lionel Jobert![3]

Considering Jobert's future activities in the United States, it seems highly possible that the Naval School may have been Jobert's own idea, presented to the new rulers of the republic for their consideration. He was also likely to have put himself forward as a qualified leader for such an enterprise based on his own training to be a sea captain and his years of hands-on nautical experience on the high seas. Having succeeded in this endeavor, it was no coincidence that the public notice of the school's creation was published just five days after Jobert's official disembarkation from the *Frédéric*. Chief among the incentives for Jobert was his new salary of 600 francs per month, a considerable 450-franc increase above his salary as a capitaine au long cours.[4]

The new Naval School director's first task was to conduct preparatory courses in advance of the formal admission examinations that were scheduled for June 15. The rest of 1859 was spent implementing the planned entrance examinations for the first cohort of cadets and commencing their formal instruction. This work appears to have been hindered by a lack of qualified young men between the ages of fifteen and seventeen able and/or willing to commit to the new institution. Nevertheless, the school progressed, and Jobert and the small contingent of first-year students were invited to a New Year's reception hosted by President Geffrard at the *Palais National* on December 31, 1859.[5]

Days after the reception a committee comprised of local authorities carried out an evaluation of the progress of the Naval School. As part of the review visit, Lionel Jobert, now described as commandant, delivered a speech during the first week of January 1860 that summarized his efforts and the current state of the school and its cadets. Among those in attendance was one of his superiors, the Haitian Admiral Lafond, whom Jobert made sure to praise. The speech reveals Lionel's strong suit: his gift for oratory.

> The navy is, for an island state, of such an importance that upon our arrival in this country we were distressfully surprised at the dilapidated state of the erstwhile Haitian fleet even if well maintained and that has cost so much money!

The revolution which was accomplished on the 22nd of December 1858 proved the uncontested need for a navy, and His Excellency the President of Haiti created, several months later, the Naval School which I have the honor to command.

. . . It is my duty to publicly compliment the Admiral for the friendly cooperation that he has offered for my work in being so obliging as to place all of the services at his command at my disposal; thus supported, I cannot but succeed. . . .

It is beneficial, however, that I speak to the Commission of the very great difficulties that I have encountered during the recruitment of the students.

The school that I command was new for the country; one presumed that entrance would be opened to young men who did not show sufficient promise for advancement. . . .

I had thus, and in the midst of many urgings, obtained forty or so youths who not only did not fulfill the fixed age requirements, but also had difficulties, for the most part, in reading and writing.

I decided, Mr. Minister of War, to fix at 12 the number of naval cadets; then, day by day, I sent back those unable to make the grade. Soon there remained but 7 students, who today form the first division. The 4 who form the second have not had, on average, more than three weeks of courses.

In spite all of these obstacles I believe that I have allowed the naval students a degree of theoretical instruction very sufficient considering the short amount of time spent at the school, and I invite the gentlemen of the Commission to examine them strictly.

. . . I am proud to have been chosen for the training of the Haitian Navy; I am happy that the government of His Excellency has avoided, in employing me, the anti-progressive pre-judgement which tends to be extended to foreigners, and that it has understood that there are men in France totally disposed to bring here the assistance of their intelligence and their specialized knowledge for the grand project of regeneration, an enterprise undertaken with such admirable perseverance by His Excellency and those who surround him.[6]

Jobert's address represents his earliest known writing. The speech is indicative of a defensiveness that would punctuate his relationships with authority and society over the coming years. It would not be the last time that he would cite less than ideal conditions so as to cover himself for possible delays or shortcomings in the performance of his duties; it would also not be the last time that his lofty promises of success would end in disappointment and scandal. The speech further reveals that, taken at his word, Jobert felt one's country of origin was not as significant as one's willingness and ability to help Haiti develop its navy. Tellingly, Jobert referred to "men in France" instead of Frenchmen; the man mattered more than his nationality. Yet the constraints of French citizenship would compel Jobert to clarify his legal status while serving in a military capacity for a foreign country. Thus, by imperial decree, "the gentleman *Jobert (Edme-Lionel-Holwell)*, capitaine au long cours, born on the 20th of October 1829 at Caen (Calvados), residing at Caen, is authorized to join the service of the navy of Haiti, without the loss of his French status; with the express requirement of him that he never, under any pretext whatsoever, bear arms against France, under the penalties as declared by the law."[7]

After the review of the Naval School in January, Jobert turned his attention to preparing the cadets for a voyage to France the following month that would involve two primary purposes. First, the students were to undergo further naval training under official French tutelage at Brest. Second, following this training they were to travel back to Haiti on board a newly completed steam gunboat called the *Geffrard* and participate in its entrance into Haitian naval service. This vessel was one of two that President Geffrard had decided to order from abroad, at significant expense, for use as armed patrol boats. The second ship was the *22 Décembre*, named in recognition of the date of Geffrard's overthrow of Soulouque. This mission would keep Jobert and the cadets away from Haiti for nearly ten months. We may track their progress during this period with a great degree of detail. Haitian and French diplomatic correspondence that survives in France and the United States provides a good picture of the events surrounding the preparations of the *Geffrard* for its transatlantic crossing, the actual three-month voyage of the gunboat, and the role played by Jobert in each stage of the saga.

Jobert arranged passage for himself and the cadets on the three-masted schooner *Créole*, captained by one Mr. Cligny; the ship departed Port-au-Prince for Nantes on February 18, 1860. Their voyage, which was also the occasion for practical training in nautical skills, was even reported in the New York *Evening Express*.[8] The *Créole* arrived at St. Nazaire, a port near Nantes, after a journey of more than two months: "On 23 April, the three-masted [schooner] from Nantes, *Creole*, belonging to Mr. Demarge, arrived at the dock; this vessel carried to France Mr. Lionel Jobert (French), commander of the Naval School of Haiti. It [also] carried to France the young Haitians who make up this school: there they will have a stay of several months, then taking [ownership] of one of the steam corvettes constructed at Bordeaux for the account of the Haitian government, and sailing it to Port-au-Prince."[9]

On arrival in France, Jobert was expected to liaise with the Haitian Legation at Paris. His primary contact there became Alexis Beaubrun Ardouin (1796–1865), the new resident minister of Haiti to France. Ardouin was a distinguished Haitian statesman and man of letters, well known for authoring *L'Histoire d'Haïti*, his multivolume history of independent Haiti. He and Jobert almost certainly had become acquainted the previous year in Port-au-Prince, and he would spend a significant amount of time with Jobert over the coming months in Paris and Bordeaux.

Late in April Jobert went to Paris, deeming it prudent to leave the youthful cadets at St. Nazaire so that they would not be distracted by all that the French capital had to offer. There he met Haitian Chargé d'Affaires Auguste L'Instant Pradine, as Ardouin had not yet arrived to take up his post as minister. Pradine noted that Jobert was "obliged to go and spend several days in Caen to deal with family matters." Lionel surely met his newborn half-brother Eon Jobert, St. Edme and Emilie's youngest child, while in Caen.[10] In the middle of May Jobert was back in Paris, decked out in the uniform of the Commander of the Haitian Naval School, as evidenced by a caricature given to him by a friend. The sketch depicts the amply sideburned and jaunty looking Jobert dangling small naval vessels on strings from one of his hands, almost like a puppet master (see figure 2.1). During this time he met, together with Pradine, the French Minister of the Navy Ferdinand-Alphonse Hamelin, a fellow native of Calvados in lower Normandy; they discussed the placement of the cadets at the training facility for ship's boys in Brest.[11]

In accordance with these plans Jobert traveled from Paris to St. Nazaire in order to pick up the Haitian cadets who were still waiting there and bring them to Brest. At Brest the cadets were enrolled "under the authority of the [French] Naval Ministry, at the Practical School for Mousses."[12] Their instruction was to take place on board the French training frigate *Thétis*, which they boarded on May 26. In late June, Jobert left the cadets at Brest and returned again to Caen to visit his father after receiving approval to do so from Minister Ardouin.[13]

In the meantime Ardouin became more and more preoccupied with preparing for the handover of the *Geffrard* to his government as well as the mounting expenses related to its streamlining and outfitting. The ship,

20 / Lionel Jobert and the American Civil War

Figure 2.1. Caricature of Lionel Jobert, printed by A. Beillet, 35 Quai de la Tournelle, Paris. The inscription reads in French, "Raynal to his friend Lionel Jobert, Paris 14 May 1860." Jobert signed and dedicated the print "Lionel Jobert d'E. to his very nice Mr. Delattre, Bordeaux, 2 Sept. 1860." The accompanying seal is that of the Haitian warship *Geffrard*. Author's collection.

constructed in Bordeaux by shipbuilder Lucien Arman, had been christened there on June 18, 1860, but the English-made engine still awaited installation.[14] In addition, during their two-month stay at Brest the Haitian cadets were to be provided with basic sustenance, clothing, and incidentals paid for by the French government that had to be reimbursed by the Haitian Legation. Finally, Ardouin had been dealing with a number of requests from Jobert for his own expense reimbursements relative to his internal travels in

France and the needs of the cadets while at St. Nazaire. Already at this early stage Ardouin did not fully agree with some of Jobert's claims, particularly after Jobert acknowledged that he had received a substantial cash advance from the government prior to leaving Haiti.[15]

It was only at this point that Ardouin was able to assure himself that Jobert had been formally tasked by the Haitian government to command the *Geffrard* on its maiden voyage from France to Haiti, and in truth this decision had been taken prior to the departure of Jobert and the cadets for France.[16] Ardouin saw this as a practical decision that was based on Jobert's previous experience in the French merchant marine and the fact that he was already engaged by the Haitian republic as commandant of the Naval School.

> I have had to think, and I still think that the government had intended that it would be Mr. Jobert who would take the command of the steam vessel at Bordeaux in order to steer it to Haiti. Besides he is a capitaine au long-cours and he could do this, in employing him in this position the Legation will avoid engaging another captain and paying the latter.
>
> So the [salary] payment that I have made tends, Mr. Secretary of State, to place Mr. Jobert at the disposition of the Legation for the moment when it will be necessary to launch the steam vessel, to maintain him in the directorship of the naval School where he may be really useful to our country. By that I think to serve the intentions and the desires of the government.[17]

Meanwhile Jobert continued to wait in Caen for the order from Ardouin to proceed to Bordeaux to make the final preparations for the gunboat's departure. Ardouin wrote to him on July 16, thanking him for contacting the commander of the *Thétis* in order to ascertain that a rumor of abuse or neglect of the cadets by the French authorities at Brest was in fact unfounded and that the French authorities were treating the young men well: "I congratulate you, sir, for your concern for the students that the Haitian government has confided to you; the approach that you have taken for assuring us of their position at Brest, after the rumor that had reached you, proves this sentiment on your part. I will account for this with the government, which has been so satisfied with the goodwill of Mr. the Minister of the Navy, Admiral Hamelin that it has published in the *Moniteur Haitien* the letter that you have written to me from Brest, on 26th May, and which I had forwarded a copy." Jobert worked to gain Ardouin's confidence, but suspected not every authority held him in esteem. In the same letter, Ardouin sought to assure Jobert that his position was not threatened by an important individual scheming to undermine him: "You are mistaken, sir, to think that a powerful person influences me against you. I know the allowance that it is necessary to make for human passions, and I don't allow myself to be guided by intrigues."[18] Regardless of the identity of that powerful person, it was Lionel Jobert's inability to manage his own human passions that would cost him both Ardouin's admiration and his job.

Ardouin received word in late July from the steamer's contractor Jerréal Silvie that, aside from the placement of the ship's guns, the *Geffrard* was essentially ready for hand over and initial tests already had been carried out on the engine. Around August 1, Jobert was in Paris where he linked up with Ardouin, and the two men then traveled to Bordeaux where they arrived on August 4. They were now kept busy recruiting a crew and other support staff, arranging their respective employment contracts, provisioning and outfitting the ship, and participating in the final evaluation of the *Geffrard*'s English-built engine and its overall seaworthiness. The latter task was to be assisted by an independent commission of experts led by a naval engineer by the name of de Gasté, whose employment Ardouin requested that Hamelin authorize, and assisted by one Mr. Labat.[19]

As the young Haitian cadets were not capable of performing most of the important nautical duties, some experienced French seamen were required. Besides Jobert's two lieutenants there was a need for engine mechanics, a blacksmith, a carpenter, and stokers. Supplemental equipment not provided by the constructors also had to be procured, as well as instruments, tools, foodstuffs, nautical flags, and other supplies. Jobert himself suggested some upgrades, and the exact nature of the ship's dinghies was still under discussion as Ardouin did not find the currently planned dinghies elegant or comfortable enough for the use of President Geffrard. Meal allocations had to be assigned based on the relative status and position of each traveler (Jobert's was the largest). The added expenses continued to mount and soon exceeded the originally budgeted figures in a number of categories. Added to all of this, the vessel could only carry a maximum of five to six days' worth of coal, which meant Ardouin and Jobert had to plot out where to stop en route to replenish fuel. Ardouin made contact with Haitian diplomatic staff and local businessmen at the available coaling stations to ensure supply could be obtained as needed. On August 5, Jobert and Ardouin toured the ship together with Monsieur Silvie, and three days later a trial run was made on Bordeaux's local river systems. John Forster, an English engineer from the manufacturer of the engine, was in charge of this operation; Ardouin soon engaged Forster for two years to serve as the chief mechanic for the vessel. A further test of the steamer brought it to the French coast at Royan on August 19–20, with the participation of the expert commission hired by Ardouin to assess the oceangoing stability of the vessel. Despite some contested reservations on the part of de Gasté as to the overall soundness of the ship's construction, Ardouin considered the ship cleared for service.[20]

Last minute delays continued to hinder the *Geffrard*'s departure. From about August 21 to 25, Jobert had to travel to Paris with Ardouin to help determine the legal status of French sailors and specialists engaged by the Haitian republic. A dispute had arisen over whether the French authorities would have any purview over their contracts—drawn up by Jobert—which were to be signed with the Haitian government, and Jobert advised Ardouin to defend Haiti's rights to the extent possible. The French Foreign Minister Édouard Thouvenel, who did not seem favorably inclined to Jobert, declined to weigh in on the matter and referred the men to Minister of the Navy Hamelin. Although Hamelin was not available, they were able to meet with the chief of Hamelin's cabinet, Garnaut, who assured them that an accommodation could be found in which the French consul in Port-au-Prince would not be granted authority over any disputes that might emerge related to the engagement contracts of the French crew after their arrival in Haiti. The contracts, which probably conformed in large measure to French law and naval regulations, were finally signed, but not before Ardouin was forced to make a further concession related to the pension and disability rights of the French crew members in the event of their death or incapacitation through accident or illness.[21]

Finally satisfied that all was essentially ready, and facing an unofficial deadline so as to take advantage of favorable weather patterns prior to the onset of autumn, Ardouin dispatched Jobert back to Bordeaux to make final preparations for departure. The little gunboat had become Ardouin's pride and joy, as evidenced by his letter to his superior at Port-au-Prince.

> When H.E. the President of Haiti and his ministers will have seen it you will better judge everything that has needed to be executed in order to make it a sturdy and beautiful warship. In addition, it attracts the attention of the public in Bordeaux which has not ceased visiting it. A citizen of our country will without doubt share in this admiration. In order to produce

a good impression in Haiti, I have condescended to the wish manifested by Commandant L. Jobert to fit it out completely, to provide him with all of the indispensable material which the government will have difficulty finding in Port-au-Prince."[22]

Jobert's Second Lieutenant G. Thomasson collected the Haitian cadets at Brest and brought them to Bordeaux during the third week of August. An accounting of the estimated thirty-five to thirty-seven crew and passengers due to travel on the *Geffrard* constituted far more than Jobert had ever commanded as a ship captain. Along with Commandant Lionel Jobert, there was Lieutenant Théodore Démost, Jobert's second-in-command; Lieutenant G. Thomasson, ship's bookkeeper and provisions manager; the boatswain (a French seaman); six mates (all French seamen); the master carpenter; the master blacksmith; chief mechanic Mr. John Forster; the second mechanic; four engine stokers (presumably all French); the twelve cadets from the Haitian Naval School; the cook; the steward/head waiter; three authorized private passengers (two of them Haitian subjects, the other the contractor Silvie); and one or two servants. Following a Catholic mass on board the ship on August 30, and the unfurling of the Haitian flag, the *Geffrard* put to sea under Jobert's command on September 3, 1860. It left, however, without Mr. Silvie, who had a last-minute falling out with Jobert and Ardouin over his desire to have control over the technical operation of the ship and its engine during the journey, to which Jobert had strongly objected. In a foretaste of Jobert's activities in the United States as a colonel in the Union Army, he clearly would brook no challenges whatsoever to his authority. At this point in time he had Ardouin's full support in this regard, plus an English chief mechanic for the engine, John Forster, already had been engaged.[23]

Meanwhile, back in Port-au-Prince the authorities had been following news of the cadets as well as the plans for the maiden voyage of their steamer. A ministerial report on the "General Situation of the Republic" observed that the "young Haitian marines, from the naval school, who have been sent to France and who will return aboard the steam corvette the *Geffrard*, have been the subject of the goodwill of the French government, and have been placed aboard a training frigate at Brest; according to the reports which have been sent back to the government by the Haitian minister resident in Paris, they have been noted for their discipline and their progress."[24] Shortly after the publication of this report the Haitian government learned of the *Geffrard*'s departure of September 3. As Ardouin put it in his dispatch of September 13 to Port-au-Prince: "At last, the *Geffrard* has departed, I believe, with the best chances for a good voyage, with good weather. Shortly before, there had been some storms, some hurricanes, which hit London and diverse other localities on the continent. It is to be presumed that it will arrive in the inter-tropical seas after the season of hurricanes, and it will be able to arrive at Haiti amidst good conditions. That is my hope and my most ardent wish."[25] Both the authorities in Haiti and Minister Ardouin in Paris now anxiously awaited news updates on the timely and safe journey of the steamer to the Caribbean.

The ship made numerous stops en route to Port-au-Prince. Using a variety of sources[26] we may create a reconstruction of the journey as shown in table 2.1. Ardouin had asked Jobert for regular reports from each port of call. Initially these were received, albeit sporadically. Over time Ardouin expressed increasing worries about the slow progress of the steamer. Originally expected to complete the journey in not more than two months, it can be seen from the itinerary that the ship did not reach Port-au-Prince until December 4, 1860. These delays were also noted with growing concern in the Haitian capital.[27]

Table 2.1. Maiden voyage of the Haitian warship *Geffrard*, September–December 1860

September 4	Arrival at Royan, France at the mouth of the Gironde estuary
September 9	Arrival at Lisbon, Portugal; took on coal
September 16	Departure from Lisbon bound for Madeira (Portugal)
ca. September 20	Arrival at Funchal, Madeira; took on coal
September 23	Departed Funchal; forced to return to Madeira due to strong wind
October 15	Second departure from Funchal
October 16	Arrival at Tenerife, Canary Islands (Spain); obtained water, victuals
ca. October 25–26	Took on coal at St. Vincent, Cape Verde archipelago (Portuguese)
ca. October 28	Departure from St. Vincent en route to the Caribbean
November 11	Arrival at Antigua (British colony); took on coal
November 19	Arrival at St. Thomas (Danish West Indies)
December 4	Arrival at Port-au-Prince, Republic of Haiti

Furthermore, Ardouin clearly was irritated by some of the expenses Jobert incurred as the journey wore on, betraying the latter's sense of entitlement to comfort and luxury whether he had the means or authority to afford such. Ardouin had advanced 4,500 francs to Jobert at Bordeaux for coal purchases and pilotage fees at the first two ports of call,[28] but soon noted some unauthorized spending and later learned of a series of drafts for British pounds that Jobert began to draw on the Haitian Legation in London. Ardouin wrote to Secretary of State Victorin Plésance on October 14.

> I know that he had to pay the pilotage costs to depart from the river of Bordeaux; that while being in this port the ship had several caulking repairs, although brand new. But I find rather high the figure of 650 f. for a similar transaction at Lisbon, unless the very short navigation to get it there seriously damaged the ship in this respect. Mr. Jobert also declared having spent 167 f. *on the [Gironde] river* and 312 f. at Lisbon for bread, fresh meat, and vegetables for the crew. It seems to me that he could have abstained from spending this 479 f., since the ship had received provisions for three months, among which conserved vegetables [and] flour, and can make bread on board. There were medications forming a pharmacy: why has he expensed the 22 f. etc.[?] Why 75¢ for *paper*, when the ship was provided with it at Bordeaux? I don't know at what price he paid for coal at Lisbon; at Bordeaux this item was at 37 f. per ton.
> ... Mr. Jobert must justify all of these expenses.[29]

In mid-October Ardouin learned of the *Geffrard*'s arrival at Funchal, Madeira around September 20. He also was informed by Jobert that the commandant had ordered the debarkation from the ship of the English chief mechanic John Forster. The specific reasons for this eviction of the Englishman were not enumerated by Ardouin, although they seem to have been tied to a dispute over authority similar to that which occurred earlier with the ship's contractor Silvie, who, according to Ardouin, had been friendly with Forster. Relieved that the steamer had safely reached Madeira, Ardouin continued to offer the benefit of the doubt to Commandant Jobert and his "justifiable" craving for control over all affairs related to the gunboat.[30]

Jobert's letter of September 22, sent from Funchal also provided a promising update on the plans for the next stages of the *Geffrard*'s journey. Ardouin paraphrased Jobert as follows:

Mr. Jobert told me "that he was going to depart (i.e., on the 23rd) for the island of St. Vincent; that he had on board coal for 7 days; that in 5 days he would be at St. Vincent; that he would replenish his coal there; that from there to St. Thomas, proceeding again for 7 days under steam, only 3 [more] days under sail would be required for him to arrive there, by reason of the distance calculated on the charts. I thought it necessary, he added, to opt in favor of this latter route, longer in appearance, shorter in reality and prudent; and God knows I must take it with my ship!"[31]

According to this reckoning by Jobert, he would be at St. Vincent (Cape Verde) by the end of September, en route to St. Thomas at the beginning of October, at St. Thomas by mid-October, and at Port-au-Prince shortly thereafter.

From this point forward there was a major lapse in communications from Jobert. On November 19, Ardouin expressed his apprehension: "I had great hopes that the [postal] steamship which arrived would have brought me news of our little steamer the *Geffrard*, which would be at St. Thomas, where it would have stopped at the end of October; but there is nothing at all, and that worries me." As a result, Ardouin was forced to make inquiries with the coal merchant G. Seidel whom Jobert had dealt with in Lisbon as well as with General A. Dupuy, the Haitian minister at London, to see if their intelligence channels could yield any updates on the whereabouts of the ship. A few days later Dupuy was able to confirm to Ardouin that the *Geffrard* had been at St. Vincent (Cape Verde) as of October 29. Although comforted by this news, Ardouin went on to tell his colleague with respect to the lengthy delay that the ship "must have been really hindered, in one way or another, to find itself still there on this date." Updating Plésance at Port-au-Prince a few days later, a clearly perturbed Ardouin wrote "neither my colleague nor I have received any others [letters] from Commandant Jobert. It is such that we do not know for what reasons the steamer still found itself at St. Vincent at the end of October, but the fact remains that it was prepared to leave for St. Thomas, since it had supplied itself with coal. If it has not had any new hindrances, I trust that it must have arrived at this moment at Port-au-Prince."[32]

More than a month passed before Ardouin learned that after departing Madeira on September 23, Jobert was "forced" for some reason to turn the ship around and return to Funchal. The Lisbon merchant Seidel informed him that Jobert had then spent "24 days there before heading to St. Vincent." Ardouin told Plésance that he "could not conceive" why Jobert had not provided any updates on the hindrances causing the delay in the *Geffrard*'s progress.[33] What exactly had happened at Madeira?

Still unknown to Ardouin, Jobert had in fact committed an astounding breach of discipline and dereliction of his duties at Madeira that would lead to his eventual downfall. The matter in question was his two-week-long dalliance with a young and already married British woman at Funchal, whom he eventually spirited away with him on board the *Geffrard*. Jobert's courting of Theodosia Augusta Lloyd, commenced in the last days of September, resulted in a three-week postponement—not to mention the inevitable added expenses—of the departure of the Haitian steamer from the Portuguese island.

In 1864 details emerged about the seduction and elopement of Mrs. Lloyd when the aggrieved husband, Thomas C. Lloyd, sued for divorce for reasons of adultery in a court in England.[34] Several British newspapers reported a summary of the events.

> In 1853 he [Mr. T. C. Lloyd] married a Miss Gordon at Madeira, and afterwards lived with her in England, on the Continent, and in Madeira. In 1859 he took a house near Funchal, and they lived together there, near the residence of the respondent's mother, until October, 1860. In that month a Haytian war steamer came to Funchal, commanded by Captain Lionel Jobert, who introduced himself into society in the town as Count Epineul [*sic*]. He became acquainted, among other persons, with Mrs. Gordon and Mr. and Mrs. Lloyd, and visited at their houses. A fortnight or three weeks after his arrival Mrs. Lloyd left her home about eight o'clock one morning, saying that she was going to see her sister-in-law, went down to the landing-place on the beach, got on board a boat, belonging to the war steamer, and commanded by the first lieutenant, and was taken on board the steamer, which immediately afterwards went out of the harbour. She took with her a box, which one of the servants had carried to the beach for her, and before embarking she took off her bracelet and sent it to her mother. About three weeks afterwards her mother received a letter from her, saying that she was on board the steamer with Captain Jobert, and that she was in great distress of mind, and was sorry for what she had done.[35]

Although Mrs. Lloyd may have been conflicted by her decision to leave her family behind at Madeira, she would remain by Jobert's side for a full two years. What the youthful Haitian cadets must have thought on seeing their commandant bring her aboard for the continuation of the journey to Port-au-Prince one can only imagine. Here we also encounter Jobert's first full usage of the title Count d'Epineuil, a moniker he would grow fond of in later years.

Toward the end of October 1860, after a stop at Tenerife on the Canary Islands, the *Geffrard* finally arrived at St. Vincent, an island in the Portuguese Cape Verde archipelago where there was a long-established coaling station. Around November 1, well after the time when the gunboat originally had been expected to arrive at Port-au-Prince, it departed St. Vincent and commenced the Atlantic crossing to the Caribbean. After a further two weeks the ship arrived at Antigua around November 15, where it took on fresh coal. Four days later it was at St. Thomas, a fact Ardouin learned when he finally received a dispatch from Jobert to this effect in mid-December.[36] Why the ship took two more weeks for the short final leg from St. Thomas to Port-au-Prince, where it arrived on December 4, 1860, remained unexplained.

The *Feuille de Commerce* noted the arrival in Port-au-Prince of the apparently fully intact *Geffrard* and cited Jobert as praising the conduct of the cadets during the voyage. Subsequently, no further notices appeared referencing Jobert in his role as commandant of the ship and the Naval School. On December 11, the steamer received its official christening in the presence of President Geffrard and with the participation of an American steamer named the *Jasper*. The president, other officials, and a Haitian military band boarded the *Geffrard* for its tour of the harbor in the company of the US vessel. Jobert, however, was not mentioned in the account of the day's events, so it is unclear whether he participated in any capacity during the festivities.[37]

Jobert's behavior relative to Theodosia Lloyd in Madeira, his "violent" ejection from the ship there of the English engineer Forster, and his alleged poor treatment of some of the French seaman, one of the cadets, and a servant soon became known to the Haitian government. Based on testimony from the crew and passengers, Jobert was formally accused, together with his second Démost, of misconduct and asked to appear before a Haitian commission of inquiry, which he refused to do. At the close of these hearings around December 15, he was dismissed as Naval School Director and "honorary Commandant" of the *Geffrard*. As this situation also would reflect poorly on France, the French consul general in Port-au-Prince, Léonce Levraud, asked Haitian Secretary of State for War and the Navy Déjoie to try to publicly downplay the investigation and its aftermath. Déjoie agreed to work with the French authorities to settle the fallout of the *Geffrard* affair in an amicable manner.[38]

Jobert was now in deep trouble with the authorities who rued their engagement of this unreliable foreigner and contemplated criminal proceedings against him. The threat of arrest, trial, and detention in prison would have been unpalatable to say the least, and days after his dismissal Jobert made the decision to flee Haiti with Mrs. Lloyd. He succeeded in convincing Captain Joseph Potter of the US brig *Baltimore*, which had arrived in Port-au-Prince five days before the *Geffrard*, to take them on board and give them passage to New York. The *Baltimore* departed the capital in mid-December carrying only two passengers: French Navy Capt. and Mrs. "Geaubeure." The personal information on the manifest for Capt. "Geaubeure" and his "wife" tallies with that which was currently valid for the two of them (aside from a claim of French nationality for Mrs. Lloyd), and the misspelling may have been a deliberate ploy on Jobert's part vis-à-vis Captain Potter to confuse his identity. Haitian officials, however, were not unaware that "Mr. L. Jobert took refuge on board an American vessel with the woman abducted from Madeira, and they have had themselves transported to the United States." The ship arrived in New York City on January 7, 1861.[39]

One can imagine the disappointment and frustration of Minister Ardouin back in Paris when the news of Jobert's behavior finally reached him more than a month after the fact: "The facts that you pointed out to me on the unimaginable conduct of this captain explains the silence which he kept towards me during his long stops, be it at Madeira or at Cape Verde. However I have good grounds for being not the least bit surprised by his refusal to present his accounts to the Government to which he is answerable."[40] He went on to declare to Plésance in a further dispatch that "I appreciate the motives which have caused the Government to dismiss Mr. Jobert whose conduct is not only reprehensible, but punishable under the laws." Nor did Ardouin shy away from accusing Jobert of fraud.[41]

The Haitian minister to France had invested a great deal of time and trust in the French sea captain, only to be betrayed and embarrassed by his antics. Now it was his duty to officially inform the French government about the circumstances surrounding the dismissal of a no-longer-to-be-trusted French subject from the service of the Haitian republic. On February 4, 1861 Ardouin wrote to French Foreign Minister Thouvenel, who it will be recalled did not seem favorably disposed to Jobert when they met in August 1860. "If I bring these deeds to your attention, Mr. Minister, it is because I have good reason to believe that Mr. L. Jobert may possibly have the intention to come to France in order to complain about the conduct of the Haitian government in his regard, or to agitate through scandalous ways to try to tarnish the reputation of this government."[42]

In the aftermath of the Jobert affair, most of the original French crewmen engaged for service on the ship had requested and been granted the annulment of their contracts with Haiti, returning soon afterward to France. Ardouin and the authorities in Port-au-Prince meanwhile would be kept busy for several months dealing with the issues and costs arising from the cancelation of these crew contracts, as well as accounting for the remaining bank drafts drawn by Jobert on the Haitian government to cover coaling expenses, and in Ardouin's estimation, to line his pockets. Determined to avoid a similar occurrence, the government would not allow the *22 Décembre* to stop at any port on its maiden voyage to Haiti.[43]

Fortunately for Ardouin's reputation, the *Geffrard* had been guided safely by Jobert to Haiti, arriving intact and fully outfitted. Despite the delay in its arrival it was able to go into patrol service immediately, although with a new provisional Haitian captain and largely local crew. The new captain was Louis Chassaing, a French subject of Haitian origin, to whom the Geffrard regime granted nationality on taking the post. The vessel stayed in service for seven more years. After President Geffrard abandoned turbulent Haiti for Jamaica in March 1867, rebels opposing the government of Sylvain Salnave scuttled the *Geffrard* to prevent its capture at Petit-Goave on September 20, 1868, the same day that Salnave's forces fired on and sank the *22 Décembre*.[44]

Added to the abuse of his authority that resulted in Jobert's dismissal, two other serious situations also may have been in play. First, Jobert appears to have left some Haitian business partners in the lurch, and avoiding their wrath may also account, at least in part, for his hasty departure from Haiti.[45] Second, and perhaps much more serious, were intimations that soon surfaced that Jobert had been in contact with the former right-hand man of the deposed Emperor Soulouque, Count Damien Delva. In October of 1859 Delva and his son were tried for organizing an assassination plot the previous month against President Geffrard. The attempt failed but resulted in the death of Geffrard's daughter. Verdicts of death for both were announced by a Haitian tribunal, but could not be carried out as the Delvas had been exiled to the safety of France following the fall of Soulouque.[46] On February 1, 1861, Ardouin came into possession of a thick envelope sent by Jobert from New York on January 19, and addressed to Count Delva via the Haitian Embassy in Paris. Ardouin could not bring himself to open the parcel, instead returning it to the director of the Paris post office while explaining that Delva was persona non grata in Haiti and therefore both Ardouin and the Legation could not forward the item to him. Without opening the envelope, Ardouin could not be certain why Jobert would have openly posted a parcel to an avowed enemy of the Geffrard regime via the Haitian Legation in Paris, but nevertheless Ardouin assumed some type of connivance between Jobert and Delva, hinting at the possibility that they may have met earlier when Jobert visited Paris several times in the spring and summer of 1860. In his letter of February 7, 1861 to his superior, the Haitian Foreign Secretary Victorin Plésance, Ardouin wrote of the same worries about Jobert attempting to extract revenge that he had expressed to Thouvenel three days earlier: "The Secretary of State for the Navy and yourself have sent to me only the *Summary* of the operations of the commission of inquest with regard to the complaints drawn up against L. Jobert, but it could come about that I will have need of the *corresponding copy* of these details, if this man comes to France and publishes defamatory articles, or brochures against the government, which would give me the right to proceedings before the [local] courts."[47]

Two days later, in a letter mainly concerning an unrelated affair involving Captain Antonio Pelletier using the US ship *William* for slave trading, an irritated Foreign Secretary Plésance reminded the United States Commercial Agent in Port-au-Prince, Joseph N. Lewis, that Haiti had followed protocol in dealing with Lionel Jobert's flight from justice: "Very recently you have had a striking evidence of the extreme anxiety which causes the government to observe and prescribe circumspection whenever its agents are under the painful necessity of proceeding against foreigners. When the arrest of Mr. Lionel Jobert, a French subject concealed on board an American vessel, against whom we had very great causes of complaint, was under consideration, did not the proper authorities officially apprise the commercial agent of the United States of their intentions?"[48] Yet the Jobert episode did not have any further ramifications for relations between Haiti and the United States. The Haitian government, treading lightly with their powerful hemispheric neighbor that had yet to diplomatically recognize the Afro-Haitian nation, soon dropped its pursuit of Jobert and turned its attention to more pressing matters.

Lionel Jobert's promising Haitian adventure had reached a sudden and ignominious end. His best-laid plans and his leadership aura had been ruined by his selfish arrogance and seriously flawed decision-making. Analogous to the trickster Sisyphus, Jobert's transitory deception of the Haitian government led to his downfall. Sisyphus was a king whose ruse nevertheless bought him many more years of life; Lionel Jobert was commandant of the Haitian Naval School whose gambit while piloting the *Geffrard* afforded him little more than a three-month adventurous high. The eloquent words of his January 1860 speech thanking the Haitian authorities for their wisdom in placing their trust in the hands of a foreigner now rang hollow. His future naval career in France was also in tatters as his behavior on the *Geffrard* and his summary dismissal by the Haitian authorities were soon to be entered on his French seaman's record. Yet true to his resilient nature, he did not waste any time in reinventing himself and looking elsewhere for fame and fortune. Less than a month after narrowly escaping the clutches of the Geffrard regime, Jobert had arrived in New York City, now styling himself as Lionel Jobert d'Epineuil, with Mrs. Lloyd as "Madam d'Epineuil." Civil war was only a few months away in the United States, and Jobert soon began exploring ways to turn the exigencies of that budding conflict to his advantage.

Chapter 3

Atlantic Sisyphus

On the frigid Philadelphia afternoon of February 10, 1861, the commercial sailing ship *John Trucks* succumbed to an encounter with floating ice and sank into the Delaware River at the Arch Street wharf. Two men were missing, including the ship's French-born steward. A diver found the steward's body by feeling his way through the murky water into the submerged cabin until his hands came in contact with the ill-fated man.[1] Workers subsequently raised and repaired the *John Trucks* rather than surrender the craft to the sea. As the American Civil War began to dismantle the nation, the Union chartered the renovated ship for duty. For almost the entire month of January and into early February 1862, the *John Trucks* carried the Fifty-Third New York Regiment, a volunteer unit established the previous summer, as part of Brigadier General Ambrose Burnside's mission to capture Roanoke Island from Confederate control. Commanding the Fifty-Third New York was another Frenchman who had arrived in New York City a month before the *John Trucks* all but disappeared into the Delaware: Lionel Jobert. Nature beleaguered the vessel once again during the Roanoke campaign, while Jobert's military career foundered in a maelstrom of his own making.

Breathlessly, Jobert had evaded incarceration in Haiti. But as the winter of 1861 transformed into spring, the erstwhile naval school director found himself jobless in America, and accompanied by a woman not his wife. He would need to establish at least the appearance of respectability if he were to succeed in the United States. Up to this point, Jobert had sparingly used d'Epineuil as a surname. Partly as a means to distance his identity from the fiasco in Haiti, and partly to impress Americans with the grandiloquence of the decidedly French name d'Epineuil, St. Edme Jobert's son resuscitated the ancestrally ephemeral appellation eschewed by his father and grandfather. In the United States, Lionel Jobert d'Epineuil wore his name as a credential—derived from noble background, should anyone ask—and as a marker of European breeding. Indeed, his signature of choice became "Lionel J. d'Epineuil," showing he favored the name that frequently tested Americans' skill at orthography and elocution over the more pedestrian *Jobert*.

The French-born population in the United States had doubled during the 1850s, reaching nearly 110,000 by 1860. Thus, life in cosmopolitan New York City, with over 8,000 French inhabitants, would be an easy adjustment for Lionel J. d'Epineuil. Among the city's residents lived Baron Régis de Trobriand. Born to General Baron Joseph de Trobriand in 1816 near Tours in France, the aristocratic Régis already had led a comfortable life in America by the time Jobert arrived, corresponding with the likes of Alphonse de Lamartine and coediting the *Courrier des États-Unis* in New York. De Trobriand stood firmly integrated into New York's elite society with his wife Mary Mason Jones, the daughter of a former president of Chemical Bank. Lionel aspired to such a life of recognition and leisure. Fittingly, he and Theodosia took up residence at the newly built Albemarle Hotel on Broadway and Twenty-Fourth Street.[2] The toney district surrounding the Albemarle in Manhattan was an ideal setting for the bicultural Jobert to make influential contacts that might prove useful. Confident in his ability to navigate English- and French-speaking circles effortlessly, d'Epineuil's New York persona became that of a cultured continental with a long military career, a gentleman of station dedicated to the Union cause. Haiti was best forgotten.

What Lionel Jobert could not ignore, however, was his need for income, and the outbreak of civil war in mid-April presented opportunities for those savvy enough to find—or create—them. While Lionel pondered the national crisis, his father, Louis St. Edme Jobert, died in Caen on June 3, 1861 at the age of sixty-five.[3] The elder Jobert left behind his household of three young children under ten years of age and his second wife, Emilie. Following St. Edme's death, Emilie cooperated in compiling an inventory of her husband's belongings. The inventory logged the existence of several documents related to Lionel's debts in Caen. Nothing indicated the amount of money owed, who the creditors were, or if the debts had been settled. But the existence of the documents shows that Lionel's father, and the notary in charge of creating the inventory, felt the issue significant enough to make a record of it.[4] Jobert's two visits to Caen during 1860, and his eagerness for pay advances while in the service of Haiti, may well have been related to attending to said debts. To avoid further such financial worries, Lionel J. d'Epineuil had to make the American war pay.

One of d'Epineuil's earliest contacts in New York was Massachusetts-born John Clark Merriam. Both men were the same age, and both had been educated in France. What is more, d'Epineuil had enough familiarity with ship engines to share Merriam's interest in engineering. Merriam had been the corresponding secretary of the American Engineers' Association that had formally organized in March of the previous year; he also served as editor of the technical journal *American Engineer*. *American Engineer* began in February 1860 as an eight-page journal emphasizing the American Engineers' Association's interest in steam engines for locomotives and steamboats. Merriam strove to make the publication a professional journal, and the association courted New York's mechanical engineering elite as members. At the end of 1860, however, none of the officers or committee chairmen of the American Engineers' Association were practicing mechanical engineers, with the exception of Merriam. Merriam advertised in the June 1861 issues of *Scientific American* that his journal had expanded to sixteen pages; he thereby hoped to attract subscribers to keep the struggling publication afloat.[5] D'Epineuil could relate. He, too, had to exude confidence while personally fretting over how to provide for himself and his consort. As the fortunes of his friend's *American Engineer* began to ebb, d'Epineuil launched his plan for the Union's effort and for himself.

Even as the memory of his time in the West Indies faded, d'Epineuil scarcely could fail to appreciate the parallel between the Haitian political upset that had provided him an opening at the naval school and the civil warfare into which the United States had plunged itself in the spring of 1861. D'Epineuil took the pulse of New York and saw that the war had made Northern businessmen increasingly anxious over Confederate piracy aimed at commercial shipping. Here again was the chance to seize opportunity amid a society in flux. In early June he submitted a plan to the Board of Underwriters in New York.[6] Jobert proposed to establish a "'Union Volunteer Squadron'" of ships to patrol the coast and eliminate Southern depredations on Northern merchant vessels. Such a patrol would allow the regular navy to more effectively deploy its forces to blockade the South—part of the wartime constricting encirclement known as the "anaconda plan." The sailors were to be trained in the methods of the French navy as an amphibious unit; d'Epineuil naturally would assume that responsibility. If the Board of Underwriters financed this proposition, then the government only needed to pay the sailors for their service in the same manner as any volunteer regiment, and the profitable trade of commercial enterprise would be safe. Jobert summarized the plan's value to all concerned in a June 18 letter to the *New York Times*: "I will conclude by stating that the squadron which I propose to form would be a new creation *of undisputable use*. I hope that I have shown it to be so; and I cannot too earnestly call the attention of the friends of the Union to this important subject, and to an act which would combine patriotism with private interest."[7]

D'Epineuil's case for an ocean police failed to motivate New York's commercial interests to fund the project. But from John C. Merriam's Brooklyn residence at 1 Garden Street, an undaunted Jobert drafted a handwritten proposal to the United States House of Representatives for the development of his Union Volunteer Squadron. D'Epineuil's audience now was the federal government, not just one state, and he pitched his plan accordingly.

> At this time when the political horizon is charged with lowering clouds, when *England*, the great naval power tacitly encouraged, by her ambiguous conduct, the culpable efforts of the rebellion & the arming of privateers (which might, more justly, be termed *pirates*,) when *Spain*, availing herself of our troubles, has taken possession by surprise of two thirds of one of the most flourishing islands of the West Indian Seas, *S. Domingue*, & tends to resume her rank as a great naval power by striving to regain her former influence in the *New world*, it appears to the undersigned that the *most vigourous* efforts should be made for the internal conservation of the "*glorious Union*" & for placing a limit to the ambitious aims of its external enemies.[8]

More so than in the proposal to the Board of Underwriters in New York, d'Epineuil emphasized the international threat in his presentation to the House, painting a picture of urgent need to protect the nation from all foes foreign and domestic. Perhaps for calculated effect, d'Epineuil dated his petition July 4, 1861 to stir patriotic enthusiasm for his plan among the House members. D'Epineuil wrote in some detail about what would be required for his Union Volunteer Squadron, the creation of which he suggested should be overseen by a committee specifically charged with that task. The force should consist of three to five vessels manned by a crew of 120 each. The men recruited should have already five years of service at sea, and the officers to be accepted by examination or suitable certification. Each man would receive a bag of strong sail cloth at a cost of $48 to $50 dollars—with that expense deducted from his pay—containing the various uniforms and clothing articles he would need. D'Epineuil specified the tonnage and engine horsepower of each vessel; drew designs for the men's coats and hats as well as a sketch of a flag for the foremast to represent the volunteer squadron; and compiled a list of costs totaling $346,975 for a squadron of five vessels, a figure consistent with the projected cost of $350,000–$360,000 he outlined in the *New York Times* article. Not least on the out-of-work Jobert's mind was the officers' compensation, as he added that the "term of the commissions delivered to the officers of the Union Volunteer Squadron will be of three years (more if necessary) after the expiration of which their welfare will be attended to *amply* & in a manner worthy of the government of the United States."[9]

Jobert's recent Haitian experience found reflection in his plan for a Union Volunteer Squadron. He had opened his January 1860 speech to the inspection commission that reviewed the progress of the naval school by commenting on the dilapidated state of the Haitian fleet. Similarly, allowing that American forts could quickly be brought up to snuff, d'Epineuil cautioned that the US Navy's "*fleet*, is it in an equally satisfactory state? The undersigned begs respectfully & *professionally* to state that it is *not*!" In both cases, Jobert positioned himself as the agent of positive change. As with his Haitian cadets, the men of the Union Volunteer Squadron would receive theoretical instruction in addition to practical experience, which Jobert would oversee. Last, while advancing himself as a driving force for needed improvement, Jobert was acutely aware of the value of showing deference to higher authority. In his Haiti speech, that meant compliments to President Geffrard and Admiral Lafond. In his proposal to the US House, d'Epineuil underscored (literally) that the volunteer squadron would be "at the *complete* & *entire disposal* of the naval department" and added a note in the section covering enlistment and pay of the men that stated "all these regulations are simply projects submitted to the decision and approval of the honorable members of the committee."[10]

Despite the comparisons between his role as commander of the Haitian Naval School and his proposed role of captain of the Union Volunteer Squadron in the United States, d'Epineuil scrupulously avoided—with good reason—any mention of his experience in Haiti. Anticipating the US government's concern as to his capacity to lead the squadron, d'Epineuil wrote that he "has the honor to hold himself quite at your service, Gentlemen, to explain to you, *by word of mouth* [emphasis added], all his plans with regard to the proposal he has made & also for the purpose of certifying his identity & his competency in the naval profession which he has exercised for seventeen years." Throughout his time in the United States, d'Epineuil would remain purposefully vague as to the specific nature of that professional experience, relying on his polished social skills to deflect any pointed investigation into his background. He signed the petition to the House of Representatives as "Lionel Jobert d'Epineuil, naval officer," and used as his address "Capn. Lionel Jobert d'Epineuil, nav. off.—1 Garden St. Brooklyn N.Y."[11] One man sufficiently impressed with d'Epineuil, Elijah Ward, a Democratic congressman from New York City, submitted the volunteer squadron plan to the House where it was referred on July 12 to the Committee on Naval Affairs.[12]

Thus, by the start of summer 1861, just six months after arriving in the United States, Lionel Jobert had begun to make a name for himself in New York and in Washington. Nine days after d'Epineuil's petition went to the House Committee on Naval Affairs, the Confederates scored their victory at Manassas on July 21. Unnerved, the Union needed to regroup and increase its forces. But Congress was not disposed to allocate funds for d'Epineuil's volunteer coastal squadron scheme. Certainly a newly arrived foreigner bemoaning the state of the American fleet and proposing that he come to the rescue must have bent some noses and prompted some scowls in the United States Navy. D'Epineuil had proposed to train and lead men who could serve at sea as well as on land, expecting that dual purposing to add appeal to his plan for an ocean police. Doubtless to his dismay, on August 5 in Washington, by authority of Secretary of War Simon Cameron, Lionel J. d'Epineuil was formally inscribed in the service of the United States to raise a volunteer *army* unit.[13] D'Epineuil's experience had been maritime, and commanding a purely land force presented a challenge that he would struggle to meet. He was not, however, in a position to turn down the best opportunity available to him. Forced outside of his comfort zone, Jobert clung to the agreement that he could at least organize, outfit, and equip his regiment in the French manner, specifically as a regiment of flamboyant Zouaves.[14]

Wasting no time on his return to New York, the newly minted Colonel d'Epineuil enrolled two lieutenants on the same day that his name was added to the rolls—August 5—in his eponymous regiment: the d'Epineuil Zouaves. One of those two men was John C. Merriam. Letting go of *American Engineer*, Merriam became first lieutenant of d'Epineuil's Company E and the regimental quartermaster. Staten Island's *Richmond County Gazette* would gush with professional pride on this last point when reporting on the regiment: "the crowning feature of their success is—we modestly announce it—in having an editor for quartermaster!"[15] The other man, Thaddeus C. Ferris, became second lieutenant of Company I. Ferris had more in common with d'Epineuil than the latter probably knew: not two years before the war, Ferris had been dismissed from the New York

City police force on a seduction charge. Securing space for his headquarters at 86 Cedar Street in New York City, d'Epineuil set to work forming his regiment and benefitted from a financial contribution from New York City's Union Defense Committee for organizing expenses.[16]

Position and prestige were Jobert's ambition, and he was determined to use his regiment to attain both. His forte was making a good first impression, and his d'Epineuil Zouaves did just that with their dramatic uniforms. Brooks Brothers of New York created the ensemble: a red fez cap, dark blue jacket, light-blue baggy trousers—all with yellow accents (see figure 3.1). Recruiting advertisements made the uniform a key selling

Figure 3.1. William P. Bosworth, private, Co. H, Fifty-Third New York Volunteers in Zouave uniform. William was twenty years old when this photograph was taken in 1861. Author's collection.

point. One ad placed as far away as Maine touted the d'Epineuil Zouaves's as the "handsomest uniform in the service." A broadside in Philadelphia heralded "the Splendid Regiment of COL. D'EPINEUIL . . . Look at the IMPOSING UNIFORM---furnished at once" (see figure 3.2). A statement made by the Fifty-Third's Company A Captain W. W. Armstrong while recruiting in Plattsburg, New York also bore indirect testimony to the striking

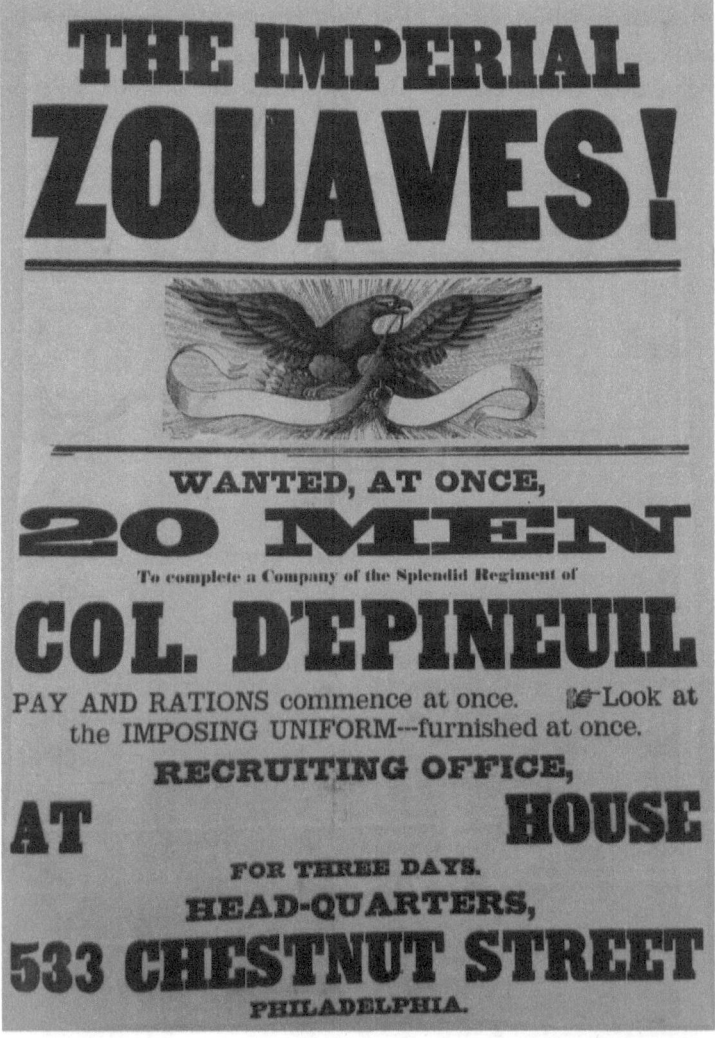

Figure 3.2. Recruiting poster for Colonel d'Epineuil's regiment. Library Company of Philadelphia.

uniform: "Some mischievously inclined person having spread the report that the uniform worn by the 'D'Epineuil Zouaves,' now recruiting here, is used as a means of entraping men to enlist, I beg through the columns of your valuable journal to contradict so ridiculous a statement." Seeing d'Epineuil's men in their uniform, one reporter observed, "it is a dress which gives to the human figure a barbaric picturesqueness, and a grace, the opposite of the stiffness of all uniforms of the Prussian type." The colonel spared no expense to look the part of a Zouave commander: Brooks Brothers charged him a substantial forty dollars for his dress suit (uniform) alone.[17]

Cutting a dashing figure certainly appealed to many recruits, but d'Epineuil also felt keenly the need to portray his regiment's leadership as an experienced group. The earliest articles in various newspapers, with the colonel himself as their most likely source, printed d'Epineuil's background as long on service in the French military. "Several officers of experience in the French Army have already offered themselves to Col. d'Epineuil," reported the *New York Times*, "who is himself fresh from the French service, in which he has been for the last seventeen years."[18] At thirty-one years of age, his seventeen years of experience stretched back to age fourteen; d'Epineuil accounted for this by including his years as a student in military school. He again emphasized his "17 years of service experience" in a letter to James Lesley Jr., the chief clerk of the War Department, avoiding mention of the sizable gaps away from maritime involvement during 1845–1846 and 1853–1855.[19] The *New York Herald* informed readers that "Colonel Lionel d'Epineuil is of one of the first families of France, the Counts d'Epineuil being well known as military officers."[20] Skilled at manipulating half-truths and selectively omitting elements of his background, d'Epineuil crafted a public image of himself that legitimized his colonelcy.

The colonel's choice of staff bolstered his regiment's reputation for qualified leadership. Lieutenant Colonel Joseph A. Viguier de Monteil indeed was a military veteran. Viguier de Monteil, born in Toulon, France in 1818, began his military service in 1835 at age seventeen. He reached his highest rank of lieutenant in a marine artillery regiment in November 1843. Disgusted with Louis Napoleon's power grab in the coup of 1851, and facing disciplinary action for his political activism, Viguier de Monteil left his native land, settling in the United States in 1853. He earned a living by teaching French in New York City.[21] D'Epineuil enrolled Monteil in his regiment on August 16, one month before Jean Baptiste Cantel reported for duty as major. Also d'Epineuil's senior by nearly a decade, Cantel had spent thirteen years in the French Army, subsequently coming to the United

States in 1855. James Lesley already was on friendly terms with d'Epineuil when Lesley introduced Cantel to d'Epineuil in a letter of September 14, 1861. Lesley asked d'Epineuil to avail his regiment of Cantel's services as a personal favor to Lesley. The colonel complied with the request, noting that Cantel had reported for duty on September 16; he formally enrolled nine days later.[22] As regimental first surgeon, the colonel warmly recommended Henry J. Phillips to New York's Surgeon General Dr. S. Oakley Vanderpool. The first sentence out of d'Epineuil's pen conveyed Dr. Phillips's experience: "I have the honor to introduce you [sic] *Dr. Phillips*, late surgeon in the *Crimean* army, medical staff." In a follow-up letter, d'Epineuil could not resist embellishing his own record, stating Dr. Phillips had "served with me in the Crimean war."[23] Both d'Epineuil and Lesley prevailed on New York Governor Edwin Morgan to accept Phillips's candidacy. "I take great pleasure in presenting to you Doct. Henry John Phillips," wrote Lesley, "whom my friend Col. D'Epineuil desires specially to have as Regimental Surgeon for his regiment." Morgan endorsed Lesley's letter, directing it to be respectfully and favorably referred to Dr. Vanderpool.[24] For recent experience with war, the colonel relied on the leadership of officers such as Thaddeus C. Ferris, James H. Sperling, Ray T. Gordon, Augustus H. Thomas, William H. Burgess, George F. Chester, and Charles W. Dustan, a group who already had seen action at Manassas as privates during a three-month enlistment in the 71st New York State Militia.[25]

In September, the state of New York took over supervision of the volunteer regiments that the War Department had authorized to be raised, and moved to bring order to the unsystematic process. Volunteer regiments had to pass the scrutiny of a Board of State Military Examiners, and undermanned regiments were to be folded into other units. All classes of volunteers, including the d'Epineuil Zouaves, were to report to the encampment at Scarsdale, New York for training; Egbert Viele, brigadier general of US Volunteers, had been commanding the camp.[26] One reporter captured the reaction of the regimental colonels to this transfer from federal to state oversight: "With a class of would-be colonels, staff and line officers, who have been presumptious [sic] enough to assume positions for which they are qualified neither by nature or education, the late transfer of the volunteer organization from the United States to the State Department is extremely unpopular, and is considered an unjust interference on the part of the governor with the patriotic volunteer movement. It is almost needless to say that these unwholesome *fungi* will be speedily squelched."[27] Colonel d'Epineuil's reaction was no exception. During the first week of September, from his new Manhattan headquarters at 66 White Street, a near-frantic d'Epineuil alternated between imploring and arm-twisting his friend James Lesley to get assurances that he could maintain a measure of independence that he felt due him under the original understanding with the War Department.

> I had, previously, made respectfully to you the two objections I had to my transfer under General *Viele* [*sic*] orders: 1° I was afraid to not be let free of organizing my regiment under our special Zouave tactics. 2° I was afraid to see, if my organization was not entirely complete in a moment, very possible, in which General *Viele* would receive sudden marching orders to see my companies taken by him & reversed in completion of other organizations.
>
> . . . you were kind enough to give me your *word of honor* that you considered my organization of true real Zouave as to produce a so good effect that I was to be sure that in Scarsdale Camp I would be under the *direct authority* of the War Department & would never be disturbed of my special organizing *without your permission*. . . .
>
> [Under a new order] I am to submit myself *though depending* directly from *you*, viz, from the *War Department*, though being a *very special* organization, to the orders of Governor Morgan whose talents in military matters I am far from denying but who having never heard of my regiment before will, very likely, oblige me to follow the regular American tactics & will break, with the best intentions, the *special object* of the *special authority* granted to *me* by *you* for a *very special organization* he can not know—& for which you have already made large & unusual expenses.
>
> In my distress, sir, I beg you to tell me what I have to do.
>
> . . . Send me authority to remain under your *direct orders* in my actual camp, Staten Island, *costing nothing to government!*[28]

Lesley's intercession on behalf of d'Epineuil, and the latter's persistence, paid off. Four days later the colonel received a personal letter of introduction from Viele to New York Governor Morgan: "This will be handed to you by Col. Lionel J. d'Epineuil of a Zouave Regt. which bears his name—and which was especially accepted by the Secretary of War, as I am informed by the Col., to introduce the true French Zouave organization & drill. Commending Col. D'Epineuil to your excellency's especial favor."[29]

D'Epineuil's missive not only provides a chronology of events, but it also reveals his emphatic desire to maintain the special French Zouave character of his unit. That character derived mainly from the French background of most of the field and staff officers, and from the regiment's uniform and accoutrements. In addition to Lieutenant Colonel Viguier de Monteil and Major Cantel, the colonel himself enrolled both Adjutant Victor Vifquain, who was born in Belgium to French parents, and Jules Dubreuil, whom d'Epineuil requested as his Assistant Surgeon. Aristide Pierard, who had recently joined the clergy at St. Vincent's Church in Manhattan, enrolled on August 10 as d'Epineuil's regimental chaplain.[30] To complement the eye-catching Zouave uniform, d'Epineuil insisted on an authentic French knapsack. Sounding a bit exasperated by his friend the colonel, James Lesley penned the following letter to Governor Morgan:

> I find that Col. D'Epineuil of the D'Epineuil Zouaves appears to be under a misapprehension with regard to his position as an independent regiment. I have written him to say that by General Order No 78, you alone are authorized to "organize and place in service" all independent regiments—of course *his own included*. Under that order, and relying upon your well known judgments & experience in public business, the [War] Department has entrusted to you the "equipment" of regiments as part of that duty.
>
> I thank you very warmly for the interest which you have taken in this regiment, which I think will be an honor to the State of New York. Colonel D'Epineuil appears to believe that, in order to make the regiment a perfect success, he should have the 'French Regulation Knapsacks,' and equipments to suit. If you deem it consistent with your own judgment, I should feel obliged if you would aid Col. D'Epineuil in this matter. If you think you have not authority to pay the extra price for the French Regulation Pattern, I leave it for your own judgment to decide whether you could not pay the same price as that paid for the American pattern—allowing Col. D'Epineuil to make up the difference himself.[31]

George Bliss Jr., an aide-de-camp on Governor Morgan's staff at the New York City Depot of Volunteers, frequently reported to the state's Adjutant General Thomas Hillhouse on the circumstances surrounding the various regiments in New York City. Bliss revealed that Lesley was no less subject than everyone else to d'Epineuil's fretting over the all-important knapsack. "Burnside will arm D'Epineuil but wants we should give him everything else, including his peculiar French knapsack with which he is partially furnished. Burnside says the Gen. Govt will of course repay their cost." Ten days later, Bliss wrote again: "D'Epineuil is still anxious about the expensive knapsacks he showed you when here."[32] For Colonel d'Epineuil, image was everything. Even certificates recognizing of each deserving soldier "that he has been diligent in his duty thus far" bore the title "Franco-American Regiment."[33] Rather than a manifestation of patriotism for his country of birth, the French Zouave motif was what d'Epineuil hoped would make his namesake regiment stand out from the others and bring him the acclaim he sought.

To be sure, the d'Epineuil Zouaves was not the only French-led or Zouave-themed regiment to participate in the war. One foreign traveler in New York City observed in late July 1861 that newly forming units reflected a potpourri of European connections, but the most popular were the Zouaves. "Everything is à la zouave here, the fashions of women . . . sweets . . . soup; it's a rage."[34] Indeed, the Independent Battalion led by Frenchman Felix Confort and known as the *Enfants Perdus* (Lost Children), Elmer Ellsworth's Zouaves, and Rush Hawkins's Zouaves were but three of the regiments that hailed from New York alone. D'Epineuil's military command in the United States had begun in parallel with that of Régis de Trobriand. Like d'Epineuil, De Trobriand descended from a titled French family; as with d'Epineuil, De Trobriand assumed the colonelcy of a New York Volunteer Infantry: the Fifty-Fifth Regiment, or *Gardes Lafayette*. As De Trobriand's regiment received orders to decamp from their quarters near New Dorp, Staten Island at the end of August 1861, Colonel d'Epineuil and his officers began assembling their regiment at the nearby community of Clifton. Even observers in Europe took note of both men's participation in the American Civil War.[35] Lionel J. d'Epineuil must have allowed himself the reverie of envisioning the soldierly grandeur these mirrored careers would achieve.

The large majority of men who became d'Epineuil Zouaves, however, were not of French extraction.[36] French names did infuse the rolls during the first month of the regiment's existence. From August 5 through September 4, sixty-three individuals enlisted, thirty-six of whom became part of Captain Ernest Fiston's Company E, and just under two-thirds of them bore French surnames. When Company E was completed, some 53.1 percent of the men came from a French background. Nevertheless, no other company came close to having that many; in fact, five of the regiment's companies had fewer than ten men with French names. Companies A, F, and H, which had the highest number of French enlistees next to Company E, had 17.5, 15.6, and 12.7 percent, respectively, French or French-American men. Captain Franklin W. Willard of Company B seems to have avoided French enlistees, placing a recruiting ad for "Men Wanted—80 Young Men, American and English, between the ages of 19 and 30, to complete Co. B, d'Epenuel [sic] Zouaves."[37] Of the ninety men for whom the place of birth is indicated in the surviving "Descriptive Book" for Company D, twenty-seven, or 25.5 percent of the company as a whole, were foreign-born, with Ireland accounting for half (fourteen) of them; only two came from France. In Company F's Descriptive Book, thirty-six were born abroad, with one third of them (twelve) born in France; the foreign-born made up 37.5 percent of the company overall.[38] The *New York Daily Tribune* estimated in mid-November that "Col. d'Epineuil may possibly have 150 of his countrymen in his command, but not more, we should judge."[39] Surveying the entire regiment, Company D's Captain George Chester averred in the latter part of December 1861 that the "Regiment is American it containing no more than eighty Frenchmen."[40] Assessing the available evidence, approximately thirteen percent of the regiment came from French families. The d'Epineuil Zouaves were more French-led and Zouave-clad than French themselves.

From August until the last day of December 1861, the d'Epineuil Zouaves mustered in nearly 1,100 men. The large majority—ninety-four percent—came from New York state, and seventy-six percent of the overall total mustered in at New York City. To fill in the ranks, recruiters culled men from out of state as well. Thirty-six enlistees came from Philadelphia; nineteen from Boston; and a collective few came from Maryland, Delaware, and Connecticut. In Company F, seven of the foreign-born men were professional soldiers before joining the d'Epineuil Zouaves, but the regiment was unquestionably a volunteer force made up of working people from a wide variety of occupations. Some men made shoes, hats, boots, watches, pianos, carriages, harnesses, trunks, bricks, and cigars; some molded iron, brass, or sugar; other jobs included engraver, doctor, saddler, carver, pastry cook, musician, butcher, farmer, boiler builder, carpenter, woolen finisher, painter, plumber, stone cutter, gardener, mechanic, teamster, baker, wood turner, peddler, stevedore, machinist, jeweler, brakeman, grocer, spinner, varnisher, caulker, and hostler. In Company D, clerk was the most common occupation (twenty-one of them) followed by farmer (ten); together they made up 29.2 percent of the company. The majority of the men were skilled laborers—not surprising given that recruiting efforts centered in New York City.[41]

Why did these men enlist? Among the myriad reasons one chose to fight, many Northern soldiers felt they were supporting the rule of law that secession contravened. The resident French population in the United States reflected local American sentiment. If in Louisiana the French inhabitants held that the South had to defend its liberty in the conflict,[42] Baron de Trobriand fought "for a great political principle, the Federal Union which can alone save this country from ruin." In the same vein, Lieutenant Colonel Monteil of the d'Epineuil Zouaves avowed, "I have always been a republican and am most anxious to distinguish myself in the actual war to help to preserve the Union and save from ruin the greatest nation of the Globe." In Captain Fiston's Company E while encamped on Staten Island, the soldiers evinced another motivation to serve, amassing a heap of construction debris at the base of which bore the French inscription "Tomb of slavery."[43] French enlistees also sought to honor French military tradition;[44] not for nothing did de Trobriand's Fifty-Fifth New York Regiment maintain the name Gardes Lafayette after the famed Frenchman who had helped the American colonies win independence during the Revolutionary War. One commentator noted this pride when observing the Fifty-Third New York,

> [When off duty, the Frenchman] brushes his clothes, pipe-clays his belts, polishes his buttons, cleans his gaiters, and blackens his shoes, in preparation for the call to drill or parade, while his Anglo-Saxon companions lounge listlessly about, play cards, or lie in their soiled clothes until the last minute, and then spring to their places in sorry personal plight. The Frenchmen in the d'Epineuil Zouaves are as easily recognizable from these regional peculiarities as those we have seen in other regiments, and in going through the camp yesterday we could not help remarking and regretting that the tidiest men about Camp Lesley were of foreign birth.[45]

French people who lived in the United States represented a cross-section of the population in France; thus, like Irish immigrants, their reasons for joining America's civil war varied widely. Irish immigrants explained their participation in terms of both their Irish and American heritage, grateful to their adopted nation for exile from their troubled yet cherished homeland. Demonstrating allegiance to the Union through enlisting also buttressed claims to future American citizenship, rejecting the dictum that anyone born a British subject stayed one for life. If some French volunteers fought for ideological reasons, some cared little about politics, simply getting caught up in the early war euphoria, proud to sport a new uniform, or eager to earn a soldier's pay. Each of these men had his reasons for joining, ignoring Napoleon III's decree that forbade any Frenchman in France or elsewhere to enlist on either side of the American conflict.[46] It was up to the former Commander of the Haitian Naval School and his officers to turn a disparate group of foreign-born and American working-class civilians into a fighting force that would help him reach the social summit held by the likes of Baron de Trobriand in the United States.

Chapter 4

A Second Ascent

The Rise of d'Epineuil's Zouaves

Colonel d'Epineuil's volunteers trained for a little over two and a half months on Staten Island at Camp Lesley, named for his friend in the War Department. Corresponding in French with Lesley in mid-August, d'Epineuil fawned, "I believe that it would not displease you too much in naming this camp *Lesley Camp*, in recognition of the kindness with which you have greatly facilitated my steps at your ministry. It would be an honor from you to my regiment, you may be assured." Lesley assented to the honor.[1] "Camp Lesley," observed a newspaperman, "where the d'Epineuils are located, is near the third landing on Staten Island. The ground has a gentle slope to a broad level below, which is used as a parade. From the summit of the slope a fine stretch of landscape with the waters of the bay as a background, is presented to the eye."[2] To this picturesque spot halfway through September the regiment had gathered together 198 mustered-in men and an additional forty-five enlistees. Recruiters employed considerable license as they strove to increase the ranks. The regiment's ad in the *Buffalo Daily Courier*, for instance, boasted that the d'Epineuil Zouaves "already numbers six hundred men, half of whom have seen service in European Wars. One Entire Company Wears the Crimean Medal."[3] No matter. Lionel d'Epineuil needed men if he was going to parlay his first impression into a lasting one.

By the end of the month the total mustered in camp had grown to 469 soldiers. Recruitment, however, was not without its challenges. D'Epineuil appeared in police court toward the end of September to file a complaint against an acting captain who had recruited about thirty men. In appreciation for his recruiting efforts, the colonel had given the man two Zouave uniforms. To d'Epineuil's consternation, the man absconded with the uniforms and with the recruits who he presented to another regiment at three dollars a head.[4] Worse still, desertions plagued d'Epineuil. Early on, unarmed camp guards did what they could with only broken-off picket fence palings to use as sticks before the regiment's Enfield rifles arrived.[5] Despite being based on an island, 119 men deserted Camp Lesley in October—nearly triple the number who had deserted in September. The record shows that by the time the regiment left New York with some 760 soldiers in mid-November, 203 men had deserted. Overall, the regiment would post a shocking official desertion rate of 32 percent, the majority (57.7 percent) of desertions happening while the regiment was encamped at Staten Island.[6] Company F, led by the impetuous Alfred Cipriani, had the highest desertion rate at 45 percent. Cipriani, at twenty-three years of age, was the youngest of all the regiment's captains. His Company F had all the recruits from Philadelphia, who, it must be said, deserted at no greater rate than those in the company who were not from Philadelphia.[7] D'Epineuil well knew that fielding a full regiment was essential for keeping it from being broken up by his superiors. The colonel, again lodging at the Albemarle Hotel, defended his unit's troop strength in the press on October 9, declaring 655 men in the regiment's camp on Staten Island, as opposed to the figure of 300 men asserted by the *New York Times*. Jobert's figure was the more accurate, as official tallies reveal—even taking into account desertions—that the regiment had 620 mustered men on the rolls through October 9, plus an additional twenty-three enlistees not yet mustered. With enough men to satisfy the authorities, the d'Epineuil Zouaves survived the review of the examiners' board intact, and in mid-October Adjutant General Hillhouse designated the regiment as the Fifty-Third New York State Volunteers, Colonel Lionel d'Epineuil commanding.[8]

    D'Epineuil could breathe a sigh of relief. His unit had weathered the transfer from federal to state oversight intact; he had been allowed to keep his regiment on Staten Island and organize it à la Zouave; and he had managed to equip the Fifty-Third New York with the prized French knapsack. In short, Lionel Jobert once again had achieved a prestigious position of authority across the pond from his native France. The colonel now had to navigate between enjoying his achievement and staying in control of it. To look sharp, he ran up his personal tab with Brooks Brothers, buying for himself a valise, a linen duster, pants, an overcoat, and an undress suit in addition to his dress uniform. He added to his account some expenses for his officers: a suit for Second Lieutenant Benjamin Ball; lace for Quartermaster Merriam's coat; and clothing and other articles amounting to $148.25 for his second in command, Lt. Col. Viguier de Monteil. For good measure, d'Epineuil also would purchase a riding suit for his "wife" from the same store.⁹ D'Epineuil haughtily reveled in the part of regimental commander. Constantly trying to keep abreast of the status of the New York regiments, a perturbed George Bliss reported, "I will try and see D'Epineuil at once. He keeps himself shut up *en privee*, with four or five sentinels at different points and no one can get access to him."¹⁰ To be granted an audience with the self-satisfied colonel was indeed an honor.

Continuing and emerging problems within the Fifty-Third, however, would not leave Lionel Jobert in peace to savor his success. Less than a month after asserting in the press that his regiment's numbers were strong, the chagrined colonel issued a less sanguine announcement: "All deserters, and all Zouaves absent without leave, are warned to report themselves at camp immediately, if they desire to avail themselves of the clemency which can now be extended to them. Those who will not return to camp before Thursday next need expect no indulgence. They will be diligently searched out, and the severe penalties which the laws provide for so serious a crime as desertion will be rigidly enforced against them."¹¹ If desertions continued to be a thorn in d'Epineuil's side, nagging fissures among his officers consumed the colonel and destabilized his regiment. D'Epineuil had endorsed both members of his medical staff, Dr. Phillips and Dr. Dubreuil. The two physicians did not get along. Phillips snorted that it "appears that Dr. Dubreuil cannot arrange with Messrs. Brooks [to purchase his own uniform]," and pointedly informed both the colonel and Dubreuil that the latter "is not in my opinion competent for the position he holds, he having no kind of authority over the men and his medical treatment is so bad that I have not the slightest confidence in him."¹² Dubreuil took umbrage at this, and promptly dashed off a retort to his colonel.

> Since, as you told it me this very morning you have nothing in common with the opinion against me expressed by your Surgeon [Genrl?] Dr. Phillips, and said opinion (It is to say that I am no longer worth any confidence) is a private one of his, I think it my duty: First: to take back the few angry words, (if there are any) of my letter dated New York the fourth inst. Second: To modify my first impulse and ask only for my removal into another regiment whatever (the Harris Cavalry excepted.) This

[A Second Ascent / 53]

determination, although most painful to me, because I had learned how to know and estime [sic] you, must be carried out within as little delay as possible, you readily understand why."[13]

Caught between the two, d'Epineuil forwarded the letters of Phillips and Dubreuil to Surgeon General Vanderpool and asked him to decide.[14] All concerned accepted Dubreuil's correspondence as his resignation, and Bernard Vanderkeift replaced Dubreuil as the 53d's Assistant Surgeon. Dubreuil, by his own admission not well-off, now found himself without a job. He pleaded with Vanderpool to be reassigned to another regiment, asserting that the colonel had turned on him, giving Phillips the advantage. "My superior Dr. Phillips," lamented Dubreuil, "whose qualities as a surgeon I am not qualified to judge acted towards me in so strange a manner that I could't [sic] stand it any longer and felt obliged to ask for my transfer into another regiment. The aforesaid gentleman had a creature of his, a certain Mr. *Van-der-kieft* whom he desired very eagerly to occupy my place." Dubreuil accused Vanderkeift of offering him $150 to buy him off.[15] The former assistant surgeon's plea went unheeded, and d'Epineuil accepted Vanderkeift as his replacement.

The most divisive issue among the officers of the Fifty-Third New York proved to be the acrimonious feud at the top. Colonel d'Epineuil and Lieutenant Colonel Viguier de Monteil waged a protracted campaign against each other that carried over into the following year. Monteil described the onset of the trouble in these words: "The Colonel of the regiment Mr. L. J. D'Epineuil had appointed me on the 8th of august [sic], and from that day I labored to help to the raising and discipline of our regiment. My Colonel who was at first always congratulating and praising me for my success, the good discipline and order of the regiment of which I, alone, had the management, for, occupied with other matters, he used to come very seldom to camp and every time to stay but a very little while, changed suddenly his conduct toward me, without any reason on my side."[16] Why did the colonel develop such antipathy for his lieutenant colonel? D'Epineuil was a man with aristocratic pretensions, and Monteil was an avowed republican in their native France. However, political differences between the two men never surfaced, and they had joined the same side in the American Civil War. One grievance d'Epineuil did make explicit regarding his second in command was that Monteil had "been completely incompetent in his way of managing my Regiment and having caused by his complete want of *tact* (so needed in a volunteer regiment) a great desertion in my camp in Staten Island, N.Y."[17] Monteil served as a convenient scapegoat for the colonel to explain the regiment's high desertion rate, and in truth, many men did not respond well to Monteil's leadership. Some officers of the 53d asserted that guard duty was lax under Monteil's supervision of Camp Lesley, and men who resented Monteil's "tyrannical" discipline voted with their feet. On one occasion not directly involving the soldiers, Monteil kicked over baskets of peanuts and apples that women were selling near the camp, and told them to go away. Such incidents created disaffection toward the lieutenant colonel. Yet other officers attributed desertions not to Monteil, but to d'Epineuil's despotic regime. D'Epineuil's conceit prevented him from accepting any blame, and his thin skin provided the main reason for his wrath: the principal cause of his enmity toward Monteil was the latter's lack of respect for his colonel, particularly as a military man. Monteil did not consider d'Epineuil to be army officer material, for the colonel knew little about military affairs, and Monteil let it be known that it was he who took care of the men and "made the regiment." This incensed d'Epineuil, stung by the truth that his military background was wanting. Most injurious to the colonel's pride and reputation was d'Epineuil's allegation the Monteil had disrespectfully referred to him as "having been nothing but a common sailor."[18] The colonel would brook not the slightest challenge—perceived or real—to his authority over the regiment that he saw as his means of advancement. Monteil had to go. Viguier de Monteil knew the truth of this as well, and in a letter of October 5, 1861, he asked Governor Morgan for permission to raise his own regiment.

> I had the honor of seeing you in Albany. . . . After perusing my credentials you told me that it was not then possible to grant the authorization, I was demanding, to raise a new regiment.
> I make bold to day to renew my demand and to make you remember that you promised to employ me when you should judge it proper, saying—"I will take notice of your demand and I will call you from the field any where you may go."
> . . . I am now the Lieutenant Colonel of the 53rd Regt. N. Y. V. but should you grant my request I would leave it not being satisfied with its organization which is not superior to that of all the other Volunteer regiments and does not answer to the expectations and need which Government has of its soldiers.[19]

As Monteil chafed under the command of a man eleven years his junior and for whom he had little regard, so too did the civilian volunteers react negatively to the culture shock of the top officers' strict rule. While the local *Richmond County Gazette* observed approvingly that the "colonel and lieutenant-colonel are experienced officers and fine disciplinarians,"[20] many soldiers and even several officers felt that d'Epineuil and Monteil too often crossed the line of propriety. The citizen-soldiers of the Fifty-Third New York expected to be treated with dignity, and especially did not expect to be subjected to corporal punishment. In this the d'Epineuils were no different than Civil War soldiers in general: demeaning treatment or abuse from superiors flew in the face of the notion that American citizenship bestowed equality among all adult white males, and the officer that ignored that idea courted open defiance from the men.[21] On a late October afternoon, an incident in Camp Lesley showed how untenable the situation had become within the Fifty-Third. At six o'clock the disgruntled men rioted at dinner. Monteil presented himself in uniform and with the aid of other officers tried to restore order. The men greeted the lieutenant colonel by bouncing plates and bread off his head. An enraged Monteil struck some men with his cane and ordered everyone to their tents. Company F's First Lieutenant Charles Jenkins recalled that "at this time the men rebelled & said they would not serve under such a Frenchman, to serve under a tyrant & be treated as slaves or niggers, or be beaten with a stick. The men threatened to desert and many did desert—& I attributed it to the superior officer the Lt. Col." Prodded by the regiment's senior captain, forty-three-year-old Franklin Willard of Company B, several officers signed a petition recommending the removal of Monteil from the regiment, and sent it to the colonel. Their reasons for signing the petition varied. Second Lieutenant Thaddeus Ferris held that Monteil understood his duty and drilled the regiment as well as anyone, but saw his manner toward the men as too tyrannical, echoing the charge of the rank and file.[22] Accusers chose the concept of tyranny carefully, for it demonstrated a violation of the first article of New York's military regulations, to wit: "Superiors of every grade are forbidden to injure those under them by tyrannical or capricious conduct, or by abusive language."[23] Captain Charles Dustan, originally reluctant to sign the petition as he had not been in camp long enough to form an opinion, eventually went to d'Epineuil's headquarters in Manhattan to add his signature; he had concluded Monteil displayed "a want of tact in governing the Regiment." Others signed the petition because they felt Monteil's departure would be the best way to restore a semblance of order among the men. First Lieutenant Henry Cocheu, who admired Monteil, stated he signed because "my motive was to preserve unanimity in the Regiment." Still other officers suspected the hand of an eminence-not-so-grise behind the push to oust Monteil.

Captain Ernest Fiston of Company E refused to sign the petition, for one thing because he viewed its charges as very vague. Moreover, Fiston added that his superior officer spoke to him in an intimidating manner, suspecting a conspiracy in Fiston's company in support of Monteil, and that if such machinations continued Fiston's men would be taken from him and put in other companies, thus leaving Fiston unemployed. Fiston named the superior officer: "This was Col. d'Epineuil."[24] The darkest view of the regiment's turmoil was taken by Captain John George Gundlack.

> I have signed a paper bringing charges against the Lt. Col. for for [*sic*] tyranny—& signed it on the representations of my brother officers as to its contents—I never read the paper. I have said that it was a plot to make the major Lt. Col. and the senior Captain Major, & said also that the major, as soon as he would be Lt. Col., he would be served in the same way the present Lt. Col. was. It seems to me that there has been a conspiracy formed here to destroy the heads of our department.
>
> A certain Officer of this Regiment, Capt. Willard stated in my presence and several ladies and gentlemen that he would be major of this Regiment before three or four days. I remarked at the time that I saw perfectly well what the end of this would be—that he would become major, and then work out the Lt. Col. & Colonel.[25]

Rife with suspicion, hostility, and intrigue, the contentious Fifty-Third New York staggered into November. Desperate to rid himself of his lieutenant colonel, d'Epineuil and his supporters within the regiment stepped up the pressure. "Once," asserted Monteil, "they offered me money, if I would resign. Another time the Colonel told me that I was sure to be murdered in making night rounds, and that the best counsel he could give me, *as a friend*, was to resign." As if that were not enough, d'Epineuil detained Monteil at Camp Lesley and held an irregular court martial against him on the specious grounds of "secessionism." D'Epineuil, Major Cantel, and two or three subordinate officers presided over the kangaroo court that "acquitted" Monteil by one vote.[26] By now, d'Epineuil's mania was evident even to those outside the regiment. George Bliss reported on November 4 that "Col. D'Epineuil was in today, *toned* down he will be all right tomorrow. Burnside told me today he was giving him much trouble." By mid-month, Bliss's opinion of d'Epineuil had crystallized into a decidedly negative one.

"I am satisfied Col D'E. is a *chevalier d'industrie*. He held a court martial in his camp and assumed to cashier his Lieut. Col. Burnside has interfered and sent the latter to Annapolis." Bliss called the colonel on the carpet about the unauthorized proceedings against Monteil, concluding that d'Epineuil "satisfied me he has held no court martial, only a sort of informal court of inquiry. The Col was very French and very excited."[27]

Monteil, too, was more than excited, and renewed his appeal to Governor Morgan for his own regiment of Chasseurs or Zouaves. Monteil asserted he had the money to raise a regiment; he had officers who could assist him in recruiting; the man he had in mind for his lieutenant colonel had 300 men already lined up; Monteil would keep vacancies open should the governor wish to place someone within the regiment; and in an oblique swipe at d'Epineuil, Monteil told Morgan he would "let you choose the uniform that will please you best from engravings I have selected. I would feel proud if you allowed me to call my regiment by your name."[28] In short, Monteil included everything he could think of that might persuade Morgan to honor his request. As if on cue, New York state Senator Francis M. Rotch (1860–1861), a friend of Company D's Captain George F. Chester, wrote to Morgan on the same day as Monteil: "The Lieut. Col of the 53d has resigned or is about to resign, and my object in writing is to urge Capt. Chester as a fit person to fill the vacancy."[29] Morgan, however, took no action. On Burnside's order, Monteil went to Annapolis ostensibly to survey the camp that the Fifty-Third New York soon would inhabit,[30] but the general's prime motive was to separate Monteil from his colonel so that both men's passions could cool down.

Citizens of the Empire State, unaware of the regiment's internal divisions, found favor with the Fifty-Third as D'Epineuil's Zouaves were to be part of New York's contribution to the patriotic task of suppressing the rebellion. The public showed their support in a variety of ways. Manhattan's Academy of Music hosted a benefit concert on November 1, 1861, to provide relief for the families of the regiment's soldiers whose departure would create hardships—financial, practical, as well as emotional—at home. The renowned Patti sisters, Carlotta and Amalia (the latter the wife of music impresario Maurice Strakosch), lent their singing talents to the program. Admiring friends presented swords to officers James H. Sperling and Ray T. Gordon; Captain Charles W. Dustan's friends gave him a sword, sash, and revolver in a ceremony at Camp Lesley. Quartermaster John C. Merriam also received an elegant sword as a testimonial from the engineers of New York and his friends.[31] On November 12, as a gift from the French ladies of New York and General Burnside's wife Mary, a delegation presented an American flag, a regimental flag, and guidons made by Tiffany & Co. to the men at Camp Lesley. The regimental flag bore the inscription "'Colonel D'Epineuil's Zouaves, Fifty-third regiment N.Y.S.V.,'" adding color to a camp already cheerfully decorated with trees, columns, and emblems.[32] Even the businesslike George Bliss was impressed by the spruced-up grounds two days prior to the flag presentation ceremony: "I was at D'Epineuils camp yesterday also. It is a beautiful sight, admirabl[y] arranged and beautified."[33] The regiment's chaplain, Aristide Pierard, blessed the colors after delivering a speech in French. Colonel d'Epineuil, with his left hand in a sling due to a fall suffered the previous day, followed Pierard's oration by graciously thanking the ladies. Assiduously cultivating a positive public perception of the unit, d'Epineuil used the opportunity to describe the flags as a "testimonial of the stability and standing of his regiment."[34]

The ceremony served as a send-off for the soon-to-depart Fifty-Third. From his headquarters in New York City, Brigadier General Ambrose Burnside and his staff had been busy assembling a fleet destined for Annapolis, Maryland in preparation for an invasion of North Carolina. The army used reinforced barges, converted commercial sailing ships, and employed passenger steamers in an endeavor to field enough vessels to transport up to 15,000 troops on the expedition. Colonel d'Epineuil's charges became part of Brigadier General John G. Parke's third brigade, one of three brigades into which Burnside divided his force.[35] Ready for duty, the Fifty-Third New York bid Camp Lesley adieu on November 16, parading through Manhattan before a throng of well-wishers. The regiment disembarked at Thirtieth Street on the North River, marched down Ninth Avenue to Twenty-Third Street, and then proceeded east to Fifth Avenue and thence down to Fourteenth Street. A reporter captured the Zouave flavor of the pageant: "Before the column came in full sight its march was announced by the half Saracenic music of the band, and the spectator almost fancying that he was about to see a battalion of Moors, had his illusion in no wise dispelled by the rich flowing Eastern garb of officers and men."[36] Colonel d'Epineuil and Major Cantel rode at the head of the procession, breathing in the adulation of the crowd. Lieutenant Colonel Viguier de Monteil was conspicuous by his absence, having been dispatched to Annapolis by Burnside to separate him from d'Epineuil for a while. From Fourteenth Street, the regiment headed down Broadway for the final stretch of the parade. Police monitored the spectacle for any Zouave who might exploit one last opportunity to desert while still in New York.[37] Such objectionable behavior notwithstanding, another crowd cheered yet another regiment prepared to represent the state in defense of the Union.

So it was that in mid-November 1861 that the Fifty-Third New York Volunteers left the state on a high note. While the celebrated d'Epineuil Zouaves were off at war, New Yorkers could dance to the "D'Epineuil Zouaves Quadrille" composed by piano specialist Pierre Eugene Chollet, or they might visit the Dodworth art studio on Twenty-Fifth Street and Fifth Avenue to admire a painting that depicted two d'Epineuil Zouaves taking leave of their loved ones. Thomas Nast, whose career would be defined by his political cartoons, drew an illustration of multiethnic military support for the Union cause titled "The Christmas Toast: 'The Union Forever.'" For the representative French figure, Nast sketched a d'Epineuil Zouave.[38] Colonel d'Epineuil was the toast of the town. As a young man in France, Lionel Jobert would not have dreamed that the opportunity to make his mark on the world would find him on the other side of the Atlantic involved in another nation's civil war. Yet as he and his regiment steamed down the coast toward Maryland, d'Epineuil must have expected that personal martial glory was imminent—a performance that would bring him the plaudits he craved.

The Fifty-Third's parade through Manhattan ended back at the North River, where they boarded the steamer *Admiral*. After spending a day anchored off Staten Island, the *Admiral* journeyed to Annapolis, arriving there on November 19. The regiment settled in at Camp Richmond and waited to play their part in the great national conflict. Amid wide streets at Camp Richmond, the soldiers set up tents spaced two feet apart, with an average of five men, some sleeping on straw, occupying each tent. Three tents served as the regimental hospital, and the men's privy was located in the woods 150 feet from the body of the camp. Surface springs and wells at a nearby farm provided water for the men. While the soldiers complained of small rations, they were served fresh meat twice a week, they ate bread baked at the Naval School, and peddlers selling food were allowed access to the camp.[39]

Many soldiers, conscious of their families back home, participated in New York's Allotment System. Headed by a three-man commission that included Theodore Roosevelt Sr.—father of the future namesake president—the allotment system allowed soldiers to designate any portion of their earnings to be sent to their families.[40] While the d'Epineuil Zouaves sent money home from Annapolis, recruiting efforts for a second battalion of the Fifty-Third continued in New York City. Governor Morgan agreed to allow d'Epineuil to form a second battalion despite the fact that the first battalion did not have a full complement of men. D'Epineuil knew that the more men he had under his command, the more important he would become in the eyes of the military leadership, and he eagerly advertised in the *New York Tribune* to attract recruits for a second battalion. This recruiting effort, however, sputtered along into December, encountering one problem after another. One snag involved Henry S. Olcott, an editor on the staff of the *Tribune*. Olcott quit his job at the newspaper and acquired a uniform on the understanding from George Bliss that he would be commissioned as a first lieutenant in Company O of the Fifty-Third's second battalion, an arrangement agreed to by d'Epineuil. General Burnside, who had wanted Olcott as his military secretary, also promoted the idea of Olcott's commission. Bliss thought he had the approval of his superior, New York's Adjutant General Hillhouse, for this specific commission, but he did not. Olcott never joined the Fifty-Third, and the state apparently resolved what Bliss termed its "awkward predicament" by permitting Olcott to accompany Burnside on his ship during the expedition to Roanoke Island.[41]

More vexing for Bliss was the fact that d'Epineuil was attempting to raise a second battalion while his first battalion was undermanned. Bliss repeatedly groused about this issue, returning to it once again in a December 4 letter to Adjutant General Hillhouse: "D'Epineuil's Second Battalion has been troubling me for some time. The fact is the Govnr. promised it and good faith must be kept, and yet it ought never to have been promised. I have today informed them that it is a *sine qua non* that the first regiment should be filled up to 850 and they have agreed to do it."[42] The d'Epineuil Zouaves' recruiting advertisement on the same day revealed its struggle to maintain its numbers: "The SECOND BATTALION of this splendid regiment will follow the first, which has left for the seat of war, with dispatch . . . all deserters who desire to join their regiment may come at once, or they will be severely dealt with."[43] Plagued by desertions, d'Epineuil himself had given up by early December on recruiting another whole battalion, and expressed as much to General Burnside: "I have the honor to write you a letter asking orders for my so called second battalion. I am still waiting & being in a hurry of raising my regt to its proper standard at 1 cont[ingent] of 1040[.] I respectfully beg to represent that a decision on that subject ought to be made at your earliest convenience to enable me to recruit for filling up my regular number. In the hope that your order in reaching me will enable me to get hold of the Cos of recruits I have now in town of NY."[44] The effort to recruit a second battalion of d'Epineuil Zouaves had waned by the end of December; desertions offset the recruits that had joined the regiment since it had left New York. Those second battalion recruits who did not join the regiment at Annapolis were transferred to other units, including Colonel Felix Confort's Enfants Perdus.[45]

The move to Camp Richmond in Annapolis did not dispel the divisiveness that continued to afflict Colonel d'Epineuil's regiment. The friction between d'Epineuil and Lieutenant Colonel Monteil did not abate, and ethnic tension developed between the non-French enlistees and their French comrades, with particular animosity aimed at the French officers. One source of that tension was the language barrier. Major Cantel criticized Monteil for sowing confusion when drilling officers before the privates, giving commands in English and explanations in French. Francis Pittman, a nineteen-year-old private in Company H, recorded two diary entries in late November that showed the difficulties Chaplain Aristide Pierard had establishing a connection with the men. "About 9 o'clock [on the morning of November 24]," wrote Pittman, "we formed a line & were marched to the chaplain tent—where we listened to a harangue in broken English—not one word of which we could understand." Pittman's entry for November 28 was similar: "at Ten o'clock fell in & were marched to the Priest's tent & stood there while he went through some ceremony—no part of which we could understand."[46] Pierard's Roman Catholicism also caused resentment among many of the Protestant faithful. To the consternation of many of the men, the regimental chaplain refused to perform a burial service for a deceased Protestant soldier. Pierard also did not hide his contempt of Protestant prayer meetings and Bible readings within the camp. Citing a " 'special' dispatch"—perhaps from one of the twenty-seven men, all in Company D, who enrolled in the Fifty-Third at Utica, New York—the *Utica Morning Herald* reported, "There certainly seems to be a necessity for some action which shall furnish this fine regiment with a congenial chaplain, or else relieve the large proportion who are Protestants from the incubus of such priestcraft."[47] Pierard tired of the circumstances as well, appealing in his resignation letter of December 31 to Colonel d'Epineuil by citing the former's dissatisfaction with Monteil: "I cannot remain in the regiment without you, under the orders of one officer, who have [sic] certainly contributed to the loss of the discipline by his bad words against you." D'Epineuil, in clear agreement with Pierard's assessment, added a marginal note to the letter: "Must be referred the chaplain being a very honest man and the heart of my poor regt."[48]

D'Epineuil's "poor regiment" suffered not only from enlisted men smarting under the discipline meted out by French officers, but also from anti-French sentiment among the non-French officers. Company I's Captain

John G. Gundlack, as shown earlier, asserted unequivocally that Company B's Captain Franklin W. Willard—who, it will be remembered, advertised specifically for American and English recruits for his company—sought to discredit Monteil so that Major Cantel would assume the vacated lieutenant colonelcy and Willard, as senior captain, would replace the major. In like manner, Gundlack asserted, Willard schemed to move his way up to the top of the regiment's hierarchy. The French-born Cantel himself opined that the "Lt. Col. hurt the feelings of the officers of the Regiment by stating how much superior the French service was (better) than the American."[49] By the end of November, the situation in Camp Richmond had grown so precarious that an alarmed Captain Charles Dustan confided to his mother that

> There is in the Rgt a horrible spirit of disaffection & mutiny against the Col Lieut Col Major & all the French officers—my Co. behave well because I have great influence with them—and also with the entire Rgt and do all I can to keep things straight where it is going to end I cant [sic] say—don't mention this to any one—not even in the family for it is not to be talked about—to me the Col & Major are as polite & kind as ever but to the poor men tyrannical & despotic in the extreme—neither *officers* or men are allowed outside the camp—a feature unprecedented in American military discipline. I much fear there will be murder done here before long the men swear horrible vengeance. Still a few of us [Captain George F.] Chester & the 71st generally (there are 18 71st officers) do all we can to check & control the spirit that pervades the camp thus far successfully how long we shall be able to do so it is hard to say.[50]

With Monteil's days in the regiment now more than ever appearing to be numbered, Captain George F. Chester's father and Chester himself joined state Senator Francis M. Rotch in promoting the younger Chester as Monteil's replacement. Chester's father, lawyer E. W. Chester, wrote to Governor Morgan toward the end of November: "it is obvious to an American that unless there is among the higher officers at least one American, difficulties will arise which foreign field officers will not know how to manage. There is a want of American common sense, & knowledge of American character. With the best feelings therefore toward Col. D'Epineuil I am desirous of seeing his first officer an intelligent American, who understands men, has tact in managing them together with the necessary military qualifications."[51]

The senior Chester had his son in mind for the job. As speculation continued to swirl in December as to Monteil's ouster, George Chester himself confided to Rotch,

> There is at present no vacancy in the field offices of my regiment. There is a pressing need of a sensible *American* in one of these offices. The Regiment is American it containing no more than eighty Frenchmen. It never can be got really into shape until an American Field Officer is appointed. It is clear also that there must be a vacancy sooner or later—from the bitter feeling against our present Lieut. Col. on the part of both officers & men. I take myself no part in these dissensions however.
>
> It is utterly preposterous to promote our present fussy little French Major . . . I have no doubt but that the Colonel thinks me the best fitted for the place of all the Captains, but whether he has any protégé in view for the place I do not know—in fact I do not care. I stand exceedingly well with him, but do not make him my confidant . . . An intimation from influential quarters to the Col. that my nomination would be satisfactory, &c. made immediately upon a vacancy occurring—might make sure of my nomination in case a nomination from my fellow officers is necessary.[52]

The Chesters' letters evoked the ethnic dissonance within the Fifty-Third. A French-led but largely American regiment had a slim chance to be cohesive, they concluded; American soldiers wanted American officers. Trying to appear above the fray, George Chester had written that he did not take part in the dissensions against Monteil, yet he had in fact been a signatory to a letter addressed by several officers to Colonel d'Epineuil urging Monteil's removal. Francis Rotch and E. W. Chester would continue to press the governor and Adjutant General Hillhouse in early 1862 to elevate George Chester within the regiment.

More than anti-French feeling, however, it was Colonel d'Epineuil's inexperience—and consequent ineffectiveness—as an army officer, combined with his example of petty uncooperativeness with his lieutenant colonel, that cost him the confidence of the men under his command and drained the regiment's esprit de corps. Ultimately, d'Epineuil's own officers would draw up a list of charges against the colonel, and the first charge was incompetency.

In this that he has not sufficient knowledge of military tactics and regulations to qualify him to command a Regiment or administer its affairs. He has repeatedly made awkward blunders when upon Parade and exhibited such incompetency as to forfeit generally the confidence even of the men in the ranks. . . . On Nov. 25th, 1861 at Camp Richmond near A[n]napolis by repeated facings & flankings he had one half the Re[g]t. right in front and one half left in front when they halted in Line. And when the order was given "Guides Posts" and *that* did not bring them right, he commanded "Front" of course one half faced *to* and one half *from* him. When that order failed he commanded—"Officers to the front & centre" after riding around to the other side of the Battallion [sic] and there scolded & reprimanded the officers in the presence of many private[s] and dismissed the parade, evidently because he did not know how to rectify the mistakes or reform the Battalion.[53]

In another instance, Monteil, more concerned with finding a way out of the regiment and into one of his own, returned late to Camp Richmond after the expiration of his furlough. "I went back," stated Monteil, "had an explanation with the Colonel in presence of General [John G.] Foster [of Burnside's First Brigade] who tried to reconcile us, and the Colonel promised to let me free to do my duties, and to act frankly and gentlemanly with me. I believed him."[54] D'Epineuil issued a written order for Monteil to resume his post on December 5, which Monteil did, however he did not sleep in camp for two days. Thus, on December 7, d'Epineuil issued a *verbal* order, passed on through the regiment's Adjutant Victor Vifquain, for senior Captain Franklin Willard to take command of the men since Monteil was not at his post, and for Willard not to cede command to anyone except the colonel or the major. When Monteil returned to camp to stay that day, December 7, he attempted to relieve Willard of command. Lieutenant Henry Cocheu recalled, "I was there the day when Lt. Col. took command Capt. Willard refusing. I never saw a man in a lady's parlor more polite than the Lt. Col." Captain Willard was not swayed, and disorder (and perhaps comedy) ensued. Willard recounted that with the regiment formed in parade in front of them, the "Lt. Col. gave orders to the battalion, I gave a counter order—I appealed to the officers—told them of d'Epineuils orders & asked which should be obeyed—good deal of confusion among men and officers." Since Willard could produce no *written* order to support his position, Monteil had Willard forcibly detained in the latter's tent, and posted a guard outside. An embarrassed and angry Colonel d'Epineuil subsequently challenged Monteil as to why he had been absent from camp twice, on the evenings of December 5 and 6, despite the order for officers not to leave without permission. Monteil replied that he was not yet fixed with the necessities to sleep in camp, and turned to leave. At that moment, Adjutant Vifquain provocatively stepped in front of Monteil to block his exit, indignant that the lieutenant colonel had "put himself as a Judge on his private conduct."[55]

The lieutenant colonel's confrontation with d'Epineuil had reached a critical stage. Monteil demanded satisfaction in the form of a court of inquiry—a request he "had been begging for since the beginning of my troubles, to answer the ridiculous and wicked accusations they were heaping on my head."[56] Brigadier General John G. Foster's Special Order 44 of December 10, 1861 authorized a court of inquiry regarding Lieutenant Colonel Viguier de Monteil to be held the next day in Annapolis. The three-man court dutifully met on December 11, with Lieutenant Colonel Thomas Bell of the 51st Pennsylvania Volunteers as president and Captain J. Merrill Linn, also of the Fifty-First Pennsylvania, as judge advocate. Lieutenant Colonel Albert C. Maggi of the Twenty-First Massachusetts Regiment—part of the second brigade of Burnside's Coastal Division under Brigadier General Jesse Reno—acted as Monteil's defense. The Fifty-Third's W. W. Armstrong, captain of Company A, submitted a list of charges against Monteil: conduct subversive of good order and military discipline, conduct unbecoming an officer and a gentleman, and neglect of duty. Colonel d'Epineuil prepared a similar list of charges and specifications, followed by a single charge, leveled by First Lieutenant William H. Burgess of Company D, that Monteil received and used stolen property from a local public school in Anne Arundel County, Maryland.[57]

The court summoned multiple officers from the Fifty-Third as well as other officers and civilians as witnesses. Three issues stood out during the court's proceedings. Had Monteil spoken disrespectfully of the colonel? Had Monteil been drunk on the night (November 19) of the d'Epineuil Zouaves' arrival in Annapolis? Had Monteil been guilty of poor leadership that contributed to the regiment's high rate of desertion? There was little doubt regarding the first issue. Many officers testified, and the court accepted as proven, that Monteil had expressed his view that d'Epineuil was not suited to command an army regiment. The court was particularly interested in determining the answer to the second issue of whether Monteil had overindulged in spirits. William S. Clark, major of the Twenty-First Massachusetts Regiment, testified "I was in my room with Col. Morse [also of the 21st Massachusetts] between nine & ten o'clock on the evening of the arrival of the d'Epineuil Regiment . . . Lt. Col. Viguier de Monteil came into the room. I saw no evidence of intoxication: did not think of it." Monteil, Major Clark asserted, was excited when talking about his Fifty-Third New York regiment, but not inebriated. In contrast, the d'Epineuil Zouaves' First Lieutenant Barry Fox of Company C stated that the night of the arrival of the Fifty-Third in Annapolis, he entered a public house and saw Monteil "in the society of a number of private soldiers, he was under the influence of liquor: he was surrounded by privates: he asked me to drink, which I refused to do. I left in company with another brother officer, Lt. Sperling. He was intoxicated, the Lt. Col. The Regt. came by sea—the Lt. Col. did not accompany the Regt. I saw him on shore upon my arrival. He was hilarious, noisy, if he had been sober he wouldn't have been in the company he was nor asked me to drink—he was decidedly drunk." With witnesses testifying on both sides of the issue, the court focused its inquiry on the hour of Monteil's alleged drunkenness. Major Clark had stated that between nine and ten o'clock at night Monteil had showed no signs of intoxication. First Lieutenant James H. Sperling maintained that it was about 11:00 p.m. when he and Barry Fox saw Monteil drinking with three Zouaves "in the house opposite our camp at St. John's College." The civilian keeper of that restaurant avowed that "I saw Lt. Col. Viguier de Monteil come into my house in the afternoon between 4 & 5 o'clock," and that the house closed at ten. When the court asked if it might have been eleven o'clock, the proprietor reasserted, "I am very sure it struck ten o'clock after my wife retired to bed with me." Faced with the totality of the evidence, Captain Armstrong withdrew the specifications of his second charge against Monteil, which included the accusation of drunkenness. Regarding the third focal point of the trial—if Monteil had been deficient in his command and thus responsible for desertions—the court determined that, despite some shortcomings in his leadership, responsibility for the high number of desertions could not be connected to the lieutenant colonel. Finally, a majority of the court found unproven Lt. Burgess's charge of Monteil's acceptance of stolen property. Charles J. Welch, secretary of the Board of Trustees of Anne Arundel School #53, testified that soldiers had taken some furniture from the school, and Monteil had expressed his regret that it had been done without first seeking permission. Monteil then got written authorization to retain the furniture, which Welch gave him, signed by one of the trustees.[58]

Beyond the specifics of the case, the trial laid bare the status distinction that officers continuously maintained between themselves and the men. Such separation, of course, served an important purpose in a military unit. The authority that rank bestowed had to be honored so that orders would be promptly carried out, thus making the regiment efficient and effective in its duties; officers fraternizing with enlisted men would break down this rigidly enforced barrier. Any hint of crossing this martial class line would be to an officer's discredit. Thus, First Lieutenant Fox, in his testimony regarding seeing Monteil sitting with privates, asserted the lieutenant colonel had to have been drunk or "he wouldn't have been in the company he was." Second Lieutenant Sperling said of Monteil: "The Zouaves drank with him."[59] Sperling did not consider himself a Zouave, although he was a member of the d'Epineuil Zouave regiment. For Sperling, the Zouave was of a class apart from and below the officers. Colonel d'Epineuil put the issue as plainly as anyone in his written charges against Monteil: on December 7, one of his officers found Monteil "sitting at the same table and dining with his own orderly, a private, conduct certainly unbecoming an officer."[60] Officers were equals; enlisted men were utterly subordinate. Graciousness toward fellow officers was a mark of a gentleman; inferiors met with an austere hand. But with civilian volunteer soldiers, the divide between officers and the rank and file was a delicate affair. If the men viewed their officers as capable, worthy commanders, even if they did not care for them personally, they could bear being sternly ordered about because they respected the officers' leadership. If the men did not respect the officers, then the dictatorial manner of the latter could ignite hostility. Captain Henry Scott of Company C echoed Captain Dustan's observation: Monteil treated Scott well, but "on account of his ungovernable temper he could not govern the men." If by the time of the trial in mid-December the spirit of the men toward the lieutenant colonel was fifty-fifty, as the regiment's Surgeon Henry Phillips maintained,[61] then half of the men would be dismayed whether the court absolved Monteil or condemned him.

Still, Viguier de Monteil's trial and the court's decision might have ended the disunity within the Fifty-Third New York Volunteers. Numerous members of the regiment got to have their say; they aired their grievances; and the court of inquiry followed the prescribed institutional procedure for settling such matters once and for all. Instead, the process inflamed the ire of Lionel d'Epineuil, who saw defeat snatched from the jaws of victory. On the eve of the trial in front of the battalion at Camp Richmond, the colonel confidently, and with smug satisfaction, declared in reference to the lieutenant colonel: " 'A man whose name I blush to mention will never trouble you again.' "62 D'Epineuil saw the court of inquiry not only as Monteil's swan song, but as a vindication for himself that would confer a seal of approval on the colonel's leadership of the regiment. Several officers had signed a petition requesting Monteil's removal; the trial would bring to light all of the lieutenant colonel's failings; and Lionel Jobert's persuasive eloquence again would serve him well. But the trial was not d'Epineuil's to control, and as the court's eleven-day process took its course, the colonel's self-assurance turned to agitated bewilderment as testimony damaged *his* reputation. Company E Private Victor Thus, for example, testifying in French through Assistant Surgeon Bernard Vanderkeift, who acted as interpreter, swore that he had never seen the lieutenant colonel drunk, and "I attribute the desertion because we did not get enough to eat and were ill treated. . . . My complaint was that I was struck with a blow on the ear with fist and with the sabre on the back by my Colonel d'Epineuil. I have been sick 13 days on account of the blows." Colonel Augustus Morse, Twenty-First Massachusetts Regiment, attested that Monteil told him he "had heard said that his Colonel did not bear a good charachter [*sic*] at home—in a moral point of view." Court: "What do you mean by at home?" Morse: "It was in his own country—France."63 Thomas Bell, president of the court, confided to his brother-in-law and sister near the end of the proceedings that "So far I'm convinced these [charges] entirel[y] trumped up by an envious set of officers determined to displace him to gain their own advancement . . . The Col. of these Zouaves was, until lately, an officer in the French Navy—is a man of fine education—a perfect gentleman & a fine musician. He is, however, nothing of a military man. Those [*sic*] regt. is about totally disorganized on a/c of their quarrels with the Lt. Col. & men are daily deserting."64 On December 21, the next to last day of the proceedings, the court met at d'Epineuil's headquarters, located in a farm house near the camp. D'Epineuil had not been able to use his most effective tool of persuasion—verbal address—so he felt compelled to write a letter to Bell and the court decrying the court's decision to give Monteil the run of the camp during the trial, thus countermanding the colonel's order of close arrest.

> I respectfully beg to state that I deeply regret to see the court giving an order contradicting *so completely* mine & my authority & without having listened to me & at least asked my reasons. . . .

> As a Colonel and as an honest man I hereby *declare* that Lieutt Col, under pretext of defending him is every day & every night going round in the tents creating what he calls sympathy for him what I call *real mutiny* & *criminal excitement* . . .
>
> My intentions in placing him in close arrest was not to stop his defence, I have proved myself alas! a too loyal adversary to him to be accused of that—but *is to save* my Regt from a complete disorganization.[65]

In the colonel's mind, the trial was a referendum on control of the regiment that bore his name as much as it was an examination of Monteil's conduct. Further, it was a zero-sum game: Monteil's exoneration would mean d'Epineuil's disgrace.

Thomas Bell signed the court's decision on December 22, but the court waited until year's end to release its findings. Meanwhile, routine life in Camp Richmond went on while the d'Epineuil Zouaves waited for orders. The commander of the Coast Division had toured the camp on December 20, and Private Francis Pittman took note of the event in his diary: "This morning at 11 we were marched down & reviewed by Gen Burnsides he is a tall rather slim bald head black whiskers & mustache looks noble on horseback, we gave him three cheers as we passed him. . . . When we returned to camp the Col congratulated his 'boys' very highly." Pittman's father, George W. Pittman, visited the camp over the Christmas holiday. On Sunday, December 21, he heard a preaching by one of the men, and attended a prayer meeting held in Captain Frederick Cocheu's tent.[66] Desertions, too, continued as a regular event, with officers itemizing what the deserter took with him. Among them, Private Giovanni Annibale of Company F fled on December 23, with his rifle and outfit. Corporal Henry Edward Gottreux also deserted, taking with him one Enfield rifle and gunsling, one cartridge box, belts, plate, one cap pouch, one bayonet, and a bayonet scabbard.[67] Soldiers often spent time in camp writing letters; the colonel and his lieutenant colonel were not the only ones to favor the military establishment with mail from the Fifty-Third New York. Sergeant Charles Price of Company I made his wishes known in a December 30 letter to Adjutant General Hillhouse: "i under stand the manual well and i am kapel of taken up the vackency of Second Liutent of my Company all of the men in the company want me to have a comishun and i ask you my dear sir for the vacency that their is to fill in the company which i am in By so doind you will oblige Seargent Price i am one of the oldest members of the company And I think I am intitle to it."[68]

The court of inquiry into Viguier de Monteil's case officially issued its judgment on December 31. Bell and the court viewed the lieutenant colonel's admitted violations, such as returning late from furlough and sleeping outside of camp, as minor infractions. While Monteil had expressed his negative opinion of d'Epineuil's leadership, allegations of drunkenness and incompetence were found to be without merit. In short, Monteil had emerged from the ordeal with his reputation and rank intact. Feeling humiliated, Colonel d'Epineuil tendered his resignation, as did several loyal officers, and they were placed under arrest. The tense moment caused no significant reaction among the men, as Lieutenant Augustus Hatch, commanding the guard that evening, reported "the camp in very good order during the night, considering the *circumstances*."[69] The next morning, January 1, 1862, Brigadier General John G. Parke allowed the officers a chance to withdraw their resignations, and they did so. For the seething d'Epineuil, the matter was not closed. In an earlier effort to frighten off his lieutenant colonel, d'Epineuil had warned Monteil that his unpopularity in the regiment would result in his murder. On January 3, that warning nearly became prophetic. General Burnside, perhaps once again trying to relieve the tension within the Fifty-Third as he had done before the regiment left Staten Island in November, ordered General Parke to "detail a field officer to proceed to New York" to revive the flagging recruiting effort for the Zouaves. Parke assigned Monteil to that duty. As Monteil rode his horse along the railroad outside of Camp Richmond, guards acting on orders passed down from the colonel to Major Cantel to Captain Alfred Cipriani fired shots at Monteil.[70] Several men recorded the confrontation in letters or journals—Charles Dustan, Henry Cocheu, Francis Pittman, and Monteil—with the details varying among the sources. Two facts were beyond question: the shots missed their mark, and d'Epineuil appeared to be coming unglued. Whether attempted murder or a scare tactic, the order to fire on the regiment's second in command revealed the desperation of a colonel unable to control himself or his regiment.

Lionel J. d'Epineuil had alienated his lieutenant colonel, instead of working out their differences, to the point that both men wanted to dissolve their military partnership. The stress that accompanied recruiting, organizing, equipping, and training a large group of volunteer civilians unused to regimental discipline further strained the relationship between the two officers. When the regiment left New York in mid-November 1861, the antagonisms and rancor that had developed at Camp Lesley went along with them. D'Epineuil could hope that, as happened with other Civil War regiments, engaging in battle might unify his charges and dispel the toxic clouds of discord that enveloped the d'Epineuil Zouaves.[71] Such hope would go unfulfilled. D'Epineuil's vehicle for personal and professional advancement—his regiment of Zouaves—would disintegrate in large part due to the actions of the colonel, leaving him, once again, without position.

Chapter 5

A Second Descent

Shattered Hope Amid Civil War

The first week of the New Year brought news that promised to dilute the volatile mixture of monotony and tension that had characterized the Fifty-Third's month-and-a-half stint at Camp Richmond. The Burnside Expedition was to be underway at last. Soldiers began to board ships in Annapolis on January 5, 1862. Brigadier General Burnside recalled how the men's spirits soared as regiment after regiment embarked. "Thank God for some change!" confided Henry Cocheu, first lieutenant of the Fifty-Third's G Company, to his diary. Cocheu, one of four brothers in the regiment born in New York to a French father and a New York–born mother, resolved with the New Year to record his experiences, thus leaving a valuable chronicle of the regiment's odyssey over the better part of the next three months. The plan called for the flotilla to depart from Annapolis, sail down the Chesapeake Bay, and rendezvous at Fort Monroe in Virginia at the bay's entrance. From there, the ships were to move south down the outer banks of North Carolina and enter Pamlico Sound through the Hatteras Inlet. Once securely inside Pamlico Sound, the expedition would proceed north toward Roanoke Island and mount an invasion. One of the ships available for use was the *John Trucks*. Burnside queried d'Epineuil as to whether the colonel thought the bark could transport the entire Fifty-Third New York regiment. On the assumption that the voyage would be just a few days in length, d'Epineuil dismissed other options and agreed to place his whole command, more than 700 strong, aboard the *John Trucks*.[1] It was a fateful decision for Lionel Jobert's military career.

The leniency of the court of inquiry and its dismissal of counts levied against Viguier de Monteil had confirmed in the colonel's mind that he did not have the absolute control over the regiment to which he felt entitled. D'Epineuil responded by commanding the regiment in an increasingly callous and arbitrary manner. The colonel struck one private on the side of the head merely because the man's beard was not to d'Epineuil's liking. Signifying his state of mind two days before the unit embarked on the *John Trucks*, an irrational d'Epineuil vented at Henry Cocheu: "I am the Colonel! I am God Almighty!! I don't like you!" The colonel's anger was stoked further by the reappearance of Dr. Jules Dubreuil. Desperate for a position after all the principals had considered his resignation a closed affair, Dubreuil had managed to board the *Admiral* and arrived with the regiment in Annapolis in November. Immediately d'Epineuil had him placed back aboard ship, and Dubreuil was obliged to return to New York. Vowing to "stand the hurricane," Dubreuil made his way back to Annapolis, keeping a low profile by staying among the men in their tents at Camp Richmond. When the regiment boarded the *John Trucks*, d'Epineuil had the persistent Dubreuil roughly evicted from the vessel. The doctor complained to Generals Parke and Burnside, but as he immediately wrote to New York Governor Morgan, they ignored him. So did Morgan, despite Dubreuil's follow-up letter to Albany on February 5, 1862, one month after he was thrown off the *John Trucks*.[2]

The colonel's reign of terror over the Fifty-Third did not cease aboard ship. Within forty-eight hours of squeezing on board the severely overcrowded vessel, the men began to voice disapproval of their commanding officer's choices. "We are packed together like a lot of sheep," wrote Private Pittman, "we have just standing room, it is impossible to find room to lie down." On the same day, January 6, Henry Cocheu recorded: "At 8 p.m. Colonel, who had been twice offered by Gen. Burnside a bigger ship, or two small ones, went below—every Co. except G yelled and groaned him. He has not a friend left among the Boys."[3] D'Epineuil allowed men to be tied to the ship's rigging even during a storm; he seized money from two men he found gambling and threw it overboard, despite the fact d'Epineuil himself gambled on board; yet another private's whiskers brought down on him the wrath of Caen—d'Epineuil yanked the hair by the roots from the man's face. None of these actions endeared the colonel to his men, who quickly became disgruntled with the living conditions and harsh discipline on the *John Trucks*. The situation only got worse. Just days after setting sail, the *John Trucks* ran aground in Chesapeake Bay. While the men literally tried to rock the boat by running from one side of the deck to the other, a steamer labored to pull the ship free. The delay put the Fifty-Third New York well behind the rest of the fleet; not until January 13 did the regiment reach Fort Monroe at Hampton, Virginia, opposite the entrance to Chesapeake Bay.[4] The still-simmering resentment between the colonel and lieutenant colonel added to the rancorous atmosphere aboard ship. After all that had transpired between them, it was impossible for d'Epineuil and Monteil to coexist on the same vessel. Monteil had written to General George McClellan on January 6, detailing the rift with the colonel, including the shooting incident three days prior. McClellan, unmoved by the affair, revoked the authorization for Monteil to raise recruits in New York and ordered him to rejoin the Fifty-Third forthwith. When Monteil presented the order to his colonel aboard ship on 15 January, d'Epineuil refused to accept it, and was more than happy to say nothing and look the other way when Monteil left the *John Trucks* and boarded the *Suwanee*, which carried the Fifty-Third's horses.[5]

Persistent stormy weather prevented ship Captain Levi Collins from maneuvering the *John Trucks* close to Hatteras. The raging tempest and treacherous sand bars affected the entire fleet. Some ships sank; several slammed into each other. The expedition's progress was delayed to the point that food rations and drinking water ran low. Gales drove the *John Trucks* out to sea, where it spent more than a week alternating between riding out the storm at anchor and attempting to progress toward Hatteras Inlet. Finally, on January 26, the Fifty-Third New York drew close to the inlet. The stalled fleet had been deepening the channel by running heavy ships over the bar and relying on the current to wash away the loosened sand. Nevertheless, the weight of the overburdened *John Trucks* caused it to float too deeply in the water, making it impossible to cross the bar into Pamlico Sound. D'Epineuil, perhaps remembering at that moment that the *Bayonnaise* had faced the same situation in Macau fourteen years earlier, left the ship to confer with Burnside, who saw little practical worth in a ship that could not navigate through the swash and help accomplish the mission. Thus, the expedition's commander ordered Colonel d'Epineuil to return with the *John Trucks* to Fort Monroe.[6]

Making their way back to Virginia, the Fifty-Third New York Infantry survived on daily rations of four crackers and a pint of water. Company F's Alfred Murden, looking back on the experience while in his mid-nineties in 1936, remembered that men coveted places under the sails at night so as to catch a few drops of moisture as the dew dripped down. Hungry, ill, exhausted, and their celebrated uniforms unraveling and infested with lice, the Zouaves signaled their distress by hoisting the ensign union down. The steamship *Ericsson* spotted the cry for help on January 29, and took the *John Trucks* in tow back to Fort Monroe. Colonel d'Epineuil went ashore two days later to report to General John E. Wool.[7] On February 1, Wool issued the following order: "Colonel d'Epineuil will with his Regiment, the 53rd N.Y. Vols., now on board the steamer [sic] 'John Trucks,' proceed without delay to Annapolis, Maryland, and report to the Commanding Officer of that station."[8]

Jobert doubtless sensed the tide had turned against his bid for military acclaim with the Fifty-Third and against his pursuit of prestige, so he shifted tactics. The colonel returned from his meeting with Wool with a box of wine as a gift for his officers. It was too late. Instead of judiciously picking his battles within the regiment, d'Epineuil had demanded unquestioned loyalty to his often capricious leadership, and the cumulative effect of months under his heavy and unsteady hand had turned many of his men against him. The *Ericsson* towed the *John Trucks* away from Fort Monroe on February 4, and the next day the ship anchored outside Annapolis. A month had elapsed since the d'Epineuil Zouaves had first embarked on the *John Trucks*, and they found themselves back where they had started with nothing but frustration to show for their efforts. Meanwhile, the Burnside Expedition succeeded in capturing Roanoke Island on February 8, without the help of the d'Epineuil Zouaves. Had the Fifty-Third New York Infantry been able to participate in the siege, Colonel d'Epineuil and his men would have had a share of both the honor accorded soldiers who engaged in battle and the glory of victory, a sure tonic to raise the men's spirits and promote cohesion within the regiment. That potential future disappeared as the overloaded *John Trucks* sailed away from the seat of war. D'Epineuil would never compile a war record such as that of the highly regarded Régis de Trobriand, who engaged in several of the war's most memorable battles at Fredericksburg, Chancellorsville, Gettysburg, and Petersburg. Nor could d'Epineuil match de Trobriand's station in life, despite his best efforts. While he struggled to keep his vision of distinction afloat as the elements lashed the *John Trucks* in mid-January, the well-established Baron de Trobriand, his wife, and their daughter Caroline enjoyed a dinner in the White House as guests of the Lincolns.[9]

The future that came to pass was far less favorable for Lionel Jobert. A determined group of officers sent a list of five charges and thirty-two specifications against d'Epineuil up the chain of command to Adjutant General Hillhouse and Major General John A. Dix on February 10. Colonel d'Epineuil, among other infractions, had engaged in conduct detrimental to order and unbefitting an officer and a gentleman. The officers poured their months of dissatisfaction with their colonel into the charges and minced no words. D'Epineuil had "an unusual alacrity in getting himself and his regiment into trouble everywhere," and "by his lack of tact and judgment, his inability to understand American character, his ungovernable temper & overbearing manner, his extraordinary selfishness and self assumption, his tyrannical disposition his inability to appreciate or recognise the separate and distinct responsibilities of different grade in the service, his lack of administrative ability and of power to maintain proper and regular discipline in fact by all his peculiarities of mind character and temperament he is unfitted to command an American Volunteer Regiment." D'Epineuil's inflated ego worked to his disadvantage in the eyes of his men. The charges asserted that "he habitually employs sergeants of his regiment as waiters and personal attendants upon himself and has them perform the most menial of services." When officers tried to quote Army regulations to him, the colonel responded "he is 'the Regulation.'"[10] From the perspective of the rank-and-file, the view was the same. Four days before the charges were submitted, Private Francis Pittman recounted the colonel's efforts to quell an agitation aboard ship. Pittman's visual description of the colonel was telling: "he came on board with a pair of navy revolvers stuck in his belt"; "he came back on the quarterdeck awhile & stood with folded arms—looking more like a king than our humble volunteer Colonel." Thus maligned by his own creation, Lionel J. d'Epineuil retreated to Washington, DC, to try to minimize the unavoidable damage to his name.[11]

Privately, Lionel Jobert had only "Madame d'Epineuil," his constant companion for nearly a year and a half, to comfort him. Born Theodosia Augusta Gordon, the daughter of an English merchant, she was only eighteen in 1853 when she married Thomas Charles Lloyd, a gentleman without occupation. The couple had two children, Minnie and Amelie. By the time Lionel Jobert arrived at Madeira in 1859 in charge of the *Geffrard*, Theodosia had grown disillusioned with her leisure-loving husband. Mr. Lloyd, Theodosia would later complain, "might easily earn an income if he chose to work instead of spending a life of idleness."[12] Torn between her familial responsibilities and the promise of a more exciting life with the debonair Jobert, she chose the latter, embarking on a two-year odyssey that few women of her day experienced. Theodosia suffered pangs of regret during the voyage to Haiti, leaving behind her daughters, one age four and the other not quite two, but the die had been cast. From the outset of her time with Lionel Jobert, starting with the Haitian

Naval School cadets aboard the *Geffrard*, Theodosia inhabited a predominantly male sphere, defiant of Victorian strictures on female comportment. In this d'Epineuil was complicit. At Camp Richmond near Annapolis, he shocked his men when "at the hour of parade he repeatedly rode about Camp Richmond in presence of his Regiment drawn up in line with Madame d'Epineuil on the same horse behind him dressed in the uniform of a private soldier."[13] Thomas Bell sketched the youthful-looking Theodosia, who presented the appearance of a self-possessed woman, her hands thrust into the pockets of her Zouave trousers, fully aware of the gender norms she was challenging, and unrepentant (see figure 5.1). Bell described Theodosia to his sister as follows:

Figure 5.1. Sketch by Lt. Col. Thomas Bell of "Madam" d'Epineuil (Mrs. Theodosia Lloyd), 1861. In Bell to Dr. & Cass, Camp Union near Annapolis, December 19, 1861, Lt. Col. Thomas S. Bell papers, Chester County History Center, West Chester, PA.

After the Court adj'd yesterday I walked down to the camp (we had been sitting at the Col's H'dqrs a farm house near his camp) with her, she being dressed in the *full* Zouave costume. I send you a little sketch of her. She wears their full rig—red fez, dark blue jacket with yellow trimmings, light blue sash & pant (made like a bag with two holes cut in the bottom) dark leather gaiters, & white linen ones for the feet. She declares she is going with us—Genl Burnside to the contrary notwithstanding. Col. says if they won't let her go as Madam d'E. or his Secty, then he will take her as the Vivandiere of the Regiment! How would you like such a trip in such a dress Cass?[14]

If Colonel De Trobriand's Fifty-Fifth New York Regiment could have a vivandière—which they did, the sister of one of the men of the regiment[15]—then so, too, could Colonel d'Epineuil.

Theodosia did indeed join the Fifty-Third regiment aboard the *John Trucks*: one woman among more than seven hundred men on a ship for a month. However, she never functioned as a vivandière or matron (nurse); she was there as d'Epineuil's confidante and lover, and she seems to have taken the harrowing journey on the *John Trucks* in stride. When a private was lashed to the ship's rigging for the prank of putting a piece of pork inside a bugle, Theodosia sat out on the deck underneath him. Henry Cocheu noted an evening of intimacy aboard ship between d'Epineuil and his paramour. Cocheu entered into his diary that after the colonel reported to General Wool on the last day of January 1862, "he returned at dark & took the Matron!!!"[16] Lionel and Theodosia would maintain the fiction of being married throughout her stay in America. In mid-March 1862, d'Epineuil scorned those "who, respecting nothing, dare reproach my noble wife with her devotion to the regiment, when, delicate as she is, she had consented to follow it, as nurse, through all its fatigues, in order to devote her care to the poor wounded of her husband's command."[17] Theodosia was not Madame d'Epineuil but, except on paper, she had long ceased to be Mrs. Thomas Charles Lloyd.

In the wake of his officers' charges against him, Colonel d'Epineuil dashed off a report of his regiment's ordeal to Brigadier General John P. Hatch in charge at Annapolis and sent a copy to United States Adjutant General Lorenzo Thomas.[18] D'Epineuil further sought to salvage his reputation by addressing the commander-in-chief: President Abraham Lincoln. Jobert informed the president of the unit's misfortune and the colonel's desire for the regiment to be put into action. On February 14, Lincoln penned a note for "the bearer" (d'Epineuil) to General George B. McClellan that summed up the tricks that Mother Nature had played on the Fifty-Third New York while aboard the *John Trucks* and asked General McClellan what he wanted to do with the now idle regiment.[19] McClellan sent one of his staff officers, Major Nelson H. Davis, to conduct an inspection of the Fifty-Third in his capacity as assistant inspector general. The condition of the *John Trucks* and the men prior to the inspection scandalized an assistant quartermaster, James C. Slaght, when they disembarked at Fort Madison in Annapolis on February 13. "The 'John Trucks' arrived here after a voyage of eight days with the 53d Regt. N.Y. Vols. on board," wrote Slaght. "They were filthy in the enlarged sense of the term—their bodies literally covered with vermin, and the vessel a perfect Lazar house."[20] On arrival at the fort, three men immediately deserted. During their court martial trials, they all cited unsanitary conditions as the reason for their desertion. Corporal John Gillard, for example, swore he had no intention of deserting. Defending his reason for absenting himself without leave, Gillard stated, "I was ill treated and the Regiment was full of *vermin*, I was going to clean myself and return." The court found Gillard guilty, and ordered that he forfeit ten dollars per month of pay, be confined at hard labor for the rest of his enlistment, and be dishonorably discharged.[21]

Major Davis arrived at Fort Madison on February 17. It was raining. At the morning report that day, Davis recorded 625 enlisted men and 34 commissioned officers in all. As Davis proceeded with the inspection, querying the men tent-by-tent, Private Pittman recalled that "Our Colonel & Major was with him & tried to scowl the men into answering falsely."[22] After a second day of inspection, Davis had seen enough and his impression was less than favorable. He noted in his report that the Enfield rifles were in bad order; bayonets only fit the rifle they came with and were so often exchanged among the soldiers that many could not fix bayonets to their rifles. Nearly all tents, recently issued from Baltimore, leaked badly. Discipline was lax. Mud had prevented drilling, but the want of instruction he observed convinced Davis that from "ignorance or willful neglect of their duties, and impropriety of conduct, *several* of the officers are *wholly unfitted* and *incompetent* to hold their positions." The inspecting officer emphasized in his remarks the deplorable infestation of lice on the men's bodies and clothing, and blamed the officers for allowing this to occur aboard the *John Trucks*. For Major Davis, the course of action to be taken was clear: "Genl. Hatch reports that about 200 men of this Regt. would enlist in the U.S. Army, and recommends such enlistments, then to transfer the balance to other Vol. Regts, and disband the officers. I concur with the Genl. in this opinion, if it can be effected."²³

Now uncertain of their future, the regiment would spend a month at Fort Madison drilling, standing inspection, and even engaging in a dress parade to keep busy.²⁴ For the soldiers who could afford it, meals available at Fort Madison were positively sumptuous compared to those aboard the *John Trucks*. Captain Charles Dustan informed his mother that

> until to day [I] have lived quite well—broiled mackerel—fried potatoes—sausages eggs &c for breakfast. Steak and *fixings* for dinner—but today I dined on boiled potatoes & boiled potatoes only—it turned out most fortunately, however for as I sat chewing & refining—entre the Major (who had been refused admittance at the only other decent mess in camp) with a request to join *my* mess—now I would not have him anyhow he eats so much & pays so little—I did not refuse—but I said "Yes—Major" "*I* take but two meals a day this is a specimen dinner sit down" "Ah, well, but, yes indeed, *no*" (*blessed word*) "I sink zat I vill alone too" said the Major and retired disgusted—it was a narrow escape though for yesterday I had roast turkey.²⁵

But the regiment's days were numbered. On the basis of his trusted staff officer's inspection report, General McClellan issued Special Order 42 from Army Headquarters in Washington, dated February 26, 1862, which set in motion the process of disbanding Lionel Jobert's regiment. The text of the order closely followed General Hatch's recommendation that Major Davis had included in his report: "By direction of the Secretary of War, such men of the 53d New York Volunteers (d'Epineuil Zouaves) as are willing to enlist in the U. S. Army, and are accepted by a recruiting officer, will be discharged the service on their so enlisting. The remainder of the men will be transferred to other New York volunteer regiments. The officers of the said regiment are discharged the service, and the regiment is disbanded, to take effect March 1, 1862."²⁶ The soldiers were a valuable asset that the army wanted to retain. Lionel J. d'Epineuil was not.

Few appear to have known of the disbanding order for a number of days, as the regiment continued to go about its routine. On February 27, Colonel d'Epineuil toured the camp, directing other companies to pattern their tent arrangements after those of Company H, with which he expressed his satisfaction. The next day, the colonel requested permission for one of his captains to go to New York to recruit for the regiment. Assistant Quartermaster Slaght informed Burnside that he had dismissed the *John Trucks* from service, and that the Fifty-Third was awaiting orders: "They are about 800 strong and are all able bodied men, and I think some disposition should be made of them."[27] But by March 3, news of the order for disbanding the regiment had leaked down to the rank-and-file. Pittman recorded the rumor in his journal; Charles Dustan did the same in a letter to his mother. "I've bad news for you," Dustan wrote, "I believe that owing to the incompetency of the higher officers of the Rgt, and the great annoyance & trouble they have caused the Authorities we are (capable & incapable guilty & innocent alike) to be disbanded that is the men absorbed into other Rgts and *all* the officers mustered out of the service." Learning of the regiment's pending dissolution, surgeons Henry Phillips and Bernard Vanderkeift requested of New York Surgeon General Vanderpool that they be reassigned to another regiment or hospital so as not to be without a job.[28] The regiment was unraveling as badly as the Zouave uniforms. Back in December, Sanitary Commission inspector J. H. Douglas, reporting on the regiment's uniforms, commented that the "men look very well." Now, in early March, inspector Dr. Robert Ware's responses to the section of the questionnaire regarding uniforms told a far different story. "Very few smart looking men," observed Ware. To the question inquiring if the men take pride in the uniform, Ware dryly wrote, "I rather think not now—they did once." Even the officers' dress shocked the inspector: "Clothing in such condition that it was difficult to say whether the disorder in dress was from necessity or choice." Ware added that the men "have but one suit of underclothing, and it was pitiful to see them on the day of my visit standing nearly naked in the March wind washing their clothing. Everything has become so infected [with] vermin that repeated washings had not cleaned the garment[s]. Uniforms must be washed as well as underclothing. Shoes very bad."[29] On March 9, the ragged Fifty-Third moved into tents at the Naval Academy in Annapolis where the volunteer soldiers turned in their arms and accoutrements, and on March 11, they were transferred to barracks at Soldiers' Rest near the railroad depot in Washington, DC. The timing of the disbanding of the Fifty-Third could not have been better for recent deserters like Corporal Gillard, because the sentences against them were not carried into execution as the regiment was disbanded before the trial results were received at headquarters.[30]

Colonel d'Epineuil and Major Cantel mustered out on March 11, and other officers followed in the ensuing days. With so many officers gone, the unit fell into relative disarray, some of them "wandering about the streets intoxicated and begging for bread."³¹ D'Epineuil bid adieu to his Zouaves in a self-exculpating address in Washington on March 15.

> You and I! we are to-day the victims of coward and underhand intrigants, who for personal motives—covered with the pompous name of so-called devotion to their country—have tried to and succeeded in demolishing one of the finest organizations ever gone from New York. . . . [My] crime, when alone, helpless—surrounded by enemies working against me, underhand, cowardly, without frankness—is to have devoted my money, my time, my health, my reputation, to make out of you all a fine regiment, and to maintain the discipline so much compromised every day by so called officers . . . My heart bleeds, my beloved boys, you Zouaves, who wear the name of my respected father, my heart bleeds when I think how glorious you would have made this name if it had been possible for us to show ourselves in any fight. My heart bleeds . . . when I see that, without any court-martial, without any plausible or apparent reason, I must see you taken suddenly away from me.³²

D'Epineuil did not face charges in a military tribunal, so the ex-colonel spoke his piece in the court of public opinion. He had given his all; any discipline he meted out was warranted; the treachery of devious subordinates undercut his efforts to make soldiers out of the recruits. Cruel circumstance—certainly not his own actions—sullied his name. A group of sergeants replied the next day with consoling remarks, affirming respect for their former commander. They, too, took the opportunity to press their own agenda, responding to a newspaper assertion of their public indecency: "we are daily hectored and annoyed by officers of other regiments, who strive to force us from our determination to be in all things sober and discreet, orderly and obedient, but firm and united in our resolve to get our honorable discharge from our own regiment, to be at full liberty of choice as to what others we will re-enlist in. We have no desire to leave the service, which has our most patriotic sympathy, but we know our rights as volunteers and freemen, and will maintain them against all hazards."³³

Some of d'Epineuil's Zouaves did indeed join other regiments. Company A, for instance, by Special Order 66 of March 8, transferred into the New York Seventeenth Infantry. Others exercised their rights as freemen and went home to stay after less than eight months in the service, thereby forfeiting the 100-dollar bounty promised them on their three-year enlistment. McClellan, as Special Order 42 indicated, did not want the enlisted men to be discharged. Carrying out McClellan's orders, on March 13, Bridagier General Silas Casey issued Special Order 72 by which 348 men of four companies from the Fifty-Third were to be distributed among other New York regiments; Casey noted the men appeared satisfied with that arrangement. On the same day, however, George Chester, now the ranking officer of the 53d NY, informed Casey that the soldiers of the regiment had since changed their minds. Chester reported

> That on visiting the quarters occupied by the 53rd New York Volunteers we found that an entirely unexpected change had occurred in the opinions and feeling of the men since we last saw them yesterday morning. They have been assured by Colonels and other officers as well as by Members of Congress &c that they are entitled to and if they insist upon it will receive their discharge and be allowed to return home—that they cannot legally be transferred against their wills. Such advice as this has had its natural effect. They will listen to no other advice from any one, but insist upon being discharged. Most of them it is true, assure us that after they have visited their homes they intend enlisting somewhere—but wish to select their own Regiments to serve in.
> The men are now organized, have fixed upon their plans & act in concert under the advice which I have mentioned.

Thus, the Zouaves won a battle after all: almost all of the more than 500 remaining soldiers of the Fifty-Third New York mustered out in Washington on March 21, lingering in the capital long enough to collect their pay.[34]

The beginning of spring marked the end of the Zouaves' winter of discontent. On their trip back to New York, 200 men of the now defunct Fifty-Third enjoyed a stopover at the Cooper Shop Volunteer Refreshment Saloon in Philadelphia, a pleasant transitional event for the many about to return to civilian life. In May, a new unit, also numerically designated as the Fifty-Third New York and to be dubbed the Vosburgh Chasseurs—which did not serve with the d'Epineuil Zouaves—began mustering enlistees. The second incarnation of the Fifty-Third New York became consolidated with the 132d New York Infantry. A small group of Native Americans from the Tuscarora Reservation in Upstate New York, so often mistakenly described as comprising a company of the d'Epineuil Zouaves, joined this second organization of New York's Fifty-Third Regiment. The names of those few men, hardly an entire company, do not appear on the roster of the d'Epineuils, who made up the first organization of the Fifty-Third New York.[35]

For all their misfortune, the d'Epineuil Zouaves returned from their ordeal relatively unscathed. The most prominent exception was the regiment's second in command: Joseph A. Viguier de Monteil. Disaffected, Lieutenant Colonel Monteil detached himself from the Fifty-Third and eventually boarded the *Virginia*, which carried Hawkins's Zouaves—the Ninth New York Regiment—thus allowing Monteil to join the fray at Roanoke Island with the rest of the Burnside Expedition. On February 8, Monteil, while leading a spirited charge, took a shot to the head and died on the spot. As a battlefield exigency, Monteil's body was wrapped in a carpet and quickly interred on Roanoke Island, the carpet serving to separate the corpse from the soil to provide what Civil War soldiers saw as a dignified burial.[36] Lieutenant Colonel Thomas Bell, who had served as president of Monteil's court of inquiry in December 1861, attended Monteil's reburial on February 16, at Roanoke. Bell somberly reflected on the suddenness of Monteil's demise: "On last Sunday in the drizzling rain I stood beside his grave while the last honors were being paid to the brave old man. His body had been exhumed in order that he might be properly buried. Poor old fellow I was talking with him just a little while before he fell. He was in the very lightest spirits. His regt not being here he was fighting with his rifle, as a private. I little thought that the shower a canister & grape that went screaming by me had killed him till I saw his dead body carried past."[37] Monteil's friend Lieutenant Colonel Albert C. Maggi, who had been Monteil's defense counsel during the court of inquiry, presided over the reburial.[38]

The death of the Fifty-Third's lieutenant colonel naturally meant the position was vacant, and E. W. Chester once again pushed for an American—clearly meaning his son George—to be promoted to the job. Echoing the earlier letters of George Chester and Francis Rotch, the elder Chester disdained Major Cantel as a replacement based on ability and social class: "The Major is utterly & wholly unfit for his present place much less for a higher one, even if he were an American & understood American character. He is uneducated . . . brother of a baker in sixth Avenue . . . It would be unfortunate for himself as well as for the Regt. to put him in a higher position. You would see what he is in three minutes conversation with him." Fourteen officers of the 53d, with Captain Franklin Willard conspicuously not among them, signed a petition addressed to Governor Morgan in support of George Chester's elevation to the lieutenant colonelcy of the regiment: "We are sure that the appointment of Captain Chester would meet the approval of all the officers who have not personal aspirations and certainly of every man in the ranks with whom he is deservedly a favourite." Chester learned of his promotion on March 6, just two weeks before the regiment disbanded.[39]

More than a month before the Roanoke engagement, diarist Henry Cocheu privately had praised his brave Lieutenant Colonel Monteil as being totally different from the rest of the 53d's leadership. Now Monteil's fortitude was known to all. Newspapers reported widely on Monteil's courage and enthusiasm in battle, and eulogized him in reverent prose. Brigadier General Burnside honored the fallen Monteil by renaming a battery after him on Roanoke Island's Shallow Bag Bay.[40] Even Colonel d'Epineuil, in a statement that may strain credulity, paid homage to the fallen Monteil. "Having been more an enemy of my Lieut. Col than a friend when he was still in this world," professed d'Epineuil, "I most positively desire to prove to every one that his high bravery has destroyed all hatred against him in my heart by doing *my best* to honor his noble & so brave memory."[41] Nearly a month after Monteil's death, his widow Marie pleaded with General Burnside to have the lieutenant colonel's remains returned to her so that he could be buried with family and friends in attendance.

> I have been expecting the remains of my husband, hoping that they would be sent to me for burial.
> Will you see, General, that my request be granted . . . He gave his life to this country—will you not give me his bones? . . . I beg you, Sir, by what you respect more on this earth to order that my wishes be complied to. There is no rest for me as long as I know that my poor dear husband is so far away and without a decent place of rest.
> Be good enough to excuse me for troubling you in the midst of your labors, and may God allow you to come back safe to those who love you.[42]

The army returned Monteil's body to New York City on March 13, and funeral services took place at his late residence, 166 East Thirty-Third Street, two days later. Four months after the entire d'Epineuil Zouaves regiment paraded through New York City without their lieutenant colonel, Viguier de Monteil moved slowly along Manhattan's streets in a procession honoring him alone. Grieving family and friends laid Monteil to rest across the East

River in Brooklyn's Green-Wood Cemetery.[43] It was the name Monteil, not d'Epineuil, that became synonymous with heroism.

The soldiers of the Fifty-Third New York Regiment never enjoyed the lasting approbation afforded other French-inflected units, and neither did their commanding officer. The antithesis of Lionel Jobert's intention had occurred: instead of becoming a respected icon à la the colonel of the Gardes Lafayette, d'Epineuil had become Baron De Trobriand's grotesque doppelgänger. Jobert had risen quickly in the summer of 1861 to command a volunteer Union regiment, but a little over seven months later he tumbled out of the service just as fast. In the regiment's final month of March 1862, the Fifty-Third's James Bryant Smith, a Company K private promoted to commissary sergeant, set to paper a long tongue-in-cheek poem—"Zouavata"—that chronicled the saga of d'Epineuil's Zouaves from beginning to end. The final stanza cedes to a future unknown.

> What became of gallant Colonel
> Muse historic must hereafter
> Tell in verses more poetic.[44]

With his means of ascent now disbanded, whither Lionel Jobert?

Chapter 6

Paternity and Performance in Philadelphia

Lionel Jobert rarely ventured out of his refuge in Washington's National Hotel during the spring of 1862. On March 28, two and a half weeks after having been mustered out of the United States service, d'Epineuil's letter to New York Adjutant General Hillhouse showed that the ex-colonel still felt the sting of his regiment's ignominious end.

> I have the honor to acknowledge I am the receip[ien]t of yr favor of this day stating that yr Dept had received, officially or otherwise, no confirmation as to the causes of the disbandg of the 53d Rt. N. Y. V[.] I had the honor to command . . .
>
> I think (without even invoking the kindness you always showed me, but only appealg to yr *sense of honor* & justice) I think the causes of my disbandg are owed to me as a right I today respectfully but most firmly claim. I think it would be a shame to yr state as well as to the g[ener]al government to suddenly disband a Regt. raised at so heavy expense by a foreigner—without giving of such a hard measure the smallest reason. When a thief—a swindler or some low class scoundrel is never condemned except on *causes* well *established* & *known*.
>
> I have to say
>
> Was I guilty? Why have I not been court-martialed?
>
> Was I incompetent? Why have I not been rejected by a board of examiners?[1]

D'Epineuil understood that once formally discharged from the military it would be hard for him to get another commission as an officer. One immediate consequence for d'Epineuil was loss of income. A volunteer colonel earned the same as a colonel in the regular army: a base pay of $110 a month, plus $54 or the equivalent in rations, $24 allowance for forage for horses, and $49 or the labor of two servants, for a total income of $237 per month.[2] Now his pay was zero. If he could not rejoin the armed forces, how would he support himself and Theodosia? His concern over finances came through in his letter: d'Epineuil had spent considerable sums to field his namesake regiment. D'Epineuil also intuited correctly, with wounded pride, that the army brass simply wanted no more to do with the colonel, summarily dismissing him as counterproductive, or at best insignificant, to the Union cause. Thus, Jobert prevailed on his ally Congressmen Elijah Ward to intercede with the War Department on his behalf. D'Epineuil addressed a letter to Secretary of War Edwin Stanton that recounted Jobert's tale of woe, adding: "*A foreigner* in a country in which he came to serve loyaly [*sic*] & win some glory in, he can not be sent away in such a manner, receiving dishonor in exchange for his money time & reputation so devotedly spent in the service of the U.S." On April 12, Ward forwarded d'Epineuil's letter to the secretary of war with the request that Stanton look into the matter.[3]

While brooding over his most recent misfortune, d'Epineuil heard tell of a quixotic escapade that involved three former officers of his disbanded Zouave regiment: Adjutant Victor Vifquain, Captain Alfred Cipriani, and Second Lieutenant Armand Dufloo. The trio of young men, all in their twenties, also had taken rooms at the National Hotel in March after mustering out of the Fifty-Third New York. Together with a fourth conspirator, Maurice de Beaumont, they plotted an unrealized scheme to kidnap President Jefferson Davis of the Confederacy. Southern authorities arrested Vifquain, Cipriani, and de Beaumont as they passed through Virginia in April; Dufloo did not accompany them as he had absentmindedly shot himself through the hand while cleaning his pistol. Subsequent to their detention, the adventurers were unable to get close to Davis, and returned to Washington. Rumors circulated that the three captives were turncoats offering their service in support of the rebels. Such was the coverage in the press that former Fifty-Third New York Captain W. W. Armstrong felt obliged to defend the integrity of his men by reminding the citizenry that his Company A had been transferred out of the d'Epineuil Zouaves and had nothing to do with the ill-conceived ploy. The three adventurers personally experienced enough contempt from others that Cipriani, on behalf of his fellows, publicly admitted their youthful carelessness in blithely moving about Virginia, but disavowed any dishonorable motives. D'Epineuil weighed in as well, refuting the allegation that it was he who had taken part in the affair under the assumed name de Beaumont.[4]

D'Epineuil's letter of June 13, subsequently published in the *New York Herald*, revealed more than his indignation at being accused of "committing all kinds of boyish actions under a false name." Jobert up to this point in his life appeared rather apolitical, but in this letter he identified himself as a legitimist. Legitimists in France were conservatives who favored traditional monarchical succession. In the context of the United States, where he could have fled to New Orleans or elsewhere in the South to escape his Caribbean crisis, Jobert viewed a legitimist's position as support for the duly constituted government of the Union, and he chose to reside in New York. Yet, in Haiti he gladly had accepted employment under the insurrectionist General Fabre Geffrard. Jobert's politics, then, were largely, if not exclusively, the politics of convenience; what he valued most was his own advancement. His missive to the *Herald* also showed that Jobert still hoped the military would be the means of that advancement, declaring "although my services have as yet met with a singular kind of reward, I trust that they may, by and by, be better appreciated, and that I may have an opportunity of distinguishing myself in the cause which I have adopted from conviction."[5] That opportunity was not forthcoming. The War Department had referred d'Epineuil's letter, sent by Congressman Ward, to the Adjutant General's Office with the directive to issue a report on the case. Adjutant General Thomas's report, dated June 16, 1862, ended the matter: "This regiment was mustered out of service because it was found to be in a demoralized condition, and according to the Inspection reports it became so through the inefficiency of the Colonel." The War Department informed Elijah Ward of this conclusion ten days later.[6]

Still Lionel J. d'Epineuil tried to cajole his way back into military service. One position d'Epineuil pursued was that of aide-de-camp. Several of the former officers of the Fifty-Third New York did the same. The day after Major Cantel mustered out of the d'Epineuil Zouaves he was the beneficiary of a warm recommendation letter from Brigadier General James Cooper to Abraham Lincoln. "Major Cantel," Cooper wrote the president, "late 53d New York volunteers, by the disbandment of the said regiment, is now without position, and is willing to take the post of principal Aid de Camp in my staff. I know Major Cantel well. He is a gentleman and soldier deserving consideration at the hands of all good and loyal men. I will gladly give him a place on my staff, as principal aid de camp." Despite this endorsement, quite at odds with the Chesters' assessment of Cantel, Cooper had no vacancies under his command of Marylanders for Cantel to fill. Captain Charles Dustan and a few of his brother officers of the defunct Fifty-Third New York also sought posts as aides-de-camp in other volunteer units.[7] To land such a position for himself, the oft-criticized d'Epineuil needed help from influential quarters. On July 23, Ambrose Burnside, now a major general, accommodated d'Epineuil with a letter of support that provided a more favorable accounting of the latter's abilities than he deserved: "This will certify that *Col. 'Lionel J. d'Epineuil'* organized a Regt of Vol. in the city of New York, in the fall of 1861. In the organization of this Regt. and in equipping the same Col. d'Epineuil *showed much skill* and in the regimental drills evinced a *thorough knowledge* of *military tactics. But owing to some unfortunate appointments of officers under him* the regt was very much injured and was mustered out of service." To strengthen his chances, d'Epineuil once again appealed to the highest authority, writing to President Abraham Lincoln. D'Epineuil's letter to the president bemoaned the disbanding of the colonel's regiment "*on the simple report of an asst. Inspector general* who has been *influenced* against me in the most hostile manner," and reproduced Burnside's letter to counter the conclusions of the inspection report. "In presence of such a summary injustice," d'Epineuil whined, "I, as a foreigner, french [*sic*] by birth, a lover of the American Union by heart—the sufferer of an undeserved shame—I do *solemnly appeal* to the *justice of the President* of a *great nation* I came to serve faithfully." The former colonel concluded with a request for his case to be reviewed by a board of inquiry that, he was certain, would allow him to "regain my reputation." Lincoln submitted d'Epineuil's letter to Secretary of War Stanton on August 7, perhaps unaware that Stanton had already had the matter investigated and closed.[8] The impatient d'Epineuil continued his crusade by meeting the president face to face on August 11. Ever the lawyer, Lincoln wrote a carefully worded memorandum on the subject: "Today Col d'Epineuil calls on me and asks me to send him to some general as aid de Camp with the rank of Colonel. I have no lawful power to appoint him a Colonel nor to appoint him an aid de Camp until he is commissioned as Colonel or to some other rank by the governor of some state. When he gets such commission *I will appoint him aid to any general who may ask for him*, provided it be lawful for me to do so."[9]

Whether at her companion's request or of her own accord, it was Theodosia who asked Kentucky Representative John J. Crittenden to recommend Lionel as an aide-de-camp to Crittenden's son, Major General Thomas J.

Crittenden. Armed with the Burnside and Lincoln letters, d'Epineuil followed Theodosia's overture by writing to the senior Crittenden.[10] Meanwhile, taking the squeaky-wheel-gets-the-grease approach, d'Epineuil convinced some fellow guests at the National Hotel to write Stanton again. The letter posited that since no law existed authorizing the mustering out of a commissioned officer other than by court martial or court of inquiry, "it is the opinion of three of the most enlightened lawyers of this city that the mustering out of Col. L. J. d'Epineuil was illegal & that consequently he has a right to consider himself still in the service of government although unemployed since the 11th of March 1862."[11] Whatever the finer points of law as they applied to discharging a foreigner who had led a volunteer regiment, they went unexamined given the exigencies of war. Even with the support of his friends and Representative Crittenden's indulgence, d'Epineuil was unable to secure another military position on anyone's staff.

The situation got worse in the latter half of 1862 for both the Union war effort and for d'Epineuil. Confederate forces defeated their Union counterparts in the second battle of Bull Run at the end of August. In October the South's General J. E. B. Stuart rode around McClellan's forces again, embarrassing the Army of the Potomac. Then in December Major General Burnside failed to dislodge the Confederates in a costly assault at Fredericksburg, Virginia. Costliness preoccupied Lionel d'Epineuil as well. Anxious to recoup his expenditure on horses that got separated from his regiment during the Burnside Expedition, d'Epineuil relied on New York merchant Stephen M. Gladwin for assistance. Gladwin wrote to the Quartermaster's Department in Washington to facilitate d'Epineuil's attempt to recover the cost of the animals, characterizing d'Epineuil's situation as "a very severe case, when taken in connection with all the other loses to him in raising and organizing this regiment, now disbanded."[12] While trying to gain compensation for the horses, Lionel Jobert's worries rapidly multiplied. The district court of Washington, DC issued a writ on October 9 for d'Epineuil to appear in response to a lawsuit filed against him by Brooks Brothers for nonpayment of his bill of more than 500 dollars; depositions in the case would be taken the following spring.[13] That same week in October d'Epineuil's two-year relationship with Theodosia came to an end. Thomas Lloyd had begun divorce proceedings in England against his wife, naming Jobert as a defendant along with Theodosia, who sailed to England so she could deal with the issue. While the divorce case took another year and a half to become final,[14] there is no indication that Lionel and Theodosia ever saw each other again. In debt and companionless, d'Epineuil's situation sank even lower. At noon on November 11, a month after Theodosia's departure, a no doubt startled d'Epineuil was arrested by the Washington, DC police. John Decatur, a former business partner of Jobert's while in Haiti, caught up with him in Washington and charged him with obtaining money under false pretense. Decatur alleged that Jobert had cheated him out of 1,500 dollars. D'Epineuil's defense counsel pleaded the statute of limitations and the lack of an extradition treaty between Haiti and the United States during his tenure as the commander of the Haitian Naval School. Justice of the Peace Charles Walter concurred, and dismissed the case.[15] Lionel J. d'Epineuil's second year in the United States could not end fast enough for him.

At the beginning of 1863, President Lincoln issued the Emancipation Proclamation, declaring free all enslaved persons in rebel territory. Jobert saw a favorable moment for a last-ditch effort to rejoin the United States military. D'Epineuil once again addressed himself to the secretary of war on March 13, 1863, this time from 460 Fifteenth Street in Washington; the National Hotel had become too expensive a residence for the cash-strapped Jobert. D'Epineuil requested "the necessary authority to raise a *brigade of colored men* accordingly to the very same rules & regulations already ruling the volunteer service . . . I hold myself at yr entire disposal Mr. Secretary to explain you [sic], if necessary, my views on this important & *radical* subject & to show you my titles if you decide to see them." His titles were his credentials authorizing his service for the Haitian government; he had commanded black men—youths, really—before. Such a gambit risked investigation into the disgraceful end of his tenure in the employ of Haiti. The War Department's prompt reply the next day informed d'Epineuil that his request had been put in the files of the adjutant general for consideration.[16] In short, filed and forgotten. Ex-Colonel Lionel J. d'Epineuil had to resign himself to the fact that he could not revive his military career.

Jobert's fruitless attempts to rejoin the US military—although he continued to employ the moniker "colonel" just in case—meant his road to advancement must lay elsewhere. Always abreast of current events, Lionel hoped that Napoleon III's imperial ambitions might present an opportunity for employment, and he was willing to quit the United States. In June of 1862, France had wrested from Annam in Southeast Asia territorial concessions that would come to form part of French Indochina. The emperor also desired to make Mexico a client state, and the latter viewed the presence of the French navy in the Pacific with foreboding. None other than *La Bayonnaise* anchored in Acapulco in late August, an arrival that preoccupied the commander of nearby Mexican forces to the point that he ordered the French corvette to leave. The tense situation abated when *La Bayonnaise* left for Panama, but not before threatening to shell the city in response to the demand that the ship depart. In January 1863, with the United States distracted by its own civil war, the French navy bombarded Acapulco.[17] Recovering quickly from the War Department's tepid reply to his overture, Jobert penned a letter on March 15 to the French secretary of the navy and of the colonies requesting a position as an auxiliary ship's ensign, prepared to serve anywhere—only in desperation did he consider venturing outside of his familiar Atlantic sphere. In the letter Jobert highlighted his imperial authorization "in 1860, to take up military service in Haiti where, over the course of two years, he has directed, with success, a *"Naval School"* which he has founded at Port-au-Prince for the Haitian government, then moved to America where very grave matters of interest detained him"; he wished "to resume service in France and profit from the opportunities for advancement that the war in Mexico and the China expedition offer to him."[18] D'Epineuil must have known that the Haitian authorities had complained to the French government about his service while in command of the *Geffrard*, but he was at the end of his rope, and hoped that French officials might have forgotten the particulars of more than two years ago. Hence Jobert's selective representation of events: he had successfully directed the naval school; he then moved—not fled—to the United States, where duty born from conscience led to his service in the Civil War and had interrupted his career as a capitaine au long cours. But the French Naval Ministry had no use for the discredited Lionel Jobert and declined to hire him. Officials even wrote a notice of the ministry's rejection in Jobert's maritime file: "the Captain solicited employment as an auxiliary ensign. He did not appear to be worthy of being admitted into the corps of ships officers."[19] Grasping at straws, the mind of a desperate man fabricated a glimmer of hope where there was none, and on May 6, d'Epineuil replied,

> You have told him [d'Epineuil] that his request "to be admitted to serve aboard the vessels of the Imperial Navy in the rank of Auxiliary Ship's Ensign cannot be accommodated at the present time."
>
> The undersigned has nothing but to submit to the decision of Your Exc., something hard for him who is informed of this decision. But the words "at the present time" seem to reserve that the refusal is nothing but temporary; he begs insistently Your Excellency, Mr. Minister, to be so good as to take note of his request so that as soon as the needs of the service will permit it can be responded to favorably.[20]

As he languished in the American capital, Lionel Jobert knew enough to consider alternatives should his native country never find itself in need of his services. Panicked New York merchants in mid-1861 had inspired Jobert to put forth his plan for an ocean police. What did Washingtonians want? The capital's streets had endured two years of punishment from legions of soldiers, horses, and wagons moving in and out of the city on a regular basis. Under such conditions, it was impossible to keep the paved thoroughfares free of mud and debris. Certainly an enterprising man could devise a solution that, if applied to all the major avenues of Washington, would bestow on the inventor both a favorable reputation and a handsome income. To that end Jobert teamed up with James Monroe Letts. Letts had served as a captain in Colonel Robert F. Taylor's Thirty-Third New York Regiment until Letts resigned for health reasons at the end of 1861. A Daguerreotype artist by trade, Letts had a penchant for inventiveness. Together, d'Epineuil and Letts came up with a design for iron street crossings, for which they received a patent in May 1863. An advertisement placed in a local newspaper suggests that d'Epineuil had begun in earnest to develop the plan as early as mid-February. The author of the ad sought office space "suitable for a draughtsman, situated as near as possible to the Patent Office"; respondents were asked to contact " 'D. J. L.' "—d'Epineuil's monogram in reverse. The idea consisted of creating a masonry- and iron-lined ditch up to five feet wide and two feet deep that ran across the street. The ditch would be covered by cast iron plates that had grooved openings in them, allowing mud, rain, and debris to fall through, thus leaving the street relatively clean. The trench was to be slightly angled from the center in both directions so that the detritus would run away from the middle of the road. The *Daily National Intelligencer* reported on and endorsed the plan that July. Benjamin Brown French, appointed by President Lincoln as the city's commissioner of public buildings in September 1861, received a dozen letters in support of the project the morning after the *Intelligencer* ran the story. French ordered the construction of an initial trench at Pennsylvania Avenue and Sixth Street—right in front of the National Hotel. Commissioner French, a veteran of the Washington political scene, thought the idea of iron street crossings a good one, but cautioned that to implement the project citywide would require significant funding.[21]

D'Epineuil sorely needed the city of Washington to adopt his idea for iron street crossings because his personal finances were under siege. Some time prior to mid-March 1863, lawyers for Thomas Lloyd had served d'Epineuil in the Lloyd v. Lloyd and Jobert case, demanding that Jobert pay the cost incurred by Thomas Lloyd in filing the petition for divorce. While this potential monetary loss threatened d'Epineuil's pocketbook, the judgment in the Brooks Brothers lawsuit put him further in arrears. Depositions in the case were taken in New York City on May 11, 1863, the deponents responding to a set of questions agreed on beforehand. The law firm of Norris and Johnson had gotten d'Epineuil off the hook in the Decatur case of the previous November, but there was little that attorney John E. Norris could do for d'Epineuil against the brothers Brooks. The evidence clearly showed that d'Epineuil had received $551.65 worth of merchandise from the clothiers, a sum that included expenditures made by d'Epineuil's old nemesis, Lieutenant Colonel Viguier de Monteil. Norris hoped to establish that an understanding existed regarding the government paying the bill, but employees testified that they knew of no agreement stipulating that d'Epineuil would procure a government contract for Brooks Brothers to furnish clothing or other equipment. When testimony ended, Edward J. Wilson of New York, the commissioner charged with collecting the depositions from the witnesses, mailed the depositions to the Supreme Court of the District of Columbia, the city of d'Epineuil's current residence. The court found d'Epineuil responsible for the entire bill, plus interest.[22]

Lionel Jobert again found himself on the wrong side of fortune. Badly in need of funds, d'Epineuil had to take a job as a first class clerk in the office of the First Auditor of the Treasury Department in October 1863. Adding insult to injury, the push to use iron street crossings in the nation's capital petered out by the end of the year. As with his coastal patrol plan two years earlier, d'Epineuil had correctly gauged the public's interest. Benjamin French's prescience, however, was well considered. Two months after French began arrangements for the first trench on Pennsylvania Avenue, the work remained pending. The project still lay moribund in December, despite the *Intelligencer* imploring Congress to support it. Whether wary stone masons blocked the use of iron street crossings, or Congress envisioned disbursing funds to more pressing endeavors, it became clear as 1863 ebbed that another of d'Epineuil's carefully thought out plans would come to naught.[23] Yet the year 1864 began with a stroke of luck for Lionel J. d'Epineuil. Avoiding appearing in court had helped him to wriggle out of responsibility for his role in the Lloyd divorce case when the prosecutors could not prove for certain that d'Epineuil was involved, although it was clear to all but the court that he had in fact been the offending party. Surprisingly, the court ruled in January 1864 that the marriage "between Thomas Charles Lloyd the Petitioner and Theodosia Augusta Lloyd heretofore Gordon spinster the

Respondent be dissolved by reason of the adultery committed since the celebration of the said marriage by the said Theodosia Augusta Lloyd with *some person unknown* [emphasis added]." The divorce became final in May.²⁴

One bullet dodged, but Jobert still cast about for some loftier means of subsistence than his dreary clerkship. Three days before ending his brief career with the Treasury Department,²⁵ d'Epineuil wrote to George McClellan on March 5 seeking consent for the exclusive right to produce a French translation of the general's report on the operations of the Army of the Potomac during his command: "I have received in due time the letter you so kindly wrote me and in which you authorize me to undertake the translation of your very remarkable military report—which I have already beggun [*sic*]. Although my object is simply to attach my humble name to yours—I should still be glad to obtain from you the *monopoly* for this translation. I am not rich, unhappily, and could not otherwise, meet the necessary expenses of *cop[y]ists* and time to be made for so serious an enterprise." McClellan had no objection to the proposal;²⁶ however, d'Epineuil must have shelved the idea and not returned to it, finding the need to secure an immediate source of income more pressing. Writing in late July 1864 from yet another new Washington residence at 275 Vermont Avenue, d'Epineuil next addressed Secretary of State William Seward for employment in the State Department as a first-class clerk. He cited former superiors, including Generals Burnside and Foster, as references, as well as Congressman Elijah Ward, his stalwart supporter. D'Epineuil dropped one more name he hoped would be of particular value on this job application: that of his brother-in-law, Edmond Breuil. Making reference to his own credentials, d'Epineuil wrote, with his habit of underscoring words for emphasis, that the "documents here enclosed might be certified by the French Chargé d'affaires, Mr. de Geofroy—with whom I have no *personal* acquaintance, but who is one of the good friends of Mr. E. Breuil, *my sister's husband*, now our French Consul at Lisbon (Portugal)." Two and a half weeks later d'Epineuil again contacted Seward, this time to ask that his credentials be returned to him, as he assumed correctly that not receiving a response from the State Department meant that his services were not required there. If the Lincoln administration lacked interest in d'Epineuil, perhaps McClellan's presidential campaign could use him to canvass among soldiers for the upcoming election. Lionel communicated that very point to McClellan at the end of August, doubtless hoping to benefit from postelection spoils should McClellan prevail, but Lincoln won reelection that November.²⁷ Approaching three years of residence in the capital, Lionel Jobert concluded that the city of Washington no longer had much to offer him. What the former colonel needed was another new beginning. The place: Philadelphia.

Jobert's near success with the iron street crossing invention in the nation's capital had the silver lining of showing him the possibilities of advancement via patents and the marketplace of ideas. Yet while Washington, DC swelled in population during the war, the city remained a relatively small urban area that had numbered just over 61,000 inhabitants in 1860. New York was the nation's largest city, but d'Epineuil's name had little purchase there anymore. So, by the spring of 1865, d'Epineuil had taken up residence in Philadelphia. Philadelphia was the nation's second-largest metropolis, growing from 565,529 residents in 1860 to 674,022 in 1870.[28] Its large market, cultural vibrancy, and geographic location between Washington and New York made Philadelphia an attractive destination for Lionel Jobert. In January and February of 1865, d'Epineuil had this advertisement printed in the *Philadelphia Inquirer*: "A Gentleman, lately an officer in the United States Army, desires to obtain a position as Civil Engineer, or draughtsman, or an accounting clerk, in any establishment requiring such services. His testimonials are of the highest character as to ability, integrity and steady habits. Address, 'Lionel,' at this office." It takes little to read d'Epineuil's desperation between the lines of this ad: *any* job would do. D'Epineuil even returned to the idea of writing, this time a history of the late rebellion. From office space he secured at 427 Walnut Street in Philadelphia, Jobert corresponded in May with functionaries in the war-born state of West Virginia, asking for copies of that state's official reports for his book on the war; he let them know, not inaccurately, that he had been "a participator in its contests."[29] The completed book project, like the translation of McClellan's report, did not materialize.

The American Civil War had all but ended in that month of May 1865. When the war began, Lionel Jobert had hoped the conflict would be his avenue to fortune and fame. By war's end, however, most people had either forgotten d'Epineuil's short time in the military or remembered it with scorn. In sharp contrast to d'Epineuil, Régis de Trobriand received a brevet to major general, the only Frenchman aside from the Marquis de Lafayette to be so honored by the United States. D'Epineuil emerged from the war years worse off that some of his wartime acquaintances, but better than others, at least insofar as he survived the conflict. Jean B. Cantel returned to civilian life in Washington, DC, after his unsuccessful bid to become an aide-de-camp to General Cooper. Cantel married Augustine Gicquel in New York City on March 19, 1862, just eight days after mustering out of the Fifty-Third New York Volunteers, and later secured work as a clerk in the Clothing Bureau of the Quartermaster General's Office. With one son and another on the way, Cantel tried to improve his situation by becoming a naturalized United States citizen in September 1864 and then applying two months later to President Lincoln for the post of United States consul to Boulogne, France. Former Maryland governor and then senator Thomas H. Hicks's letter in support of Cantel's application revealed some of the politics that could factor into doling out government jobs: Hicks pointed out to Secretary of State Seward that Maryland had but four such appointments abroad, while Rhode Island had seven. Hicks failed to sway Seward. As with d'Epineuil's attempt to secure a similar post, Cantel did not get the position in Boulogne; instead, he was transferred in February 1865 from the Quartermaster General's Office to a clerkship in the Office of the Commissary General of Subsistence. In the fall, Cantel returned to his prewar position teaching French to young ladies at the Patapsco Institute in Ellicott City, west of Baltimore.[30] D'Epineuil's co-patentee, James Letts, worked during the war for the Treasury Department. Supported by men of influence such as United States Minister to Mexico Thomas Corwin and Michigan Representative Francis W. Kellogg, Letts landed the post of US commercial agent at Saint-Marc, Haiti, a duty he began in 1865. Captain-cum-Lieutenant Colonel George Chester of the d'Epineuil Zouaves managed to stay in the military, becoming the colonel of the 101st NY Regiment and participating in the Battle of Fredericksburg. Not all of d'Epineuil's former colleagues from the Fifty-Third New York Volunteers fared as well. In June 1863, Henry Cocheu was killed in action with the 173d NY at Port Hudson, Louisiana, one of the hundreds of thousands of examples of the nation's harrowing sacrifice. Second Lieutenant Thaddeus C. Ferris reenlisted with other regiments, including the Enfants Perdus. He died in October 1864 while fighting as part of the 90th New York Infantry at Cedar Creek, Virginia, and was buried in the same Brooklyn cemetery, Green-Wood, as Joseph A. Viguier de Monteil. As for Monteil's widow Marie, she married the martyred lieutenant colonel's friend, Albert Maggi, in Boston in 1864.[31]

It was not until mid-June of 1865 that d'Epineuil finally landed a job of some duration, but to do so he had to create it himself. A small advertisement in the *Philadelphia Inquirer* announced his latest venture: "THE UNDERSIGNED HAVE THIS DAY formed a co-partnership for the purpose of carrying on the business of Patent Right Brokerage, Engineering, etc., under the style and title of D'EPINEUIL & EVANS.

LIONEL J. D'EPINEUIL, CHARLES H. EVANS. June 14, 1865."[32] The firm, located in the heart of Philadelphia, at 435 Walnut Street, bought and sold patents, helped people obtain patents for their ideas, worked to refashion rejected patent applications, pursued cases of patent infringement, and gave engineering advice to aspiring inventors. Charles Evans, a patent attorney, handled the legal matters. To promote their company, d'Epineuil and Evans ran advertisements mostly in Philadelphia papers, but also in places such as Washington and other Pennsylvania towns. Early ads courted investors, offering a "rare chance" to acquire rights to a worthy patent or to contract with the firm. Other notices sought agents to canvass communities to drum up business. The proximity of one notice placed in the same newspaper column nine ads below a d'Epineuil and Evans advertisement in 1866 surely appeared to the great chagrin of the former colonel: the *John Trucks* was for sale. For the broadest transatlantic appeal, d'Epineuil and Evans collected information on foreign patents and billed themselves as an "American & European Patent Agency" on company letterhead that prominently displayed references "By Special Permission," with Ambrose Burnside and Elijah Ward still among d'Epineuil's supporters.[33] His job as a patent solicitor gave Lionel J. d'Epineuil a chance for success; he became a fixture in the City of Brotherly Love for the next five years.

D'Epineuil witnessed several patents handled through his firm. None is more revealing than the March 5, 1867 patent for an improved broom and brush head. Two facts stand out about this otherwise mundane patent. The first is that the inventor was George T. Reed of Philadelphia, d'Epineuil's soon-to-be business partner. Keeping up-to-date with literature relevant to his business, Jobert counted among the readers of *Scientific American*. Indeed, one year before the March 1867 patent, d'Epineuil had written a letter to *Scientific American* about ordnance used in the Crimean War. The appeal of editing his own trade paper led d'Epineuil to begin weekly publication of *Scientific Journal* in the spring of 1867. Jobert's coeditor and co-owner of *Scientific Journal* was patent agent George T. Reed. The journal catered to inventors, manufacturers, patentees, and all those interested in developments in the world of science and engineering. To edit the publication, d'Epineuil likely drew on knowledge gained from his friend John C. Merriam's experience editing *American Engineer* at the beginning of the decade and modeled his *Scientific Journal* on the well-established *Scientific American*. Both publications, typical of nineteenth-century periodicals, used a sixteen-page, three-column format. The pages from one issue to the next were numbered sequentially, with the expectation that the issues would be bound together in a volume. "The Cover Sheet for the First Volume of the SCIENTIFIC JOURNAL is not yet ready for publication," d'Epineuil and Reed announced to their readers in the second issue. "We submitted it to the best sketcher and engraver in the United States, Messrs. Geo. T. White & Lauderback. No pains or expense will be spared to obtain a most stylish and artistic cover." Like *Scientific American*, *Scientific Journal* presented articles on inventions and general science, followed by a list of the most recent patents, and then a back page or two given to advertisements. The *Scientific Journal*'s earliest issues prominently displayed an ad for Novelty Broom and Brush Works, not surprisingly, as that company served as the exclusive maker of George T. Reed's brooms and brushes. D'Epineuil even used the paper's name recognition value to refer to his establishment as the "Scientific Journal" Patent Offices.[34]

The other noteworthy fact about Reed's broom and brush head patent was that Jobert witnessed it as Francis d'Epineuil—the only time he signed his name as "Francis." There was no Francis Jobert or Francis d'Epineuil in Philadelphia, and d'Epineuil's full name was Edme Lionel Holwell Jobert. Why did he use the masculine form of his mother's name in this instance? D'Epineuil's deliberate semi-obscuring of his name coincided with his relationship with a woman who conceived his child in 1867. The only other reference to Jobert as "Francis" appears on the child's birth record—in Scotland. Mary Faulkner, giving a married name of d'Epineuil, registered the birth of her child Frederick John D'Epineuil in Pollokshaws, Eastwood Parish, Renfrew County, Scotland, on July 18, 1868. Frederick was born June 9, 1868, precisely nine months after Mary claimed she was married in Philadelphia, America on September 9, 1867. Mary gave the boy's father's name and profession as Francis d'Epineuil, newspaper editor.[35] There is no marriage record in Philadelphia between Mary Faulkner and Francis d'Epineuil, because Lionel Jobert never wed the mother of his child, just like Theodosia Lloyd was not his wife, despite his references to her as such.

While Frederick was being raised in his maternal grandmother's home in Scotland, Lionel d'Epineuil's business continued apace. George T. Reed had sold his interest in d'Epineuil's patent business and in *Scientific Journal* in May 1867, after which Jobert changed the name of his company to d'Epineuil & Co. The business had moved from 435 Walnut Street to 411 Walnut by 1868—just a few doors down from the d'Epineuil Zouaves' former Philadelphia recruiting office at 403 Walnut—and transferred their model and pattern-making workshop to the third floor of the same building. Jobert easily could walk in less than fifteen minutes from his residence at

120 Pine Street to his office on the 400 block of Walnut where lawyers, insurance businesses, oil companies, and real estate agents predominated. As the company's proprietor, d'Epineuil witnessed patents ranging from improved water coolers to harnesses; from gas engines to a rocking swing; from a spinning machine to halter clasps.[36] Jobert continued to publish *Scientific Journal* as well, adding translations of French and German articles to the paper. Charles H. Evans moved on to a job with a different weekly industrial journal produced in Philadelphia, *The American Engineer*, as editor of the paper's department of engineering and patent law. William O'Shea Dimpfel, young scion of steam boiler manufacturer Frederick P. Dimpfel, replaced George T. Reed as d'Epineuil's partner on *Scientific Journal* while pursuing his engineering studies.[37] Even a fire that broke out in the mailing room of *Scientific Journal* on the morning of December 26, 1869 did not interrupt publication of the paper. D'Epineuil described the aftermath of the fire with his usual flourish, proclaiming that the business would soldier on despite the calamity.

> The smoke was very thick, greasy and so dense and penetrating that all our five rooms are literally ruined and must undergo a complete and costly refitting. All the books of the firm, our library, and almost all our papers are so much damaged, and in some instances blackened, as to be almost illegible. Nearly all the "copy" prepared for this [*Scientific Journal*] issue, was either destroyed by smoke or water, and the second number must be written hastily and in the midst of an inevitable and sad confusion. However, and in spite of our losses (which, to us, are heavy, especially at the start of this new series), we will continue our publication as though nothing had happened to delay or mar it.[38]

A local newspaper matter-of-factly reported that the insured building itself "was somewhat damaged."[39] The journal did indeed press on. Rowell's *American Newspaper Directory* printed a full-page advertisement for *Scientific Journal* in 1870, and the latter publication responded with collegial reciprocity by praising the efforts of George P. Rowell & Co.'s newspaper advertising agency.[40]

With the war long won and victorious General Ulysses Grant as the nation's president, Lionel J. d'Epineuil could hope that his public reputation bore the stamp less of the failure of his earlier regimental leadership than of his standing as a businessman. Author Scott Sandage has posited that the ambition of mid-nineteenth-century American businessmen "required a mastery of social and commercial masks," and that personal magnetism operated independently of character.[41] D'Epineuil fit this description, pursuing his ambition by deftly projecting himself as socially engaged and his business as commercially sound. The first image masked the part of his character that was willing to ignore a moral compass if doing so would make life easier for himself, and the second hid his growing financial difficulties. D'Epineuil most publicly displayed his involvement in Philadelphia society by indulging his passion for performing in musical theater. "Science, Music and Art are sisters, why should they always be kept apart?" queried d'Epineuil and Dimpfel rhetorically on New Year's Day, 1870.[42] As early as 1861, Thomas S. Bell, who presided over the contentious court-martial case of the Fifty-Third New York's Lt. Colonel Viguier de Monteil, noted d'Epineuil's musical prowess. D'Epineuil put that skill on display in mid-May 1869, performing at the Amateur Drawing Room on Seventeenth Street near Chestnut in Philadelphia. Opposite the renowned Philadelphia belle and songstress Emilie Schaumburg, d'Epineuil played the role of Jean in Victor Massé's comic opera *Les Noces de Jeannette*. Lionel may well have seen *Noces* in Caen when it was first performed there on October 20, 1853—his twenty-fourth birthday. Given Jobert's personal life, the role was not without its irony. The character of Jean is a French country-dweller who falls in love with Jeannette. However, at the moment of signing the marriage contract Jean balks, singing "wedlock is but a jail." Jeannette tracks him down at his residence and gets him to sign a marriage contract as proof of his intent to marry her, so that this time she can publicly refuse *him* and save face. Jean, having indulged in spirits, inks the contract without knowing what he has signed, and when Jeannette reveals that it is a marriage contract he flies into a rage, smashes up the furniture, and retires to sleep off his intoxication. Jeannette arranges to replace Jean's demolished belongings, and when Jean comes to and sees Jeannette's efforts his countenance softens and he agrees to marry her.[43]

The performance had as its object the raising of funds to aid a local "Female Beneficial Association." Lionel doubtless expected demonstrations of noblesse oblige to enhance his reputation. Early in January 1868 d'Epineuil had resigned from the French Benevolent Society of Philadelphia on the grounds that the organization's constitution did not, in his estimation, sufficiently require the society's officers to direct, through a clearly purposed staff, as much of the association's funds as possible to ameliorate "the sufferings of the unfortunate French population." Both d'Epineuil and Miss Schaumburg were subscribers to the Philadelphia Fountain Society, an organization founded by Wilson C. Swann in 1868 to provide free, fresh drinking water to the city's inhabitants, and d'Epineuil kept *Scientific Journal* readers informed about the Fountain Society's activities.[44] For d'Epineuil, conscientious charity and public beneficence could compensate for his failings and uphold his image as a gentleman. Indeed, the editors of *Scientific Journal* commented at some length on the social value of the theater arts in an article promoting the idea of building a new auditorium to replace the outmoded Amateur Drawing Room:

> it is undeniable that private theatricals, when conducted with propriety, improve the taste for literature, the classics, good elocution, give grace and ease to the adepts, and are, after all, an innocent yet very instructive recreation. Private operatic performances also develope [*sic*] the taste and critical artistic power among us; as we all know that music sung on the stage to an orchestra, requires deep, serious study of all the parts of the score, and the success of the performers will necessarily create an ambition and artistic emulation among the gifted ones of the audience. . . . The object of an Amateur Drawing Room is not solely to gratify private amusement, but most especially to enable charity to render private talent productive in a way compatible with the exigencies of the dignity of private life.[45]

D'Epineuil offered to provide the proposed new theater with a system of his own design for quickly transforming the flooring of the sitting room into a dance floor. In response to a reader's letter that denounced the plan for a new hall as a wasteful absurdity—and Jobert's movable floor idea as a stupidity—d'Epineuil published a biting retort: "We do not know our correspondent, nor do we care much to make his acquaintance, which, if we judge from the unkind intention of his letter, would not prove very agreeable; but we fancy him an old grumbling, disappointed, gouty fellow, who, unable to take any longer his share of the pleasures of this world, is ready to object to and snap at any thing new which may be projected for the amusement of others."[46]

Performing at the Amateur Drawing Room and contributing to charitable causes allowed d'Epineuil to demonstrate a commitment to enriching the culture and improving the social welfare of Philadelphia. Through such pursuits he hoped to showcase his worth to the community, but running a thriving business counted for at least as much when it came to establishing respectability. Recurring legal problems, however, hamstrung d'Epineuil's pursuit of business success. Between 1867 and 1870, d'Epineuil alone or with his business partners was a defendant in half a dozen lawsuits and plaintiff in two more. To promote his patent business, d'Epineuil had purchased advertising space in newspapers and local city directories, including the cover of *Gopsill's Philadelphia City and Business Directory for 1868–69*. As he had done with Brooks Brothers in New York, d'Epineuil had promised payment but had not delivered. He offered no defense in the first two lawsuits against him, one in 1867 and the other in 1868, and the combined damage assessed against him by the court totaled a sobering $807.04—or $14,550 in 2019 dollars. The following year, 1869, the publishers of Philadelphia's city directories brought suit to collect from d'Epineuil yet again, this time enlisting the aid of banker Anthony J. Drexel, later senior partner to financier J. P. Morgan and founder of Drexel University, as garnishee.[47] The legal expenses involved in these cases drained Jobert's efforts to keep d'Epineuil & Co. and *Scientific Journal* as going concerns.

As legal costs piled up, Lionel Jobert sought solace in the far more agreeable atmosphere of the theater and, it was remembered in years afterward, under the protective wing of Emilie Schaumburg. "Few romances in late years," *The Times* of Philadelphia recalled, "have stirred Philadelphia like that of her devoted cavalier for many years, Colonel or Count d'Epineuil, whose cause she espoused against the almost united antagonism of Philadelphia society. If people wanted her they had to receive him and, despite the declarations of social leaders everywhere that they would not recognize him, they had to receive him while he remained in her favor."[48] Indeed, on d'Epineuil's behalf, Emilie's father James W. Schaumburg wrote to the adjutant general in Washington on October 10, 1868, to ask for Jobert's military record. Mr. Schaumburg handed the returned letter and reply to d'Epineuil; it stated that based on the February 1862 inspection report of his regiment the colonel's inefficiency had been the reason for the demoralized state of the men and the disbanding of the Fifty-Third New York. D'Epineuil, who had been enduring the scorn of Philadelphia society, then addressed the adjutant general in order to get a copy of the inspection report so as to defend his reputation: "as I have been suffering by the malicious detractions of my enemies, and such an official report may have been the ground for their slander." D'Epineuil eventually received a copy of the inspection report the following spring.[49] The report notwithstanding, the Philadelphia belle continued to stand by Lionel Jobert. Miss Schaumburg and d'Epineuil reprised their roles in *Noces* at the Union League Theatre in New York City during the spring of 1870 in a benefit concert given to raise money for a monument to the American composer and pianist Louis Moreau Gottschalk who had died the previous December. On the same Saturday as d'Epineuil's performance, May 21, 1870, Carlotta Patti had been slated to perform at Steinway Hall but demurred due to fatigue. She was the same Miss Patti who had sung at a benefit concert for the families of the d'Epineuil Zouaves on November 1, 1861, a few days after the first American performance of *Les Noces de Jeannette*.[50] Perhaps d'Epineuil and Patti greeted each other that weekend in 1870; it would not have been their last meeting. Jobert again garnered plaudits for his portrayal of Jean, such as this reviewer's assessment: "Mr. d'Epineuil, as Jean, also showed great talent and experience, both as an actor and singer, and throughout the entire performance his conception of the part was worthy of the highest commendation, particularly in the scene when he wakes from his supposed sleep and finds everything changed around him; his movement in sitting down on the stairs, as if to collect his thoughts, and the expression of his face at that moment, would have done credit to any of our best actors."[51] The *New York Times* reviewer was more critical of Jobert's talents, but remarked that after the show "the singers, however, were both recalled, amid great applause."[52] For a brief weekend Lionel Jobert exacted some acclaim from the Manhattan citizenry that had little reason to cheer his military efforts of eight years earlier.

Philadelphia, for Lionel Jobert, represented an opportunity to live the life he desired: that of a gentleman who could spend his time engaged in intellectual pursuits and be admired for his social graces. But the persistent bane of having to finance a life of leisure constantly nipped at his heels. D'Epineuil admired men of industry and achievement in business, but as much as he would have liked to match their accomplishments, he could not. Shortly after the completion of the transcontinental railroad in 1869, d'Epineuil wrote to the president of the Union Pacific Railroad Company to request information for a series of articles he planned to write on the feat. D'Epineuil marveled at "this one more instance of the admirable *go aheadism* of the American engineer,"[53] a trait he could not translate into commercial success for himself. In the spring of 1870, d'Epineuil attended commencement exercises for the French language students of his old friend Jean B. Cantel at the Patapsco Institute in Maryland. The son of Caen's melancholy came through in an autobiographical introduction to his description of the event.

> At the age when one begins to comprehend life such as it is, the mind loves to dwell upon the times of early school life, leaving off all the little disagreeable incidents, and replacing them, in our imagination, by the pleasant thoughts of our first affections, spontaneous and evanescent as they were, of our first struggles for superiority—remembrances always pleasant—for in reviewing our first efforts we also think of our first pride, we feel that innermost gratification of our own importance, originating in the consciousness of having accomplished something, of having filled a place in our little world, of having done our duty, one of the great sources of real happiness in our after life.[54]

At age forty, life such as it was for Lionel Jobert had been one of unrewarded striving for comfort and ease amid the respect of his peers. He had endured plenty of disagreeable incidents, often of his own doing; his successes were evanescent. The fact that he, a cultured and educated descendant of the Count d'Epineuil, had to struggle for superiority galled him, and the debacle in Haiti, the inglorious disbanding of his Civil War regiment, the failure to make his way in Washington, and his legal difficulties in Philadelphia all forced him to face his overblown sense of his own importance.

D'Epineuil clung to what remained of his social standing in Philadelphia until he could do so no longer. The Franco-Prussian War provided him with his last high-profile foray into the city's social consciousness. Two days before France declared war, d'Epineuil editorialized in *Scientific Journal* that "[France] owes it to herself to repel this aggression even at the cost of war, though we do not believe that Prussia will venture the experiment, bold and daring as she is." Prussia did venture the experiment, and once the conflict was underway d'Epineuil called on the French residents of the city to organize a patriotic demonstration in support of the fatherland. D'Epineuil saw that the opportunity for American businessmen to profit from the war would prove irresistible, "as soon as the war cloud now gathering on the Rhine shall have burst in earnest." The actor fancied himself a dramatist: like the reference to "lowering clouds" in his petition to the House of Representatives for a Union Volunteer Squadron nearly a decade earlier, he employed a vivid metaphor of ominous natural portent to add weightiness to his commentary. The pro-Prussian sentiment he perceived around him gave d'Epineuil more soapbox fodder for public consumption: "the simple fact that Prussia holds a much larger proportion of our securities, does not add a whit to the justice of her cause, but nations, like individuals, are apt to be selfish, and the prospect of immediate gain makes the American people forget the part which France took at the cradle of their liberty."[55]

Despite this surge in civic discourse, d'Epineuil's monetary and legal woes had become overwhelming as plaintiffs leveled three lawsuits against him during his last months in Philadelphia. The disagreeable incidents had become too many. Lionel J. d'Epineuil's American script now called for a final scene. "The awful war now raging in France compels me to go back to my native land," d'Epineuil disingenuously wrote on September 18, 1870, to Secretary of War William Belknap. The former colonel sought an honorable discharge from the United States Army to complement his collection of recommendations that vouched for his integrity, including a recent one: "my friends and numerous clients have, to day, presented me with a letter bearing testimony to my abilities, good conduct & morals both as a gentleman of the world and an engineer, for the last *seven* years that I have been practicing here." "As I am to sail very early," he concluded, "I would very respectfully request that you would be so kind as to have this matter answered immediately." The reply, coming from the Adjutant General's Office, was that only discharges specifying they are dishonorable are such, and thus no further documentation need be solicited.[56] Peering under the social mask that d'Epineuil's missive represented, one would find little moral or gentlemanly behavior toward Mary Faulkner; one would not come across an engineering degree; and one would note that he practiced his profession in Philadelphia during the last five-and-a-quarter years, not seven as he underscored. In the pages of *Scientific Journal* that year, d'Epineuil had donned one of his commercial masks and pronounced that "Thanks to the public and our friends' kind patronage, and in spite of the unprecedented dullness of business, we are pleased to say that the Scientific Journal is succeeding very well," and he praised his journal's printers, McCalla and Stavely. The compliment did not deter the latter gentlemen from suing d'Epineuil and Dimpfel.[57] Before the curtain fell on 1870, d'Epineuil fled the city.

D'Epineuil's life after the Civil War, just as during the conflict, displayed the curious mixture of character traits that largely defined him. Vain but enterprising, unscrupulous yet cultivated, he aspired to prove to himself and to others that he was worthy of esteem. The public and private d'Epineuil waged an internal struggle like Dr. Jekyll against his alter ego. He could give of his talents for worthy causes yet willfully ignore his debts. On balance, Jobert's actions in the years he spent in the Americas revealed the dominance of his own Mr. Hyde. The future, however, provides everyone with an opportunity for at least some redemption. For Lionel Jobert d'Epineuil, the decade about to dawn would give him that chance—but neither in Philadelphia nor in Washington; not in New York or in Haiti. He crossed the Atlantic again, and did not return to America.

Chapter 7

The Count and Countess d'Epineuil

London-based A. Lynes and Son, merchant clothiers and outfitters, published a series of seasonal brochures showcasing their clothing lines and included short stories in the brochures to make them more attractive to the public. Their summer 1871 issue, *Wit and Wear*, presented a story called "The Naked Truth." The story's protagonist, Simon Fluffywick, repeatedly fell victim in his youth to those who sought to take advantage of him. Such incidents affected the mature Simon to the degree that "If telling a falsehood served his ends better than telling the truth, or saved him trouble, he invariably shut the door at truth, and opened the window for falsehood to enter." In a dream, a fairy came and cast a spell to make Simon tell the truth. He did so, but tactlessly, insulting friends and acquaintances and airing their skeletons in public. His wife had him committed to an asylum, "Hopeless House," when a doctor certified him as insane. The fairy eventually returned in another dream and lifted the spell, admonishing Simon to be delicate when telling the truth. After his release from the asylum, "Simon made himself the most agreeable host that ever lived" at a welcome back party thrown by the friends he had insulted.[1] Simon *made* himself be agreeable; it was an act. The message of the tale is that falsehoods and semitruths—such as things we say to be polite instead of what we are really thinking—are a common part of human social relations; how one manages such interaction is a measure of one's character.

The author of "The Naked Truth" was Sir Horatio Henry Wraxall, a British baronet and writer of light literature. Wraxall was Lionel Jobert's contemporary, just two years younger than Jobert. Also like Jobert, the titled Wraxall had a maritime background, having started as a teenage apprentice merchant navy seaman in 1845. Performing in theatrical productions served as Jobert's artistic escape and writing was Wraxall's. Jobert and Wraxall proved adept at truth-bending when it served their needs, just like Wraxall's character Simon Fluffywick. And perhaps most significantly, both men faced the decade of the 1870s in financial distress: Jobert fleeing debt obligations in the United States and Wraxall squandering his wealth by betting unsuccessfully on horse racing.[2] Comparing the latter to d'Epineuil shows us two facets of nineteenth-century Atlantic history. One is that the era had its share of confidence men and opportunists; men like them were not outliers, but rather representative of a subset of the population who cared more about personal advancement than about the great issues of the day. Another is that Jobert's mobility around the Atlantic region allowed him to evade the more severe consequences of misleading the authorities and acting against the law, whereas Wraxall's permanence in Great Britain allowed government officials to contain him more effectively.

When St. Edme Jobert died late in the spring of 1861, his first child Clémence and her husband Edmond Breuil were living in Civitavecchia in the Papal States where Breuil served as French consul first class. The French government promoted Breuil to Lisbon in 1862, where he and Clémence lived for seven years. During that period, Breuil's career proceeded upward. He received the rank of officer of the Legion of Honor in 1867, having been made a chevalier of that society in 1856 while serving as consul first class in Rio de Janeiro. Monsieur Jobert's second child, Lionel, had just established himself in New York City at the outbreak of the Civil War in 1861 and stayed in the United States throughout the remainder of the decade. Clémence and Lionel appear not to have known that their father held assets in England at the time of his death, or knew them to be of relatively little value, for it was not until late in 1870, more than nine years after St. Edme Jobert had passed, that Lionel went to London to attend to the details of his father's English estate. Clémence and Edmond had moved to California in 1869 as the latter assumed the duties of consul general in San Francisco.[3] Thus, over the course of less than two years, Clémence crossed the Atlantic in one direction while her brother Lionel crossed in the reverse. The fortunes of Louis Edme Jobert's eldest children likewise would develop along opposite paths for the rest of their lives.

The assets left by his father may have been one factor that attracted d'Epineuil to England, but evading the pressure of his mounting problems in Philadelphia best explains the timing of his arrival in London. On October 5, 1870, the *New York Herald* reported that "Lloyd Epernil, of Philadelphia" was staying at the New York Hotel. While the *Herald* reporter, or the hotel desk clerk, may have mangled his name, it is just as likely that d'Epineuil gave a false name, as he had done before, in order to disguise his flight from legal troubles in Philadelphia. The now former proprietor of *Scientific Journal* actually had left the United States aboard the *City of Baltimore* on October 4; it was the same ship on which his paramour Theodosia Lloyd had departed America eight years before. When he arrived in Liverpool thirteen days later, Lionel Jobert had become Le Comte d'Epineuil, the name he would use henceforth.[4] His contemporaries in France would have regarded his use of the title as little more than a *titre de courtoisie*, but Jobert counted on it to impress English acquaintances. D'Epineuil could have returned to his native France, and he allowed people in the United States to think the reason for his abrupt departure was to participate in the Franco-Prussian War, a conflict about which he had been so vocal. But at age forty-one and accustomed to civilian life, he did not move to France. The cachet of being a foreign gentleman in England appealed to Lionel Jobert, and he checked into London's Castle and Falcon Hotel on Aldersgate Street. Count d'Epineuil received official sanction to administer his father's estate on November 4, 1870, precisely one month after fleeing America. Two and a half weeks later, Lionel obtained the same regarding his mother's estate and secured more permanent lodgings that month at 14 London Street in Hyde Park. Ever on the lookout for a chance to earn some money, d'Epineuil was one of the seven initial investors who formed the Milford Bank late in 1870, despite none of the men being known as bankers or financiers. One of the other seven original shareholders was Horatio H. Wraxall.[5]

Despite moving to London, Jobert maintained continuities between his life in the United States and in England. For one, he identified his occupation as "Late Colonel U.S. Army" in the census of early April 1871. Although he had not been in the US military for nine years at that point, Jobert felt the title of colonel more prestigious, and potentially more advantageous, than patent solicitor or practical engineer. Another continuity was his fondness for musical theater. Jobert performed at the Bow and Bromley Institute in March 1871, opposite composer and singer Elizabeth Philp in the duet "I'm an Alsatian" from Jacques Offenbach's operetta *Lischen et Fritzchen*.[6] An American soprano, Cornelia Stetson of Boston, also sang—another connection that spanned the Atlantic for d'Epineuil. As with his performance in New York the previous season, the March 1871 effort was a benefit concert, this time to aid the distressed French peasantry. Once again d'Epineuil charmed his audience: "M. le Comte d'Epineuil, a distinguished amateur, created also a great impression by his spirited singing of Gounod's drinking song, 'Qu'ils sont doux.' "[7] D'Epineuil even rated an invitation to a formal reception on May 13, given by Queen Victoria, who herself approved the guest list of eminent noble, diplomatic, and military personages. "By command of the

Queen a Levée was held on Saturday at St. James's Palace, by his Royal Highness the Prince of Wales, on behalf of Her Majesty," Londonites read two days later. "Presentations to his Royal Highness at this Court are, by the Queen's pleasure, considered as equivalent to presentations to Her Majesty." True to form, Jobert had fast become known in his latest adopted city. D'Epineuil followed this honor with another performance in the last week of June, beginning an association with the Polish composer and pianist Anton de Kontski. Both men had caught the attention of London society enough to be invited in early November by the Lord Mayor and the Lady Mayoress to a dance at the Mansion House, attended by royals Prince Edward of Saxe-Weimar and Prince Alfred, the Duke of Edinburgh. In fact, Jobert had attended the Mansion House soirée the previous Friday, too.[8] Count d'Epineuil, just a year removed from the patent business in Philadelphia, shone in London as a musical talent, a bon vivant, and a man-about-town.

Being a gentleman of leisure, however, required considerable expense, and d'Epineuil soon ran through his assets. D'Epineuil's financial situation was the key element that always mitigated against his pursuit of a consistent standing and recognition as a gentleman. Consider author David Hancock's description of the emerging British gentleman in the eighteenth century, one that still held true in the 1870s: "a deportmental rather than a hereditary or professional definition of gentility gained currency: one was a gentleman if one looked and acted the part. Certain characteristics of behavior became marks of gentlemanly status: a good education, 'a genteel dress and carriage,' refined external behavior, and the financial wherewithal to support this polished style of living." Hancock adds that superior accomplishments, purchase and display of cultural products, and promoting amenities for the community also were the mark of a gentleman.[9] The suave Lionel J. d'Epineuil had many of these traits. If he could not point to superior accomplishments, he was an educated man and certainly looked and acted the part of a gentleman. One even recalls his support for the Philadelphia Fountain Society and its promotion of free, fresh drinking water as a community amenity. For good measure, d'Epineuil employed the title Count to help cover his deficiencies. But it was his lack of wealth, and particularly the unethical ways he dealt with that circumstance, that repeatedly cost him the reputation of a gentleman. The latest in a series of lifelong transgressions inspired by low cash reserves was d'Epineuil's solution in England: marriage by mendacity.

Count d'Epineuil set his sights on Georgiana Hester Cornelia Somerset, a woman nearly nineteen years his junior and the daughter of a respected

British family. Her father was Colonel H. C. C. Somerset, the grandson of the fifth Duke of Beaufort. Georgiana's mother, Elizabeth O'Connell, was the granddaughter of William Bligh, captain of the famed ship *Bounty*.[10] After a brief courtship, d'Epineuil proposed in August 1871, but Georgiana refused him. Lionel saw a golden opportunity about to slip through his fingers, so he resorted to histrionics, feigning illness to gain Georgiana's sympathy. The next month, d'Epineuil dined with Georgiana's social circle in Gloucester, determined to impress. Among the dinner guests was John Dearman Birchall, a successful merchant who had a brief flirtation with Georgiana's sister Caroline. Birchall's diary entry for that evening reveals d'Epineuil's ingratiating modus operandi: "Sept 13. Dined at Dr Ancrum's to meet Count d'Epineul [*sic*] a marvelous fellow reminding one strongly of the Count of Monte Christo, in spite of his recent illness, which had caused him to faint twice today, he was the life of the party and amongst plenty of play and wonderful tricks he caused umbrellas and sticks to stand both perpendicularly and obliquely on the carpet without touching. I never was more surprised in my life." A few days later, Georgiana related to Birchall a tale dreamed up by Lionel to embellish his background.

> Georgie Somerset gave me a most interesting account of the Count's grandfather who had a post at the French Court with Louis XVI at the outbreak of the revolution. He was aged 24, and offered to get the Count d'Artois out of Paris and seek help from the King of Prussia[.] They both passed as actors a role in which they were especially fitted from acting in the court plays at the Trianon. At Lyons they had to give a play before the police. At a later period Count d'Epineul [*sic*] returned to Paris and was seized by *Les Sans Culottes* and was only saved by one of them who had been his gardener and recognized him. The next day this honest fellow was guillotined for his kindness. The Count escaped and died in 1836 in London.

The story was vintage Lionel Jobert, a mixture of truth and fiction. Lionel's grandfather Pierre Jobert was age twenty-two in 1789, and a military supply dealer at the time of his marriage in Caen in 1795; he died in Caen in 1839. D'Epineuil had Georgiana and Dearman Birchall enthralled, but Lionel's lies eventually caught up with him. Caroline, protective of her younger sister, seems to have seen through d'Epineuil before anyone, commenting to Birchall in mid-August that Lionel "is the best of fellows, I fear

I may prove to be his murderer." Georgiana's parents checked d'Epineuil's background, and before the year was out, they had learned the truth. Birchall's diary entry cannot be improved on in summing up the situation.

> Dec 31. Walked home with Col. & Mrs. Somerset. They told me Georgie was defiant, praised her as being an angel; but lamented she was going to throw herself away on an adventurer. From Philadelphia they have received news that he is not known as a Count, but as a business man. When he left he was in debt, and writs and warrants have been issued against him during the last month. He is not known in society in England. He assumed the title finding that a card with 'Count' paid amongst the English. Col. Somerset does not think he has any right to the title. Georgie says when they thought he was rich and had a title they urged her to marry him. "I agreed with reluctance. When I find he is poor I stick to him. If I do find he is worthless it will be my mission in life to reform him". So the melancholy sacrifice is to be consummated on Thursday, because no-one can come forward and prevent a steady young lady from throwing herself on a regular scape grace.[11]

Forty-two-year-old Lionel and twenty-three-year-old Georgiana married on January 4, 1872, at the Anglican church of Saint Clement Danes in Westminster on the Strand in London (see figures 7.1 and 7.2). Adeline

Figure 7.1. Watercolor miniature of Count d'Epineuil, ca. 1872. Chanter Family Collection.

Figure 7.2. Georgiana Somerset, Countess d'Epineuil, ca. 1872. Chanter Family Collection.

Montagu Bryant, who was the sister-in-law of Louisa Newcomb-Bryant, Georgiana's cousin on her father's side, and Benjamin Humphries Tromp, a solicitor acquaintance of Lionel's, served as witnesses. Thenceforth known as the Count and Countess d'Epineuil, the newlyweds soon had less money to count. Not coincidental to his recent nuptials, d'Epineuil was adjudged bankrupt on February 23, 1872, only fifty-one days after ending his perennial bachelorhood.[12]

Lionel had moved about as a single man, from 14 London Street to 2 Albert Mansions SW, then to Norfolk Street near the church where he and Georgiana wed. Lionel and his bride took up residence at Bridge House in

Saint John's Wood, Middlesex. Despite his financial difficulties, d'Epineuil remained a public presence in London, even as his bankruptcy case wound its way through the courts. D'Epineuil performed in a de Kontski comic opera on March 11, just three days prior to being obliged to appear before his creditors at the London Bankruptcy Court. The court appointed one of its registrars as trustee of d'Epineuil's property on May 13; that weekend Jobert repeated the previous year's duet with Elizabeth Philp in a concert with the Chevalier de Kontski at St. James's Hall. Myron W. Whitney (1836–1910), noted American basso, numbered among the performers. Two days after d'Epineuil stood public examination on June 13 at the bankruptcy court, he performed in another de Kontski concert, this time at St. George's Hall. The headliner was none other than Carlotta Patti—once again associated with Lionel Jobert, and on both sides of the ocean.[13] More than just a creative outlet or hobby, concerts and the attendant applause served the amateur d'Epineuil as an emotional salve for an ego wounded by pecuniary woes. His military and business past did not give Jobert the quality of recognition he felt he deserved. Yet every season from 1869 to 1873, in the United States and England, his connection with the celebrity of Schaumburg, Philp, Stetson, de Kontski, Whitney, and Patti contributed to the grand illusion of a level of social stature to which d'Epineuil aspired but could not maintain, a seductive mirage simultaneously bolstering his self-image while masking his shortcomings, and all the while fueling his ambition to convert his elusive dream into reality.

Keeping up appearances amid insolvency continued throughout 1873. The Count and Countess d'Epineuil were among those noted in attendance at a memorial in London for the exiled Napoleon III, who died in January. When the Franco-Prussian War commenced in 1870, Jobert's editorial in *Scientific Journal* had praised the French leader's stewardship of France and derided Prussian Prime Minister Otto von Bismarck as "*Mis*-Count *Mis*-Marck." D'Epineuil took the stage again in April, singing for the Royal Albert Hall Amateur Orchestral Society.[14] But d'Epineuil understood that he needed income and that he and the countess could not live solely on her reserves. Jobert did receive $200 from the United States Government in 1872 as payment for an unspecified Civil War-related matter. He also drew on his American postbellum experience to obtain a March 1873 patent in London for an improvement on stoves.[15] Even so, d'Epineuil needed to dedicate less time to amateur theater and mount a concerted effort to find a consistently reliable revenue stream. An opportunity presented itself in September 1873. The Khedive of Egypt, Ismail Pasha, effectively ruling independently even though officially under the suzerainty of the Ottoman Empire, regularly had his fleet of steamships repaired in England. The president of the Egyptian Marine Department, Admiral Fedrigo Pacha, and John Fowler, the Khedive's consulting engineer, invited several civilians to accompany them on a test run of the refitted steamer *Charkieh* along the Thames River. D'Epineuil was on board, networking with those in the employ of Egypt and "some well-known engineering men."[16] Meanwhile, Jobert's bankruptcy case was drawing to a close. In mid-November, the trustee of d'Epineuil's property reported to the bankruptcy court that d'Epineuil had no property, and had acquired no property, that could be used to satisfy his debts. Eager to secure gainful employment and put the distasteful business of bankruptcy behind him, d'Epineuil sailed for Alexandria, Egypt aboard the *Hydaspes* on November 27. Since no creditors came forth to oppose, the court closed the bankruptcy case of M. le Comte d'Epineuil on January 19, 1874, with the insolvent count out of the country.[17]

The *Hydaspes*, a steamer belonging to the Peninsular and Oriental company, carried d'Epineuil first to Gibraltar where it arrived on December 2. The steamship continued on to Alexandria by way of Malta across the Mediterranean Sea, ultimately bound for Bombay, India.[18] Georgiana followed in January to meet her husband in Alexandria. Five months later, in June 1874, English engineer Waynman Dixon encountered the d'Epineuils at Shepheard's Hotel in Cairo, their financial status still precarious.

> At the Hotel we are only three permanent & an odd one or two now & then. The two besides myself who make up the three are a Count & Countess d'Epineuil, a man who calls himself an Englishman, altho really French, who has married an English lady of very good family. He speaks English perfectly & is very well informed & agreeable—as well as his wife—but there is a certain mystery about them, no one knows what his business is or what he is doing here,—some sort of negotiation with the govt.—but since they cannot get him to pay his Hotel Bill I think it is most probable they stay here because they can't raise the means to go anywhere else. He is not exactly a sort of Count Fosco type but is gentlemanly, quiet, retiring & does not attempt to borrow money or apparently to make it so that at table,—the only place where I meet them they are very pleasant company.[19]

Thus began what one might call d'Epineuil's "blackout period." From Dixon's letter of June 1, 1874 to d'Epineuil's name appearing on the list of registered voters in Ashford, England, in July 1879, evidence of his activities is nearly nil. French naval officials, having no record of Jobert's activities since an outdated 1865 notation that he was living in New York, closed the books on Jobert's maritime career in February 1878, declaring him "absent without news."[20] Likewise, recounting the d'Epineuils' lives after their marriage, one observer in 1879 wrote that the "pair slipped out of sight and memory, and became as though they had never existed."[21] But, two of only three known photographs of Lionel J. d'Epineuil were taken in Port Said, a city to the east of Alexandria along the Mediterranean coast of Egypt, near the northern end of the Suez Canal. The photographer, Frenchman Hippolyte Arnoux, operated his studio in Port Said during the 1870s. For both of Arnoux's photos, Count d'Epineuil gazed to his right, a fez perched gently askew atop his head (see figure 7.3). On the *Hydas-*

Figure 7.3. Count d'Epineuil. Photograph taken in Port Said, Egypt ca. 1875. Chanter Family Collection.

pes, all crew members, regardless of rank, wore a fez. The 1879 voter list that marked his reemergence in English sources listed him as "D'Epineul [*sic*] Captain."[22] Had d'Epineuil convinced Egyptian officials to hire him in his old capacity as a ship captain, shuttling passengers and mail around the Ottoman Empire and beyond? Did he try to insinuate himself into a position for yet another country trying to modernize and improve its standing in the international community, offering European know-how as he had in Haiti? Was there a connection between the Khedive's fall from power in June 1879 and d'Epineuil's reappearance in the documentary record that same July? However—and however long—he spent his time in North Africa, it served as a watershed between d'Epineuil's first three years of carefree gaiety in England and the more sober years that followed. After his return from Egypt, Jobert ceased his stage performances. Quite possibly connected to his time in Egypt, he became an owner of the newspaper the *British Mail*, which began publication in January 1875. A monthly advertising medium for merchants and inventors, the *British Mail* covered news, published current commodity prices, reported on recent inventions, and even reviewed books. The newspaper sold at an initial cost of six pence per issue and circulated around the globe. It could be found in d'Epineuil's old haunts—the Albemarle Hotel in New York City and the National Hotel in Washington, DC.[23]

D'Epineuil's name as the proprietor does not appear in the pages of the *British Mail*. Thus, it is difficult to pinpoint when he became associated with the paper or to ascribe to him the editorials that favored free trade and trumpeted the civilizing influence of Britain on India. By mid-1880, however, d'Epineuil was a member of the firm Whiteley & Company. William A. Whiteley had been one of the partners that owned the *British Mail* under the firm Sladden Bros. & Co., who were export merchants. Sladden Brothers dissolved in September 1878 and subscription checks for the *British Mail* became payable to Whiteley & Co. with the October 1878 issue. The *British Mail*'s office also had moved to 40 Chancery Lane, London, which was d'Epineuil's office address in 1880.[24] Jobert's acquisition of a stake in the newspaper clearly echoed his proprietorship of *Scientific Journal* during his years in Philadelphia, and he doubtless hoped that the *British Mail* would provide him with the steady income that he desperately needed. Trying to hedge his bets, d'Epineuil partnered in a short-lived business as a colonial commission agent offering to represent other companies abroad. The firm, L. Holwell & Co., used Jobert's middle name to avoid scaring away potential clients who might associate the name d'Epineuil with his earlier bankruptcy.[25]

As d'Epineuil's star sank over the course of the 1870s, that of his sister and brother-in-law rose. Clémence and Edmond Breuil enjoyed the latter's tenure in San Francisco, California, as consul general of France throughout the first half of the decade and into 1876. Their stay on the West Coast was marred only by an unbalanced Frenchman's assault on Breuil in June of 1872. As Breuil strode down Kearny Street, the assailant delivered a severe blow with a slungshot—a sailor's tool that could double as a blackjack—to the consul's head. The perpetrator was apprehended, and Breuil recovered. Promoted to his final diplomatic post in New York City in 1876, Breuil represented France in centennial celebrations on the East Coast. Breuil served as the commissioner general on behalf of the French government at the International Exposition in Philadelphia and presented Bartholdi's statue of the Marquis de Lafayette, which stands in Union Square Park, to New York City in September of 1876. After a dozen years of service in the United States, his compatriots feted Breuil at Delmonico's Restaurant in New York on his retirement in 1881.[26]

Across the Atlantic in England, 1881 began with Lionel d'Epineuil's affairs having the appearance of being on the mend, his time filled indulging his interests and living in quiet comfort among his neighbors. The Count and Countess d'Epineuil now resided in Ashford, a small village twenty-five kilometers west of central London. In 1879 they had occupied the property known as the Elms, and by 1880 they had moved to the more expensive Red House. At Red House d'Epineuil employed a cook and a footman, as befitting a man of means, and in June 1880 he joined a Masonic lodge that met in nearby Walton-on-Thames. A week after marking their ninth wedding anniversary in January 1881, the Count and Countess d'Epineuil joined the well-wishers who presented gifts to a local newlywed couple. A few days earlier, identified in a *British Mail* article as "Capt. D'Epineuil, Consulting C.E." (civil engineer), he had been one of the attentive observers at a demonstration of a ventilation system at the London Custom House.[27] This veneer of normalcy, however, obscured some troubling undercurrents. D'Epineuil had contracted in July 1880 with a builder to make home repairs at an expense of 150 pounds. The builder received weekly installments of the agreed price while he worked on the house throughout the rest of the summer and into October. D'Epineuil and the builder—Mr. Lack—did not get along well and the cost of the repairs ran over the original agreement. Reminiscent of his imperious demeanor aboard the *John Trucks*, d'Epineuil accused Lack of stealing paint, and had the builder arrested. For more than three days Lack remained in detention despite the fact that d'Epineuil was in error, for Lack had not taken the paint. The court dismissed the charge on November 9. Lack, in turn, took d'Epineuil to court, alleging slander and malicious prosecution. The case began at the end of May 1881, and on June 1, Lack agreed to accept a 50-pound settlement from d'Epineuil rather than have the court see the case through to the end.[28]

D'Epineuil's fortune, in every sense of that word, continued to deteriorate as the year wore on. An intelligent, sophisticated man, Count d'Epineuil sought the privilege of voting, an honor not extended to all British men of the era, or to most women. In late September, the local Liberal Party objected to d'Epineuil's claim on the basis that Jobert was a foreigner who had not been naturalized and thus was not entitled to vote. D'Epineuil's lack of British citizenship made the decision to deny his claim an easy one for the barrister presiding over the revision of the local list of voters.[29] This blow to his ego exacerbated the mounting stress that d'Epineuil was under due to his insolvency. The debt-ridden count, with the consent of his wife, in a letter dated October 7 and addressed to his frequent creditor E. T. Tadman, pledged to Tadman monies due the countess under the will of her maternal grandmother, Dame Mary O'Connell (the daughter of Captain Bligh). D'Epineuil further promised to Tadman "'all my present and future personalty to secure to him any sum or sums I may be indebted to him at the time he may choose to make use of the above charge.'"[30]

The following Monday was October 10. Lionel Jobert stood ten days away from his fifty-second birthday, and he was broke. Again. Moreover, he had just signed over even future assets to satisfy his financial obligations. Strained and humiliated, d'Epineuil suffered an apoplectic stroke and expired. His remains were interred in Ashford on October 14, with the local vicar, Frederick Binley Dickinson, presiding over the burial. Despite his rejected claim to be counted among the local voters, Count d'Epineuil's name appeared on the 1882 polling list published for the parish of Ashford. His name was crossed out, and replaced with a simple handwritten note: "dead."[31]

Until the end, Lionel Jobert always had relied on his persuasive arts, rather than time-consuming formal training, to shepherd his schemes to success. George Bliss Jr. knew this in 1861 when he so accurately assessed d'Epineuil as a chevalier d'industrie, a duplicitous sort who worked to maintain the appearance of being a gentleman but had less to his credit than he would have one believe. Yet Jobert usually had at least something to his credit. A grain of truth served in Jobert's mind as sufficient justification for his first overture to New York, and then to the United States Congress, to head a coastal patrol squadron. His time as a capitaine au long cours provided some relevant background for the position, but a single ocean crossing as captain of the *Geffrard* constituted little experience indeed in command of a military vessel, let alone a whole squadron. Lionel's patent office enterprise and publishing of *Scientific Journal* were legitimate businesses, yet when debts piled up, he felt bound by neither ethics nor law to pay them, and avoided doing so by finding safe harbor, not for the first time, on other Atlantic shores.

The business model of d'Epineuil's contemporary Horatio Wraxall, by contrast, evinced a different approach to the same problem of insolvency: dishonesty by design. Wraxall ran afoul of the law on several occasions in London during the 1870s when he posed as a stock dealer. In 1875, he and his partner James Bland Hawkes took money entrusted to them by a customer to purchase Egyptian bonds, but they used the money for themselves. Hawkes was convicted; Wraxall evaded justice by not answering the court's subpoena.[32] Three years later, the Central Criminal Court found Wraxall guilty of conspiracy to obtain money under false pretenses. Wraxall's desperation for funds made him easy to arrest this time, as testified to by the landlord who had rented Wraxall and his new partner an office:

> I wrote a letter to the bank stating that I had three registered letters addressed to Wraxall, and I did not know his address, and on the Saturday afternoon, the 24th [August, 1878], Wraxall rushed into the office and the policeman put his hand upon him and took him off—I saw him at the Bow Street station about half an hour afterwards—I asked him about the rent, and he said "If you give me those three registered letters with the money in, I will break them open and pay you the rent out of the money"—I asked him if he had authority to break them open—he said "Yes, I have"—those three letters only existed in imagination, it was done to catch the fellow.[33]

After his incarceration, Wraxall was committed to an asylum, mirroring in real life the fate of his fictional character in "The Naked Truth." He died in April 1882, six months after d'Epineuil's demise, thereby completing the rather parallel trajectory of their lives. Both Horatio Wraxall and Lionel Jobert sought shortcuts to a standard of living they adjudged appropriate to a baronet and a count, respectively. If Wraxall's criminal record put a more damning stamp on his activities than could be placed on Jobert, both men were prisoners of an unquenchable, and in their cases unsustainable, pursuit of the good life. The *London Truth*'s editorial comment about Wraxall applied equally to Jobert: "[A noble] title, if there is no wealth to support it, is an encumbrance, and not unfrequently an absurdity."[34]

In the immediate aftermath of d'Epineuil's death, his reputation lacked luster. His name became recognizable in English legal circles for years to come as the case of *Tadman v. d'Epineuil* established an oft-cited precedent: a promise in favor of a creditor of all present and future property was valid only regarding the property that belonged to the debtor (d'Epineuil) at the date of the agreement.[35] Thus, he had avoided some liability once again, but the name d'Epineuil became firmly associated with debt long after his final attempt to manage it. In comparison to the memory of his father, there was not much that was positive to say about Lionel. Less than four months before St. Edme Jobert died, he had given a speech remembering a fellow firefighter who had passed. When St. Edme expired in June 1861, he was memorialized in turn by a comrade in glowing terms: "Another very significant loss for us: our former captain, the brave and good Jobert, has just left us. I will not attempt here to give his eulogy; we all knew the courage and tireless intrepidity of this generous and devoted man who, always the first at the height of danger, was for us a guide and model."[36] St. Edme's children by his second marriage, having lost his personal papers (to the great disappointment of the twenty-first-century researcher), wrote to the grand chancellor of the Legion of Honor in 1893 to request a copy of their father's certificate. His daughter Ernestine summed up the reason: "Having four boys, we would be happy that they have proof before their eyes of the evidence of the fine conduct of their grandfather, who was decorated, after several acts of courage and devotion."[37] Instead of a record of achievement, Lionel's gravestone epitaph in St. Matthew's churchyard in Ashford bears a resurrection hymn's promise of salvation, the hope of all sinners.

> To the
> Dearly loved memory of
> Edme Lionel Holwell Jobert
> 7th Count of Epineuil
> Who died Oct 10th 1881
> To that brightest of all meetings
> Bring us Jesu Christ, at last;
> By thy cross through death and judgment
> Holding fast[38]

The simple cross atop a three-tiered plinth may seem to be mismatched with the lofty title displayed in raised stone letters beneath his name. Yet it is apt. In life, his grandiose facade served as a gilded mask that concealed a man of more ordinary circumstances. In death, it is the reverse: the plain design of the small monument overshadows the pretense. The honorific did provide one final flicker of prestige: an advertiser in 1882 listed Count d'Epineuil among the impressively titled individuals whose homes had been supplied with the Sanderson and Company solid indestructible copper tape lightning conductors.[39]

In America, most did not remember Lionel J. d'Epineuil fondly. The case of Count de Naux illustrates the foregoing point. In 1879, a Haitian-born man who had been posing as Count de Naux attempted to swindle the director of a failing theater in Rouen, France, out of a substantial sum of money.[40] Newspapers in New York and Philadelphia ran the story in the second week of November, nine years after d'Epineuil left the United States, and leapt to the erroneous conclusion that Count de Naux and Count d'Epineuil were the same person. The articles presented a fascinating mix of truth, plausible assertions, and errors. The long *New York Times* article, with the place line Paris and without identifying him by name, recounted real aspects of d'Epineuil's life: he had a maritime background; he had raised a volunteer corps "whose uniform made a sensation" during the Civil War; he had been a government clerk; he had lived in Philadelphia; he had sung at concerts in London, specifically St. George's Hall; he had quit America after the outbreak of the Franco-Prussian War; and he had married in England. All this was true. Other assertions not corroborated elsewhere seem quite plausible. The article told of an incident in which a Philadelphia tailor, upset that d'Epineuil had not yet paid for an overcoat, took the coat off of d'Epineuil in public on Walnut Street where the latter worked. The *Times* writer further offered that d'Epineuil had served as an acting tutor to his new wife, hoping that she might establish a career as a performer. After a description of the exploits of Count de Naux, the writer rhetorically concluded, "I ask, if he be the same who sang '*Les Noces de Jeannette*' in Philadelphia private theatricals 10 years ago, what Beauty [Emilie Schaumburg] and her friends will think of their protégé?"[41] The Philadelphia *Times* also used "Beauty" to represent Schaumburg when telling of her support for d'Epineuil during his years in that city, and described him as "a bright particular star, being really a very clever actor (there was no doubt about that!), a pianist of very much more than average ability, a most entertaining talker, possessed of charming manners and of a rarely handsome person and face."⁴² A week later, the *Times* retracted the claim that d'Epineuil was Count de Naux, stating the paper had learned "'the Count d'Epineuil now resides a few miles from London, England, with his wife, Georgiana Somerset, the daughter of Colonel Somerset.'"⁴³ Like the contributor to the *New York Times*, the author of the Philadelphia *Times* articles had many facts correct. Prominent Philadelphians recollected d'Epineuil well, but not kindly. The latter journal offered another tantalizing item of scuttlebutt in an article seven years later. Wanting to bar d'Epineuil from future social gatherings, a "committee of clubmen went to France and secured his record and the fact that he had been in the galleys was proved by a deeply plotted scheme in which his shoulder was bared and the brand disclosed. But even when the bottom facts were gleaned it could only be proved that his offense was a political one and that, although he had led an adventurous career, he really belonged to a French family of distinction."⁴⁴ If true, the record in question would have been his novice seaman record, which does not survive, and his punishment would have been for some infraction aboard *La Bayonnaise*. The elite so despised socializing with a man they felt unworthy of a noble title—a chevalier d'industrie—that some men were willing to cross the Atlantic for the express purpose of determining the background of Lionel J. d'Epineuil in order to discredit him and avoid associating with him further. That reveals more about the Philadelphia social set of the 1870s than it does about d'Epineuil, but it is to that society that d'Epineuil desperately wished to belong.

In the half century that followed the disbanding of the first organization of the Fifty-Third New York State Volunteers, Americans recalled the d'Epineuil Zouaves in either neutral or negative terms. At best, some found humor in mispronunciations of the colonel's surname, as in this tale from 1871.

> The *modus operandi* employed in the construction of these popularized French names may be illustrated by an incident that occurred during our late war. When Colonel D'Epineuil's zouave-corps of French residents went to join the Army of the Potomac, the people in the districts through which it passed inquired of the men, as usual, what regiment it was. One individual, in particular, was assiduous in gaining the desired information. Having obtained it, he came back, with the look of one conscious but not proud of his superior knowledge, and finally, in answer to numerous inquiries, condescended to explain that they were the "Death-knell Zouaves."⁴⁵

The Fifty-Third's commanding officer fared poorly in an article penned for a Utica, New York newspaper in 1896. Replete with errors—probably to spice up the story—the article offered that the regiment was led "by the most cowardly colonel in the Federal army"; that d'Epineuil made the captain of the *John Trucks* run aground so as to avoid having to engage in the battle of Roanoke; and that soon after the disbanding of the Zouaves d'Epineuil "left the country and died in Paris."[46] In 1909, a wholesale liquor salesman and former Company C private in the Fifty-Third, Charles E. Stone, without identifying his prior affiliation, rather sheepishly inquired the following of the editor of the *National Tribune*: "Please let me know something about the 53d N.Y. I see so much about other regiments.—C. E. Stone, 10 Sargent Ave., Somerville, Mass."[47] The editor replied with only a brief, matter-of-fact statement containing basic information on the regiment's organization, its mustering out, the colonel's name, and the number of deaths. Three years later, the ten-volume work titled *The Photographic History of the Civil War* was equally dismissive: "The D'Epineul [sic] Zouaves, French and would-be Frenchmen, in the costliest costume yet devised, and destined to be abandoned before they were six months older."[48]

Thus, the general public's collective memory of d'Epineuil and his Zouaves remained anything but positive, and the colonel himself was the biggest reason why. As to how those directly connected with the d'Epineuil Zouaves remembered Lionel Jobert when they looked back on the events of 1861–1862, we are never likely to learn. What we do know is that they, like the rest of the nation, moved on with their lives, indelibly marked by the experience of the Civil War. John C. Merriam, d'Epineuil's early American contact and quartermaster of the Fifty-Third New York Regiment, spent most of the 1870s in Italy, returning to the United States in 1880. He lived out his last days with his wife in Brooklyn, where he died in 1884 at age fifty-four. D'Epineuil's friend Major Jean Baptiste Cantel lived much of his postwar life in Washington, DC; he died in October 1887. Captain Frederick Cocheu, whose lone signature accompanied the charges drawn up by officers of the Fifty-Third against d'Epineuil, became a fixture in Brooklyn. His 1881 divorce decree from his wife Lydia, in the customary manner granted by the New York Supreme Court on the allegation of her adultery, declared that Cocheu could remarry as if Lydia were dead, but she was not allowed to remarry until Frederick died. Cocheu passed away on New Year's Day, 1897, the same year that saw the death of Régis de Trobriand, who had retired to a life of ease in New Orleans. Theodosia Lloyd, who, judging by the surname she bore at the time of her demise, never remarried, lived to see the turn of the century. She died in Paris in February 1903, her eldest daughter Minnie's lawyer handling the particulars. Among the longest-lived members of the Fifty-Third New York State Volunteers was Company H Private William Bosworth, a Brooklyn confectioner who moved across the country to Los Angeles between 1903 and 1904. Writing to the Commissioner of Pensions, G. M. Saltzgaber, in 1920, Bosworth related the financial challenge faced by Angelinos even today: "I am in my 80th year not able to work confined to the house most of the time. I hav a wife to supporte the only support I hav comes from pension department the cost of living is so high is hard to make ends meet." His letter did not result in an increase in pension over the $30 per month he was then receiving. Two years later, William Bosworth died at age eighty-one in Santa Monica, California.[49]

The person who remembered d'Epineuil most fondly was the one closest to him. True to her word, Georgiana Somerset stuck with the count, her husband for nearly a decade. Her parents disapproved of d'Epineuil once they had learned of his past in Philadelphia, and the marriage had social consequences for Georgiana. When she attended her sister Carrie's wedding in August 1872, for instance, some potential guests refused to come on account of the presence of the Countess d'Epineuil.[50] In spite of such snubs, Lionel and Georgiana had made a life together, to which surviving artifacts attest. Georgiana's brother Raglan kept a calendar book, a gift from his mother for Christmas 1878, as it is so inscribed. Noted on its pages are birthdays and anniversaries. On a page titled "Family Birthdays," the list contains fourteen names, including his sisters Carrie and Georgie, using those diminutive forms of endearment, and "Lionel 20 October." Lionel was thus, for better or worse, a member of the Somerset family. The d'Epineuils maintained ceramic dinnerware, crafted by Haviland & Limoges, each piece bearing an ornamental letter "E" topped by a coronet with nine silver balls, or pearls, on raised stalks—the formal headpiece of a French count.[51] Such mementos and memories, however, were all the countess had left after the untimely death of her husband, with his accounts in arrears. Lawyer Sydney Gater Warner attended to outstanding claims against d'Epineuil's estate in 1882, while Georgiana mourned her loss. When one knows the circumstances, the impersonal, business-like listing of names in the Ashford directory for that year takes on a forlorn quality: "d'Epineuil Countess, The Red house."[52]

The widowed Georgiana was still a young woman of thirty-three at the time of her husband's death. Unlike the Pleiad Merope, hiding her shame for marrying Sisyphus, Georgiana continued to self-identify as the Countess d'Epineuil. Surely she liked the noble title, but given the fact that the surname had become a liability in some social and financial circles in England, the choice also demonstrated a loyalty to the memory of Lionel Jobert. In 1884 the intensity of her sadness had diminished enough that she joined a pleasure excursion aboard the yacht *Tyburnia*. The voyage retraced the Atlantic odyssey that her husband had undertaken with another woman long before he knew Georgiana Somerset. Accompanying her aboard ship was her younger cousin by seven years, Arthur Somerset, the son of her uncle Fitzroy M. H. Somerset.[53] Seizing the day, the passengers enjoyed an adventure in early December.

> The British pleasure bark Tyburnia arrived at Madeira yesterday with a pleasure party on board, including several ladies. On account of some petty infringement of customs regulations the vessel was under threat of seizure by the custom house authorities. The captain, not wishing to have the party under his charge detained for an indefinite time, got under weigh at midnight. The fort opened fire, but the Tyburnia ran the gauntlet, keeping well in shore. A custom house steamer, which was on the watch to see that the Tyburnia did not attempt to get off, threatened to sink her, but he was answered by derisive cheers from the lady passengers on board and the captain and crew, who kept on deck, acknowledging each shot by dipping the British ensign.[54]

Once across the Atlantic, news leaked out about tempers having flared among the devil-may-care excursionists: "At Trinidad, Mr. Arthur Somerset was fined £10 for having caned Lord Howard de Walden, whilst Captain Kennerly, in command of the yacht, was fined £1 for having told Lord Howard that he was a liar. The captain's defence was that he was 'the protector of the lady passengers on board, whom Lord Howard traduced.'" Addressing his apology to Arthur Somerset, Walden announced, "'I hereby withdraw all or any statements that I have made regarding the reputation of the ladies on board the Tyburnia . . . With regard to your cousin, the Comtesse d'Epineuil, I have unfortunately stated that she had been divorced. I find that this is not the case, and express my sincere regret at having made the statement.'"[55] Arthur's fiery response hinted at more than upholding his cousin's honor, but just what else lay behind his fury remained a closely guarded secret for the rest of the countess's life.

Six years after the incidents aboard the *Tyburnia*, Georgiana lived in England with her brother Raglan and their mother in Chelmsford in the county of Essex. Raglan worked as the local deputy chief constable. His next-door neighbors were Chief Constable Edward MacLean Showers and his wife Mary. In addition to Raglan, Georgiana, and their mother, the Somerset home housed a young visitor, one Pansy Somerville, age five, born in New York. Mary Showers died in December of the following year, and in time a romance blossomed between the widower chief constable of Essex and the widow Countess d'Epineuil. As the relationship intensified over the course of 1894, Constable Showers maintained a determined correspondence with lawyers in New York City. Georgiana had confided to Edward—and only to Edward—her secret: she and her cousin Arthur had conceived a child together. From Trinidad, the *Tyburnia* had made its way to New York City where their daughter was born in 1886.[56] To maintain appearances, they had done what Lionel Jobert and Theodosia Lloyd did a quarter century earlier, namely, they masqueraded as husband and wife for a time in New York City.

The marriage-minded top lawman of Essex had as the object of his letter-writing campaign the establishment beyond any doubt that Arthur and Georgiana were not married. Showers's initial inquiry centered on whether a divorce could be obtained given the circumstances. New York City attorney W. L. Bond, from his office at 137 Broadway, replied that the law held that persons saying they are married, rearing children, and gaining the reputation of having been married, are considered as such, and thus a divorce could indeed be obtained. In response, Showers promptly began paying the required legal fees and emphasized to Bond that the process must be carried out with the utmost discretion: "The lady will not consent to the slightest publicity either in England or America," the constable wrote authoritatively, "especially in England as she has sundry relations & friends in both countries and they are not aware of her unhappy position."[57] Arthur, however, had to be formally notified of the divorce action against him. Bond reassured Showers: "We can bring the action just out of the City, where no stir would ruffle the waves of gossip." Again, Bond demonstrated the peculiar qualities of his profession: "the summons will be served by order of Publication, in two papers out of town, where no one is apt to see, such as is often done."[58] Showers was equally keen to expedite the matter as the countess's emotions began to crack under the strain of the drawn-out process. Speeding up the bureaucracy cost money; Bond intimated that under-the-table payments to cut through red tape meant incurring unforeseen expenses in an attempt to hurry things along. By late May, the countess was on the brink of not following through with the suit. His nerves frayed from mediating between his distraught Georgiana and the exigencies of a remote legal system, an agitated Showers wrote to Bond that "I told you in my last letter how very important it was that Mrs. Somerville should go abroad in June. In fact, it is only at my most earnest request that on Friday the time it would take that she continued the action at all."[59] Bond, taking offense at the insinuation that he was not doing his job well, responded in measured tones to a letter from Georgiana: "Dear Madame: Yours kindly received and Capt. Showers; while I appreciate your letter, still I am some what surprised at the contents; I am very careful in my manner of doing business, never misrepresent and do all we can to make matters satisfactory . . . Now as to the expense we are doing the best we can for you, and although you do not understand how we have hastened this matter and the time we have put in the same, still it has been done."[60] Finally, on August 21, 1894, the justice of the New York State Supreme Court presiding over the case issued findings of fact, conclusions of law, and a decree of divorce. Arthur and Georgiana Somerville (so named throughout) "married" on September 1, 1885; their daughter Effie May (Pansy) was born September 16, 1886; divorce was granted on the grounds of Arthur's infidelity perpetrated in London; the plaintiff Georgiana could remarry "as though the defendant were actually dead"; and Georgiana received custody of Pansy.[61]

Edward Showers married the Countess d'Epineuil in London on August 15, 1894, six days before the court across the ocean issued the divorce decree. Georgiana shielded her secret even from Pansy, raised as an adopted daughter. When Pansy married in 1919, she gave her father's name as Arthur Somerville, the false name used since her birth. Yet the real circumstances of Effie May's origin did not in any way diminish the countess's love for her child. Pansy moved abroad with her husband in 1919, and her voluminous and tender correspondence with her mother continued unabated until Georgiana's death, at age seventy-seven, on January 29, 1926. If Georgiana had kept mum about being Pansy's biological mother, she made no attempt to hide her first marriage. From her signature on Pansy's marriage record, to when she received mention in newspaper articles, to the name on her calling card, she was the Countess d'Epineuil, her marriage to the obliging Mr. Showers notwithstanding.[62] The hierarchy of identifiers on her grave marker in the Holy Trinity churchyard in Chelmsford gives priority to an all-but-forgotten Frenchman.

> Georgiana
> Countess d'Epineuil
> Widow of Captain E. M. Showers
> Daughter of Col. H. C. C. Somerset
> Beloved Sister of
> Raglan Somerset
> Died Jan. 29th 1926
> "Life cannot end—So love knows no farewell."

After Georgiana passed, there was no one living who had known d'Epineuil well. What remains are documentary traces that lie scattered around the Atlantic region where he spent his life. No small irony accompanies the fact that Lionel Jobert's own descendants had not even the opportunity to remember him. There is nothing to suggest that Frederick De Pineuil ever knew, or was acknowledged by, his father. Frederick left Scotland for Philadelphia as a young man, perhaps hoping to find some trace of his father there, and spent the rest of his life in the United States. The inconsistency in census and vital records regarding Frederick's place of birth, his father's name, his father's place of birth, and even Frederick's surname bears poignant witness to a man never certain about some of his basic biographical data that others take for granted. Table 7.1, for instance, shows the uneven evolution of Frederick's last name. Frederick and his descendants all bore among the most unique of surnames in the United States. Family members rendered their name as De Pineuil, DePineuil, or Depineuil, never knowing the man who bequeathed it to them. Frederick died in Southern California in 1960 at age ninety-one, one week short of his ninety-second birthday, having lived a life four decades longer than Lionel J. d'Epineuil.[63] Today, in Biloxi, Mississippi, one of Frederick's great-grandsons organizes fishing excursions that customers enjoy on his boat. He is the captain.

Table 7.1. Surname variation for Frederick John De Pineuil (1868–1960)

Name	Year	Source
D'Epineuil	1868	Birth Record, Scotland
Epineuil	1871	Census, Scotland
De Penuiel	1881	Census, Scotland
Depineuil	1900	Census, United States
De Pineuil	1910	Census, United States

Conclusion

Lionel Jobert's Atlantic identity grew from the intertwining sprouts of two seeds planted in his boyhood. He absorbed from his French father and English mother a facility for two languages that allowed him a flexibility in later life not enjoyed by the monolingual. He spoke and wrote well in both languages and used those skills to his advantage in the francophone and anglophone Atlantic. Lionel also became linked to the ocean at a tender age, first haltingly as a ship's boy in Brest, followed by his credentialing and occupation as a master mariner. For Haitian officials like Alexis Ardouin, Jobert was foremost a capitaine au long-cours; in America Jobert presented himself as a man of military experience; over in England he was the titled Count d'Epineuil. Even in Cairo, Waynman Dixon recounted that Jobert referred to himself as English. While all, including Lionel, understood him to be a French national, that never served as the defining aspect of his identity. Linguistically, residentially, occupationally, Lionel Jobert must be seen as an Atlantic individual.

If Lionel Jobert kept a diary, or corresponded regularly with family as did Régis de Trobriand, those sources are not extant. Such records can reveal one's innermost thoughts, and sometimes unflattering sides, as when de Trobriand used the insensitive phrase "this flash of jewry" to describe the actions of a chaplain who charged soldiers in the field a fee for carrying money back to their families in New York during the Civil War.[1] Musing over a hypothetical diary, d'Epineuil might have written that the best of us are not so good and the worst of us are not so bad. Despite the lack of such documents, Lionel Jobert's actions spoke volumes. Unlike de Trobriand, d'Epineuil had little time for causes other than himself. D'Epineuil perceived and seized opportunity within the tumultuous political circumstances of the Atlantic in the second half of the nineteenth century. Clearly he cared far less for Haiti's struggle to maintain a stable nation in the first two years of Fabré Geffrard's presidency than he did for his self-aggrandizement at the Haitian government's expense. The fight to deny sovereignty to the Confederacy and preserve the Union, a cause in which many Americans so strongly believed, merely served Jobert as a chance to develop his social standing in the United States.

Jobert, however, did not achieve lasting success in the Caribbean or in North America. When faced with unpleasant legal or pecuniary realities, he sailed to another Atlantic Coast, far from the reach of those he had aggrieved. Yet he could control neither others from sharing information about him over the vast expanse of the ocean nor the resulting consequences. John Decatur, Jobert's business partner in Haiti, tracked him down in Washington, DC, and got d'Epineuil arrested, if briefly. French officials knew of his exploits while working for Haiti, and refused to employ him thereafter. Members of Philadelphia society traveled to France in order to research Jobert's past to confirm in their eyes that he was not worthy of association. His future father-in-law, Colonel Somerset, learned of Jobert's flight from financial troubles in Philadelphia, which tarnished the social reputation of Lionel's bride Georgiana. Thus, steam vessels and space had given Jobert great freedom of action, but that freedom was not absolute.

Like Sisyphus, condemned in the underworld to labor eternally at a task without fulfillment, Lionel Jobert repeatedly ascended to positions of stature only to lose control and be compelled to start again. But the mental and practical boulder he shouldered, composed of vanity and debt, did not countenance beginning at the bottom and undermined his pursuit of prosperity. He felt a sense of entitlement—his great-grandfather's legacy—but lacked the discipline to acquire the resources that would allow him to sustain a life of leisure. His reach ever exceeded his impatient grasp, and his pride always preceded what the early mythmakers saw as an inevitable fall.

Appendix

*Edme Pierre Jobert, First Jobert to be
Count d'Epineuil, and Selected Descendants*

1. Edme Pierre Jobert, born St. Gervais, Paris, died by 1789
1. married (m.) August 16, 1761 Catherine Claude Baroche, died 1772
    2. Marie Catherine Edme Jobert, July 25, 1762–?
    2. Anne Sophie Jobert, August 2, 1764–?
    2. Edme Pierre Jobert, January 31, 1767–March 21, 1839
    2. m. February 26, 1795 Marie L. Olympie Turpin, ca. 1768–?
        3. Louis Edme Jobert, December 11, 1795–June 3, 1861
        3. m. October 4, 1826 Frances H. Birch, ca. 1793–August 20, 1846
            4. Clémence Edme Jobert, June 6, 1827–May 30, 1884
            4. m. November 3, 1847 Edmund Breuil, May 9, 1820–1902
                5. Louise Henriette Edme Breuil, 1849–?
                5. m. 1873 Paul Babut, September 11, 1834–May 29, 1895
                    6. Edmond Babut, ca. 1874–?
                        7. Marie Louise Eliane Babut, 1910–?
                5. Marie Clémence Edme Breuil, 1852–?
                5. m. 1878 Pierre Joseph Decrais, 1846–1914
            4. Edme Lionel Holwell Jobert, October 20, 1829–October 10, 1881
            4. m. January 4, 1872 Georgiana Hester Cornelia Somerset, July 11, 1848–January 29, 1926
            4. Edme Pierre Ambroise Jobert, January 7, 1832–July 19, 1851
        3. m. April 3, 1852 Emilie Ernestine Floreska Mathieu, June 9, 1831–June 25, 1889
            4. Ernestine Jobert, July 31, 1854–?
            4. m. April 7, 1870 Jules Michel, December 30, 1842–?
                5. Jules Ernest Edme Michel, September 3, 1887–April 12, 1946

    5. Juliette Philomene Edme Michel, June 25, 1892–September 20, 1893
   4. Edme Louise Henriette Jobert, October 18, 1857–?
   4. m. February 5, 1880 Georges Joseph Pigeon (divorced July 22, 1889)
    5. Léontine Louise Pigeon, July 5, 1880–?
   4. Eon Jobert, January 29, 1860–August 25, 1926
   4. m. August 31, 1893 Augustine Avet, September 19, 1860–?
    5. Germaine Andrée, recorded 1893–?
   4. m. December 12, 1911 Marthe Marie Garnier
  3. Edme Charles Ambroise Jobert, September 3, 1797–December 20, 1860
  3. m. 1838 Julia Elizabeth Danjon
   4. Elizabeth Rachel Jobert, June 23, 1840
   4. m. June 27, 1870 Guillaume Francois Eugene Eudes Deslongchamps
    5. Emma Deslongchamps
    5. m. Alexandre Bigot
     6. Jeanne Bigot
     6. m. Pierre Henry
      7. Paul Henry
     6. Louise Bigot
     6. m. Pierre Henry when sister Jeanne died, and had four children by him
   4. Marie Mathilde Jobert, February 26, 1847–August 25, 1906
   4. m. October 23, 1880 Marie J. Eugène Bieth, September 13, 1840–October 31, 1907
 2. Edme Balthazar Jobert, b. March 3, 1768–?

Sources: Minutes et répertoires du notaire Abraham Jacques Silvestre, November 20, 1758–1770, MC/ET/XLVI/385, Archives Nationales, Paris; Registres de tutelles, Paris, accessible at http://en.geneanet.org/archives/registres/; Mairie de Paris, État Civil de Paris, accessible at http://canadp-archives enligne.paris.fr/archives_etat_civil/index.php; Registres d'Etat Civil, Archives Départementales du Calvados, Caen; *Journal de Genève*, May 31, 1884, 4, col. 1; Mariages de Paris et ses environs, France, 1700 à 1907, accessible at ancestry.com; Ouest France, http://www.ouest-france.fr/le-chateau-de-mathieu-souvre-pour-la-premiere-fois-660403; Archives Départementales du Val-de-Marne, Saint-Mandé, Décès 1906, no. 247 accessible at archives.valdemarne.fr; Légion d'Honneur file for M. J. E. Bieth, accessible at http://www.culture.gouv.fr/public/mistral/leonore_fr.

Table A.1. United States Patents Witnessed by Lionel J. d'Epineuil's Firm.

Patent Subject	Patent #	Inventor	Date
Broom and Brush Head	62,686	George T. Reed	Mar. 5, 1867
Steam-Drying Apparatus	68,239	William Ryner	Aug. 27, 1867
Stove-Pipe Drums	70,961	Jesse Conover	Nov. 19, 1867
Gas Engines	73,816	W. H. Laubach	Jan. 28, 1868
Valves for Water-Closets	74,896	Wm. S. Cooper	Feb. 25, 1868
Water-Closets	75,375	Wm. S. Cooper	Mar. 10, 1868
Harness	76,369	Wm. S. Wood	Apr. 7, 1868
Enameled Water-Coolers	77,106	C. C. Savery	Apr. 21, 1868
Registers for Railroad Cars	79,339	P. S. Gerhart	June 30, 1868
Rocking Swing	79,401	Thos. Sanders	June 30, 1868
Bolts for Trunk, etc.	85,617	Henry Simons	Jan. 5, 1869
Self-acting Spinning Machine	86,156	H. Holcroft, et al.	Jan. 26, 1869
Cement Roofing	89,186	C. G. Von Tagen	Apr. 20, 1869
Halter Clasp	96,164	E. H. Stewart	Oct. 26, 1869
Preventing Incrustation in Steam Boilers	98,173	Geo. W. Lord	Dec. 21, 1869
Cotton Gins	101,610	R. R. Gwathmey	Apr. 5, 1870
Self-recording Surveying Machine	103,479	Henry Manger	May 24, 1870
Chair and Lounge	105,677	M. P. Harley	July 26, 1870
Hair-Puffs or Rolls	110,782	J. D. Oppenheimer	Jan. 3, 1871

Source: United States Patent and Trademark Office, http://patft.uspto.gov.

Notes

Introduction

1. Nicholas Canny and Philip Morgan, "Introduction: The Making and Unmaking of an Atlantic World," in Nicholas Canny and Philip Morgan, eds., *The Oxford Handbook of the Atlantic World, c. 1450–c.1850* (Oxford, UK: Oxford University Press, 2011), 16.

2. David Armitage, "Three Concepts of Atlantic History," in David Armitage and Michael J. Braddick, eds., *The British Atlantic World, 1500–1800* (New York: Palgrave Macmillan, 2002), 16.

3. Emma Rothschild, "Late Atlantic History," in Canny and Morgan, eds., *The Oxford Handbook of the Atlantic World*, 646.

4. Don H. Doyle, "The Atlantic World and the Crisis of the 1860s," in Don H. Doyle, ed., *American Civil Wars: The United States, Latin America, Europe, and the Crisis of the 1860s* (Chapel Hill: University of North Carolina Press, 2017), 3–6.

5. D'Maris Coffman, et al., *The Atlantic World* (London: Routledge, 2015), 2.

6. Among the works that discuss the d'Epineuil Zouaves are Richard A. Sauers, *"A Succession of Honorable Victories": the Burnside Expedition in North Carolina* (Dayton, OH: Morningside House, 1996); Don Troiani, et al., *Don Troiani's Soldiers in America, 1754–1865* (Mechanicsburg, PA: Stackpole Books, 1998); William L. Burton, *Melting Pot Soldiers: The Union's Ethnic Regiments*, 2d ed. (Bronx, NY: Fordham University Press, 1998); Michael P. Zatarga, *The Battle of Roanoke Island* (Charleston, SC: The History Press, 2015); Farid Ameur, *Les Français dans le Guerre de Sécession, 1861–1865* (Rennes, France: Presses Universitaires de Rennes, 2016). The earliest scholarly treatment of Jobert and the Fifty-Third New York Regiment is Gerald E. Wheeler, "D'Epineuil's Zouaves," *Civil War History* 2, no. 4 (December 1956): 93–100.

Chapter 1

1. Marianna Eliza d'Lamartine to Fanny Jobert, Mâcon, France, December 8, 1829, Bancroft Library, University of California-Berkeley. An early twentieth-century

biographer of Alphonse de Lamartine asserted that Marianna was "more versed in orthography and the intricacies of French grammar than her illustrious husband," yet she omitted a written accent here in *sincèrement*. See H. Remsen Whitehouse, *The Life of Lamartine*, vol. 2 (Boston: Houghton Mifflin, 1918), 14.

    2. The family relationships of John Zephaniah Holwell may be viewed at http://kindred.stanford.edu/#/path/full/none/none/I91/I829/; Naissances 1829, no. 828, Archives Départmentales du Calvados, Caen (hereafter ADC).

    3. Jobert, September 22, 1774, Registres de Tutelles, Paris, Centre Historique des Archives Nationales à Paris, accessed at http://en.geneanet.org/archives/registres/view/?idcollection=12439&page=231; *Procès-Verbal des Séances de L'Assemblée Provinciale de L'Isle de France, Tenues à Melun, en Novembre & Décembre 1787* (Chez la Ve. Tarbé & Fils, Impr. De l'Assemblée Provinciale, 1788), ix, 4; *Annuaire Statistique du Département de L'Yonne, Année 1847* (Auxerre, France: Ed. Perriquet, Imprimeur-Lithographe, Editeur), 85; *Annuaire Historique du Département de L'Yonne, 1852* (Auxerre, France: Perriquet, Imprimeur-Libraire, Éditeur, 1852), 361; Décès 1839, no. 328, Naissances 1795, no. 234, and Naissances 1796–1797, no. 1188, ADC.

    4. "Avis Important," *Journal Politique et Annonces Judiciaires du Département du Calvados*, August 12. 1821, 2, col. 1; *Archives des Découvertes et des Inventions Nouvelles* (Paris: Treuttel et Würtz, 1822), 402; "Les Matériaux de Constuction et d'Entretien des Routes," *L'Ordre et la Liberté*, February 8, 1855, 2, col. 3; *Journal Politique et Annonces Judiciaires du Département du Calvados*, May 2, 1824, 4, col. 1; the quotation comes from "Avis," *Journal Politique*, July 17, 1828, 4, col. 2; just one example of the many notices showing goods shipped to or from Monsieur Jobert is "Port de Caen," *Journal Politique*, May 24, 1829, 4, col. 2; Séb. Bottin, *Almanach du Commerce de Paris, de la France et des Pays Étrangers* (Paris: Bureau de L'Almanach du Commerce, 1833), 130; *Catalogue des Produits des Arts du Département du Calvados* (Caen, France: Société Royale d'Agriculture et de Commerce de Caen, 1834), 19.

    5. Register of Marriages in the House of His Britannic Majesty's Ambassador to the Court of France, no. 506, 90 (169 originally), Records of the General Register Office, marriages and deaths of British subjects abroad, RG 33/63, National Archives, Kew, United Kingdom; Naissances 1827, no. 530, and Naissances 1832, no. 22, ADC; Louis Edme Jobert's Legion of Honor file is found at http://www.culture.gouv.fr/public/mistral/leonore_fr; *Journal des Débats Politiques et Littéraires* (Paris), August 3, 1843, 3, col. 1.

    6. Alphonse de Lamartine, *Jocelyn: An Episode, Journal Found at the House of a Village Curé*, trans. Frances Henrietta Jobert (Paris: Baudry, 1837), 3; *Fraser's Magazine for Town and Country* (London), 18 (August 1838): 173.

    7. *Annuaire des Cinq Départements de L'Ancienne Normandie* (Caen, France: l'Association Normande, 1840), 488.

    8. Caen, Recensement 1841, ADC; Campbell Gibson, *Population of the 100 Largest Cities and Other Urban Places in the United States: 1790 to 1990* (Washington, DC: U.S. Bureau of the Census, 1998), table 7; "Ville de Paris: Population & Density from 1600," http://www.demographia.com/dm-par90.htm.

9. Inscription Maritime, Rouen, Matricule de Gens de Mer, Registre de Mousses, Paris, première série, 1826–1849, 231, no. 920, Archives Départmentales de Seine-Maritime, Rouen (hereafter ADSM).

10. *Journal de Caen*, March 25, 1846, 3, col. 1; *Bulletin des Lois du Royaume de France*, IX série, Partie Supplémentaire, tome douzième (Paris: l'Imprimerie Royale, 1838), 824–31; *Annales des Ponts et Chaussées, Mémoires et Documents Relatifs a l'Art des Constructions et au Service de l'Ingénieur; Lois, Ordonnances et Autres Actes Concernant l'Administration des Ponts et Chaussées*, 2e série (Paris: Carilian-Goeury et V. Dalmont, 1843), 484–89; *Journal du Palais, Jurisprudence Administrative*, Tome X, 1845–1849 (Paris, 1851), 159.

11. *Journal de Caen*, August 10, 1846, 3, col. 2; Décès 1846, no. 705, ADC; Registre Matricule des Marins provenant du Recrutement de 1846, 2 M 17, Service Historique de la Défense, Cherbourg. The author thanks the Service Historique de la Défense at Cherbourg for this last citation.

12. Edmond Jurien de la Gravière, *Voyage de la Corvette La Bayonnaise dans les Mers de Chine* (Paris: Henri Plon, troisième édition, 1872), vol. 1, 5, vol. 2, 382; "Bahia en 1847: Deux Lettres de M. Forth-Rouen," *Journal de la Société des Américanistes de Paris* (Paris: Société des Américanistes de Paris, nouvelle série, tome IV, 1907), 71.

13. Jurien de la Gravière, *Voyage de la Corvette La Bayonnaise*, vol. 1, 11, 14–15.

14. Jurien de la Gravière, vol. 1, 179; vol. 2, 382.

15. Jurien de la Gravière, vol. 2, 382.

16. Inscription Maritime Syndicat de Caen, Matricules officiers mariniers, matelots, 1850–1865 (R_3377), no. 70, Lionel Jobert and Mariages 1847, no. 239, ADC; *Annuaire Diplomatique et Consulaire de la République Française pour 1881* (Paris: Berger, Levrault, 1881), nouvelle série, tome II, 143–44; Inscription maritime, quartier de Havre, Novices (partie 3), 1850–1865, 6P5/99, folio 900, no. 3561, Edme Pierre Ambroise Jobert and Inscription maritime, quartier de Havre, Rôles de Bâtiments de Commerce, 1849, desarmement no. 195, ADSM.

17. Jurien de la Gravière, *Voyage de la Corvette La Bayonnaise*, vol. 2, 382; *La Presse* (Paris), February 12, 1850, 3, col. 6; *Statistique de la France* (Paris: Imprimerie Nationale, 1850), 92–93, 124–25; "Conseil Municipal de Caen," *Le Pilote du Calvados*, May 8, 1847, 1, col. 2; "Nouvelles Locales," *Le Pilote du Calvados*, August 8, 1848, 2, col. 3; *Calendrier Maçonnique du Grand-Orient de France* (Paris: 1852), 235; "Inspection des LL. de l'Ouest de la France 1843," in F. Henri-Wentz, *Opuscules Maçonniques* (Grand Ordre de France, 1864), 78; Register of Marriages in the House of His Britannic Majesty's Ambassador to the Court of France, no. 506, 90, National Archives, Kew.

18. *Mémoires de la Société Royale d'Agriculture et de Commerce de Caen* (Caen, France: 1827), tome II, 315–16; "Salle de Spectacle de Caen," *L'Intérêt Public*, October 30, 1838, 4, col. 1.

19. "Théatre de Caen," *Le Pilote du Calvados*, May 6, 1847, 3, col. 1; "Théatre de Caen," *Le Pilote du Calvados*, April 3, 1849, 4, col. 1.

20. Anaïs Fargueil to M. Jobert, Caen, October 10, 1847, Bancroft Library, University of California, Berkeley; St. Edme Jobert on behalf of Sophie Méquillet, undated, Bancroft Library. Méquillet performed in Caen on several occasions between 1845 and 1851, the likely time frame for this letter.

21. England Births and Christenings, 1538–1975, 106, accessed at familysearch. org; Port of London, no. 68, January 16, 1851, England, Alien Arrivals, 1810–1811, 1826–1869, accessed at ancestry.com; *Annuaire Diplomatique et Consulaire de la République Française pour 1881*, tome II, 143–44.

22. Inscription maritime, quartier de Havre, Rôles de Bâtiments de Commerce, 1851, desarmement no. 50 and Inscription maritime, quartier de Havre, Officiers mariniers et matelots (8ème série), 1850–1865, 6P5/111, Edme Pierre Ambroise Jobert, #1103, ADSM; Inscription Maritime Syndicat de Caen, Matricules officiers mariniers, matelots, 1850–1865, Lionel Jobert, ADC.

23. Mortimer Chambers, et al., *The Western Experience Since 1600*, 3d edition (New York: Alfred A. Knopf, 1982), 828; "Caen," *Le Suffrage Universal* (Caen), September 19, 1851, 1, col. 1; Victor Hugo to Adele Hugo, February 8, 1852, in La Librairie Ollendorf, ed., *Victor Hugo: Correspondance*, vol. IV (Paris: Albin Michel, 1952), 214; Victor Hugo to Madame Hugo, February 14, 1852, La Librairie Ollendorf, *Victor Hugo: Correspondance*, vol. II (1950), 65–66; marriage record of Louis Edme Jobert, Mariages de Paris et ses environs, France, 1700 à 1907 and birth record of Emilie Floreska Ernestine Mathieu, Paris, France and Vicinity Births, 1700–1899, ancestry.com.

24. Inscription Maritime Syndicat de Caen, Matricules officiers mariniers, matelots, 1850–1865, Lionel Jobert, ADC; Inscription maritime, quartier de Havre, Rôles de Bâtiments de Commerce, 1852, desarmement no. 341, ADSM; *Annuaire Diplomatique et Consulaire de la République Française pour 1881*, tome II, 143–44; *Morning Post* (London), January 2, 1851, 3; *Morning Post*, January 18, 1851, 5.

25. Inscription Maritime Syndicat de Caen, Matricules officiers mariniers, matelots, 1850–1865, Lionel Jobert, ADC; Orlando Figes, *The Crimean War: A History* (New York: Picador, 2012), xxiii.

26. Matricules de Gens de Mer, quartier de Rouen, Paris district, 2d Series (1850–1864), Capitaines au long cours, Jobert, folio 85, ADSM.

27. Caen, Recensement 1856, Caen-Est, Quai de Abattoirs (image 136), Naissances 1856, no. 746, and Notarie de Caen, étude Beaujour, inventaire mobilier après décès de Louis Jobert, 1861, 8E_8738, ADC. Papers related to the sloops are identified in classification items 59 and 60 within the inventory.

28. Inscription Maritime, quartier de Havre, Rôles de Bâtiments de Commerce, 1857, desarmement no. 476, ADSM.

29. Vital Records, Civil State Files, Commune of St. Pierre, Colony of Martinique, France 1857, Entry 373 (image 130), http://anom.archivesnationales.culture.gouv.fr/cao-mec2/pix2web.php?territoire=MARTINIQUE&commune=SAINT-PIERRE&annee=1857&typeacte=AC_DE.

30. "Ports Français," *Journal de Rouen*, December 24, 1857, 4, col. 6; Inscription Maritime, quartier de Havre, Rôles de Bâtiments de Commerce, 1858, no. 489, ADSM.

31. Inscription Maritime, quartier de Havre, Rôles de Bâtiments de Commerce, 1858, no. 489 and 1859, no. 249, ADSM.

Chapter 2

1. Inscription Maritime, quartier de Havre, Rôles de Bâtiments de Commerce, 1859, no. 249, ADSM.

2. Inscription Maritime, 1859, no. 249; see also A. Mellinet, French Consul and Chargé d'Affaires in Port-au-Prince to [French] Minister of the Navy, Port-au-Prince, March 2, 1859, Correspondance avec le Ministère de la Marine, Port-au-Prince, vol. 30, Ministère des Affaires Étrangères, Nantes (hereafter MAEN).

3. "Advice of the Secretary of State for War and the Navy," *Feuille de Commerce* (Port-au-Prince; hereafter FdC), March 19, 1859, 2, col. 4.

4. Alexis B. Ardouin, Resident Minister of Haiti in Paris, to A. Dupuy, Resident Minister of Haiti in London, Paris, November 24, 1860, box 34, reel 28, vol. 174, Eugene Maximilien Haitian Collection (hereafter EMHC), Schomburg Center for Research in Black Culture, New York Public Library.

5. E. Heurtelou, "Haiti," in *Revue des Races Latines* (Paris) 18, no. 2 (February 1860): 636. One of the other guests at the reception was A. Beaubrun Ardouin, soon to be Haitian Minister to France. He would play a key role in the events to be described later in this chapter.

6. The original French-language transcript of the speech is found in Jules Neff, "Examens de l'Ecole Navale," FdC, January 7, 1860, 2.

7. *Bulletin des Lois de L'Empire Francais*, 11th Series (second half of 1860), supplemental vol. XVI (Paris: 1861), 304. The decree, dated July 28, 1860, was officially gazetted on September 10, 1860.

8. See the government communiqué and the list of Port-au-Prince ship departures published in FdC, February 18, 1860, 3, col. 4 and 1, col. 1 respectively; "From Port-au-Prince," *New York Evening Express*, April 6, 1860, 4, col. 8.

9. "Chronique departmentale—Nantes," *Revue des Races Latines* 21, no. 49 (July 1860): 278. See also the arrival notices in the *L'Union Bretonne* (Nantes), April 24, 1860, 3, col. 5 and April 25, 1860, 3, col. 2. In the latter notice Jobert is referred to as capitaine au long cours francais.

10. Ardouin to Victorin Plésance, Haitian Secretary of State for Foreign Relations, Paris, June 14, 1860 and the quotation is from Auguste L'Instant Pradine, Charge d'Affaires for Haiti in France, to Plésance, Paris, April 30, 1860, box 34, reel 28, vol. 174, EMHC; Naissances 1860, no. 94, ADC.

11. Ardouin to Plésance, Paris, May 28, 1860, box 34, reel 28, vol. 174, EMHC.

12. *La Presse* (Paris), June 1, 1860, 2, col. 4. This article refers to twelve cadets, which tallies with Jobert's target of twelve as stated in his speech of early January. In that speech Jobert reported eleven current students; he must have admitted an additional cadet prior to leaving Port-au-Prince for France in February.

13. Ardouin to French Minister of the Navy, Paris, June 22, 1860 and Ardouin to Jobert, Paris, June 21, 1860, box 34, reel 28, vol. 174, EMHC; *Morning Courier and New York Enquirer*, July 18, 1860, 3, col. 5.

14. *L'Industrie* (Bordeaux), July 22, 1860, 2. Ardouin identified Mr. Arman as the builder of the *Geffrard* in Ardouin to Plésance, Paris, April 7–13, 1861, box 6, reel 5, vol. 28, EMHC.

15. Ardouin to Plésance, Paris, June 23, 1860, box 34, reel 28, vol. 174, EMHC.

16. Mellinet to French Minister and Secretary of State for the Department of Foreign Affairs, Port-au-Prince, February. 24, 1860, 246, Haiti, correspondance politique, vol. 23, 1859–1860, P 17233 (microfilm), Archives des Affaires Etrangères, La Courneuve, France.

17. Ardouin to Plésance, Paris, June 23, 1860, box 34, reel 28, vol. 174, EMHC.

18. Ardouin to Jobert, Paris, 16 July 1860 and Ardouin to Plésance, Paris, July 30, 1860, box 34, reel 28, vol. 174, EMHC.

19. *L'Industrie*, July 22, 1860, 2. Testing of the engine had commenced by mid-July. Ardouin to Mr. Silvie at Bordeaux; Paris, July 20, 1860, Ardouin to Plésance, Bordeaux, August 11–14, 1860, Ardouin to Minister of the Navy at Paris [Hamelin], Bordeaux, August 7, 1860, and Ardouin to Mr. Labat, Engineer of the Imperial Navy at Bordeaux, Bordeaux, August 27, 1860, box 34, reel 28, vol. 174, EMHC.

20. Ardouin to Silvie, Bordeaux, August 5, 1860, Ardouin to Plésance, Bordeaux, August 11–14 1860, and Ardouin to Plésance, Paris, September 15, 1860, box 34, reel 28, vol. 174, EMHC.

21. Ardouin to Plésance, Bordeaux, August 29–31, 1860 and Ardouin to Plésance, Paris, September 13, 1860, box 34, reel 28, vol. 174, EMHC.

22. Ardouin to Plésance, Paris, August 29–31, 1860, box 34, reel 28, vol. 174, EMHC.

23. Ardouin to the [Vice] Admiral and Maritime Prefect at Brest [Odet-Pellion], Bordeaux, August 15, 1860 and Ardouin to Plésance, Paris, August 29–31, 1860, box 34, reel 28, vol. 174, EMHC.

24. "Exposé de la situation générale de la République, présenté au Sénat le 27 Septembre 1860," FdC, September 29, 1860, 2.

25. Ardouin to Plésance; Paris, September 13, 1860, box 34, reel 28, vol. 174, EMHC. The typical transit time for diplomatic correspondence sent between Paris and Port-au-Prince via packet boats was around three weeks.

26. In addition to the Ardouin correspondence in the New York Public Library referenced throughout this chapter, see "Movimento Marítimo," *O Parlamento* (Lis-

bon), September 14, 1860, 3, col. 4; *A Flor do Oceano* (Funchal), September 29, 1860, 2, col. 3; "Sección Marítima y Mercantil," *Eco Del Comercio* (Santa Cruz de Tenerife), October 20, 1860, 2; FdC, October 27, 1860, 2, col. 3, December 1, 1860, 2, col. 3, and December 8, 1860, 2, col. 4; *St. Thomae Tidende*, November 21, 1860, 3; *Army and Navy Gazette* (London), January 26, 1861, 53, col. 3; Lloyd v. Lloyd and Jobert, Divorce Case File L53, ref. J77/33/L53, the National Archives, Kew, United Kingdom.

27. FdC, December 8, 1860, 2, col. 4, October 27, 1860, 2, and December 1, 1860, 2.

28. Ardouin to Plésance, Paris, September 1, 1860, box 34, reel 28, vol. 174, EMHC.

29. Ardouin to Plésance, Paris, October 14, 1860, box 34, reel 28, vol. 174, EMHC.

30. Ardouin to Plésance, Paris, October 14, 1860 and Ardouin to Plésance, Paris, October 18, 1860, box 34, reel 28, vol. 174, EMHC. Forster later requested compensation for his dismissal by Jobert from the Haitian government. See Ardouin to Plésance, Paris, March 31, 1861, box 34, reel 28, vol. 174, EMHC.

31. Ardouin to Dupuy, Paris, November 19, 1860, box 34, reel 28, vol. 174, EMHC.

32. The three quotations come, respectively, from Ardouin to Dupuy, Paris, November 19, 1860, Ardouin to Dupuy, Paris, November 24, 1860, and Ardouin to Plésance, Paris, November 26, 1860, box 34, reel 28, vol. 174, EMHC.

33. Ardouin to Plésance, Paris, December 31, 1860, box 34, reel 28, vol. 174, EMHC.

34. Lloyd v. Lloyd and Jobert, Divorce Case Files, The National Archives, Kew.

35. *Liverpool Mercury*, January 30, 1864, and *Belfast News-Letter*, February 1, 1864. The "1st lieutenant" who rowed Mrs. Lloyd to the *Geffrard* likely was Jobert's no. 2 aboard ship, Théodore Démost. Mrs. Lloyd's letter to her mother was probably sent from the island of St. Vincent (Cape Verde).

36. Ardouin to Plésance, Paris, December 15, 1860, box 34, reel 28, vol. 174, EMHC.

37. FdC, December 8, 1860, 2, col. 4 and December 15, 1860, 2.

38. Ardouin to French Minister of Foreign Affairs [É. Thouvenel], Paris, February 4, 1861, box 34, reel 28, vol. 174, EMHC; Léonce Levraud to Minister of the Navy and of the Colonies [Chasseloup-Laubat], Port-au-Prince, December 17, 1860, Correspondance avec le Ministère de la Marine, Port-au-Prince, vol. 31, MAEN. Jobert's second, Démost, apparently was exonerated by the inquest commission, and reportedly later became, at least for a time, the captain of the *Geffrard*. See F. D. Légitime, *Une année au ministère de l'agriculture et de l'intérieur* ([Paris?] 1883), 233.

39. Ardouin to French Minister of Foreign Affairs, Paris, February 4, 1861; FdC, December 1, 1860, December 1 and 22, 1860, 1; *New York Tribune*, January 8, 1861, 8, col. 6; Ship Manifest for the Brig Baltimore, District of New York, Port

of New York, January 7, 1861, accessed at ancestry.com. The *Baltimore* had been cleared for departure from Port-au-Prince on December 17. The December 22 and 29, 1860 issues of FdC, issued after the *Baltimore* left Haiti, made no mention of Jobert or any scandal surrounding him.

40. Ardouin to Haitian Secretary of State for War and the Navy [T. Déjoie], Paris, January 28, 1861, box 34, reel 28, vol. 174, EMHC.

41. Ardouin to Plésance, Paris, January 28, 1861 and the assertion of fraud appears in Ardouin to Plésance, Paris, February 13, 1861, box 34, reel 28, vol. 174, EMHC.

42. Ardouin to French Minister of Foreign Affairs, Paris, February 4, 1861.

43. For an example of the issues related to the *Geffrard* in the wake of Jobert's dismissal, see Ardouin to Dupuy, Paris, March 31, 1861, box 1, reel 1, vol. 6, EMHC; "Faits Divers," *La République* (Port-au-Prince), February 28, 1861, 1, col. 3.

44. Levraud to Minister of the Navy, Port-au-Prince, January 24, 1861, Correspondance avec le Ministère de la Marine, Port-au Prince, vol. 31, MAEN; J. N. Léger, *Haiti: Her History and Her Detractors* (New York: Neale Publishing, 1907), 211–14.

45. This case is discussed below in chapter 6.

46. "News from Hayti," *New York Herald*, November 15, 1859, 1.

47. Ardouin to Plésance, Paris, February 7, 1861, box 6, reel 5, vol. 28, EMHC.

48. Plésance to F. [*sic*; Joseph] N. Lewis, commercial agent of the United States at Port-au-Prince, February 9, 1861 (U.S. House of Representatives Documents, 40th Congress, 2nd Session, Ex. Doc. No. 260).

Chapter 3

1. "Sinking of a Ship," *Philadelphia Inquirer*, February 11, 1861, 4, col. 6; "On the Ocean's Bottom," *Daily Saratogian*, March 31, 1880, 1, col. 4.

2. United States Census Bureau, *The Statistical History of the United States From Colonial Times to the Present* (New York: Basic Books, 1976), 118; Michael R. Haines, "French Immigration to the United States: 1820 to 1950," *Annales de Démographie Historique* 1 (2000): 346; William B. Styple, ed., *Our Noble Blood: The Civil War Letters of Régis de Trobriand, Major-General U.S.V.* (Kearny, NJ: Bell Grove Publishing, 1997), vii, ix; Marie Caroline Post, *The Life and Memoirs of Comte Régis de Trobriand, Major-General in the Army of the United States* (New York: E. P. Dutton, 1910), 216–19; "Personal Intelligence," *New York Herald*, March 31, 1861, 1, col. 5.

3. St. Edme Jobert's brother Charles had died the preceding December at age sixty-three. See décès 1861, no. 590 and décès 1860, no. 1246, ADC.

4. Notarie de Caen, étude Beaujour, inventaire mobilier après décès de Louis Jobert, 1861, 8E_8738, ADC. Documents relating to Lionel Jobert's debt are referenced in classification item 163 within the inventory.

5. Charles H. Pope, comp., *Merriam Genealogy in England and America* (Boston, MA: Charles H. Pope, 1906), 608; "American Engineers' Association," *New York Daily Tribune*, April 5, 1860, 8, col. 1; David P. Forsyth, *The Business Press in America, 1750–1865* (Philadelphia, PA: Chilton Books, 1964), 205; Monte A. Calvert, *The Mechanical Engineer in America, 1830–1910* (Baltimore, MD: Johns Hopkins Press, 1967), 107–8. For one of Merriam's ads, see *Scientific American*, new series 4:24 (June 15, 1861), 383, col. 3.

6. "Suppressing the Privateers," *New York Times*, June 10, 1861, 2, col. 5.

7. "A Volunteer Squadron to Look After Privateers," *New York Times*, June 18, 1861, 2, col. 1.

8. Petition of Lionel Jobert d'Epineuil, July 4, 1861, HR37A-G9.5, 37th Congress, Record Group 233, Records of the U.S. House of Representatives, National Archives, Washington, DC (hereafter cited as NARA I); *Lain's Brooklyn City Directory for the year ending May 1, 1862*.

9. Petition of Lionel Jobert, July 4, 1861.

10. Petition of Lionel Jobert, July 4, 1861.

11. Petition of Lionel Jobert, July 4, 1861.

12. *Journal of the House of Representatives*, July 12, 1861, 67.

13. *A Record of the Commissioned Officers, Non-Commissioned Officers and Privates, of the Regiments which Were Organized in the State of New York and Called into Service of the United States to Assist in Suppressing the Rebellion* (Albany, NY, 1864), 381.

14. "A Regiment of French Zouaves," *New York Herald*, August 4, 1861, 1, col. 6.

15. *Richmond County Gazette*, October 9, 1861, 2, col. 3.

16. "The Police Commissioners," *New York Times*, September 24, 1859, 1, col. 6; "The War," *New York Herald*, August 18, 1861, 6, col. 2; "Operations of the Union Defense Committee," *New York Daily Tribune*, September 23, 1861, 7, col. 6.

17. "Volunteers, Attention!," *Daily Advertiser* (Portland, ME), October 15, 1861; "Imperial Zouaves!" poster, Library Company of Philadelphia; *Plattsburg (New York) Republican*, October 12, 1861, 3, col. 1; "The D'Epineuil Zouaves—Fifty-Third Regiment N.Y.S.V.," *New York Daily Tribune*, November 15, 1861, 7, col. 1; Brooks Brothers bill, Case Papers, 1802–1863, January Term 1863, Civil Trials #626–675, box 1025, NC-2, entry 6, folder Jan. Term 1863, Trial #662, Record Group 21, Records of District Courts of the United States, NARA I.

18. "The French Zouaves," *New York Times*, August 11, 1861, 8, col. 5.

19. Lionel J. d'Epineuil to James Lesley, New York, August 20, 1861, D139, M221, Letters Received by the Secretary of War, Registered Series, 1801–1870, NARA I.

20. "The D'Epineuil Zouaves," *New York Herald*, August 7, 1861, 1, col. 3.

21. Dossier of Joseph Viguier, GR 3Ye 9057, Service historique de la défense, Vincennes, France; A. J. Viguier de Monteil to Governor E. D. Morgan, New York,

October 5, 1861, box 36, folder 22, New York Adjutant General Correspondence, New York State Archives (hereafter cited as NYSA); *Fifth Annual Report of the Chief of the Bureau of Military Statistics* (Albany, NY, 1868), note on 45–47.

22. "Fifty-Third New York State Volunteers," *New York Herald*, November 28, 1861, 5, col. 1; J. Bapt. Cantel, passenger on ship *Catherine*, September 15, 1855, New York Passenger lists, 1820–1891, familysearch.org; James Lesley Jr. to Colonel d'Epineuil, War Department (Washington, DC), September 14, 1861, Consolidated Correspondence, file 1794–1915, box 270, J. B. Cantel folder, Record Group 92, Records of the Office of the Quartermaster General, NARA I.

23. D'Epineuil to Surgeon General Vanderpool, New York, September 18, 1861 and d'Epineuil to [Vanderpool], New York, September 26, 1861, box 3, folder 1, Office of the Surgeon General Correspondence, NYSA.

24. James Lesley Jr. to E. D. Morgan, War Department (Washington, DC), September 27, 1861 and d'Epineuil to Morgan, New York, September 29, 1861, box 3, folder 1, Office of the Surgeon General Correspondence, NYSA.

25. The National Park Service website, https://www.nps.gov/civilwar/soldiers-and-sailors-database.htm.

26. "Local Military Matters," *New York Daily Tribune*, September 11, 1861, 8, col. 3 and September 12, 1861, 8, col. 2.

27. Local Military Matters," *New York Daily Tribune*, September 12, 1861.

28. D'Epineuil to Lesley, New York, September 6, 1861 (no box or folder number), Adjutant General Correspondence, NYSA.

29. Egbert L. Viele to Edwin Morgan, New York, September 10, 1861, the Gilder Lehrman Institute, New York City.

30. Victor Vifquain, *The 1862 Plot to Kidnap Jefferson Davis*, Jeffrey H. Smith and Phillip Thomas Tucker, eds. (Lincoln: University of Nebraska Press, 2005), xv; d'Epineuil to [Vanderpool], New York, September 26, 1861; *Metropolitan Catholic Almanac, and Laity's Directory, for the United States, Canada, and the British Provinces, 1861* (Baltimore: John Murphy), 6.

31. James Lesley Jr. to E. D. Morgan, War Dept. (Washington, DC), October 6, 1861, box 36, folder 10, Adjutant General Correspondence, NYSA.

32. Bliss to Hillhouse, New York, October 25, 1861 and Bliss to Hillhouse, New York, November 4, 1861, box 33, folder 17, Adjutant General Correspondence, NYSA.

33. Certificate of William Bosworth, Co. H, 1861, author's collection. Even this preprinted form misspelled d'Epineuil.

34. Maurice Sand, *Six mille lieues à tout vapeur* (Paris: Michel Lévy Frères, 1862), 162.

35. "Military Movements in New York," *New York Herald*, September 1, 1861, 1, col. 5; Richard M. Bayles, ed., *History of Richmond County (Staten Island) New York: From Its Discovery to the Present Time* (New York: L. E. Preston, 1887), 304; *Innsbruker Nachrichten* (Austria), April 7, 1862, 2.

36. Only some surviving regimental records specify the soldiers' place of birth, thus I make the assumption that men named George Boulanger and Jules Beaumont, for example, came from a French cultural and linguistic background. This approach, I readily acknowledge, is an informal assessment, and yields suggestive, but not definitive, numbers. Statistical tabulations are based on *Annual Report of the Adjutant-General for the State of New York. For the Year 1900* (Albany, 1901), 525–652. This source lists 1,097 men belonging to the 53d New York Regiment, first organization (d'Epineuil Zouaves), with six of them rendering no service, so 1,091 is used here as the total for purposes of computation.

37. *New York Sun*, September 4, 1861, 3, col. 4.

38. Book Records of Union Volunteer Organizations, 53rd New York Infantry, Descriptive Book, Companies D, F, and G, Record Group 94, Records of the Adjutant General's Office, NARA I. Twenty-four percent of all Union soldiers were foreign-born. On this last point, see McPherson, *For Cause and Comrades: Why Men Fought in the Civil War* (New York: Oxford University Press, 1997), ix.

39. "The D'Epineuil Zouaves," *New York Daily Tribune*, November 15, 1861.

40. Geo. F. Chester to Hon. Francis M. Rotch, Camp Richmond, near Annapolis, December 21, 1861, box 37, folder 20, Adjutant General Correspondence, NYSA.

41. *Annual Report of the Adjutant-General . . . For the Year 1900*, 525–652; Descriptive Book, Companies D, F, and G, Record Group 94, Records of the Adjutant General's Office, NARA I.

42. McPherson, *For Cause and Comrades*, 18–20; Farid Ameur, *Les Français dans le Guerre de Sécession, 1861–1865* (Rennes: Presses Universitaires de Rennes, 2016), 53, 110, 137.

43. "The D'Epineuil Zouaves," *New York Daily Tribune*, November 15, 1861; the de Trobriand and de Monteil quotations come, respectively, from Régis de Trobriand to [daughter] Lina, Upton's Hill [VA], September 30, 1862 in Styple, *Our Noble Blood*, 74 and de Monteil to Morgan, New York, October 5, 1861, box 36, folder 22, Adjutant General Correspondence, NYSA.

44. Ameur, *Les Français dans le Guerre de Sécession*, 101.

45. "The D'Epineuil Zouaves—Fifty-Third Regiment N.Y.S.V.," *New York Daily Tribune*, November 15, 1861.

46. Ameur, *Les Français dans le Guerre de Sécession*, 21–22, 109; Susannah Ural Bruce, *The Harp and the Eagle: Irish-American Volunteers and the Union Army, 1861–1865* (New York: New York University Press, 2006), 3, 52; Paul Quigley, "The American Civil War and the Transatlantic Triumph of Volitional Citizenship" in Jörg Nagler, Don H. Doyle, and Marcus Gräser, eds., *The Transnational Significance of the American Civil War* ([London:] Palgrave Macmillan, 2016), 42–43; *Executive Documents Printed by Order of the House of Representatives during the Third Session of the Fortieth Congress, 1868–'69*, vol. 1 (Washington, DC: Government Printing Office, 1869), 293–94.

Chapter 4

1. Colonel L. J. d'Epineuil to James Lesley [New York, undated (August 1861)] and Lesley to d'Epineuil, Washington, DC, August 17, 1861, D120, M492, Letters Received by the Secretary of War, Irregular Series, 1861–1866, NARA I.

2. "The D'Epineuil Zouaves," *New York Daily Tribune*, November 15, 1861.

3. "D'Epineuil Zouaves!," *Buffalo Daily Courier*, September 16, 1861, 2, col. 4.

4. "A Volunteer Captain Blamed for Jobbing," *New York Daily Tribune*, September 26, 1861, 7, col. 6.

5. Testimony of Sergeant John C. Bates, Court Martial Case Files, 1809–1894, box 319, folder II889, Viguier de Monteil, Record Group 153, Records of the Office of the Judge Advocate General (Army), NARA I.

6. The desertion rate during the Civil War among Union soldiers was about 9.6 percent, and about 13 percent for the Confederacy. James M. McPherson, *Ordeal by Fire: The Civil War and Reconstruction* (New York: Alfred A. Knopf, 1982), 468.

7. *Annual Report of the Adjutant-General . . . For the Year 1900*, 525–652.

8. "Arrivals in the City," *New York Times*, October 8. 1861, 8, col. 5; "Local Military Movements," *New York Times*, October 9, 1861, 8, col. 3; "Local Military Matters," *New York Daily Tribune*, October 16, 1861, 8, col. 1.

9. Brooks Brothers bill, Record Group 21, Records of District Courts of the United States, NARA I.

10. Bliss to Hillhouse, New York, October 26, 1861, box 33, folder 17, Adjutant General Correspondence, NYSA.

11. "D'Epineuil Zouaves, Fifty-Third Regiment N.Y.V.," *New York Herald*, November 3, 1861, 7, col. 3.

12. Phillips to d'Epineuil, November 4, 1861, box 3, folder 1, Surgeon General Correspondence, NYSA. Phillips later would "certify that Dr. Dubreuil resigned from the d'Epineuil Zouaves 53d Regt. NYV because he had not means to procure the necessary uniforms &c," in Henry J. Phillips [unaddressed], Annapolis, November 20, 1861, Surgeon General Correspondence, NYSA.

13. Dubreuil to d'Epineuil, Camp Lesley, November 5, 1861, box 3, folder 1, Surgeon General Correspondence, NYSA.

14. D'Epineuil to Vanderpool, New York, November 6, 1861, box 3, folder 1, Surgeon General Correspondence, NYSA.

15. Dr. J. Dubreuil to Vanderpool, NY, November 24, 1861, box 3, folder 1, Surgeon General Correspondence, NYSA. The individual who recorded the date on the back of the letter inaccurately rendered it as October 24, 1861, not recognizing Dubreuil's shorthand "9ber" for November; d'Epineuil and Monteil also used this shorthand on occasion. The context of the letter—particularly the reference to the Fifty-Third Regiment's departure on the steamer *Admiral*—also makes clear that it was not written in October.

16. Monteil to McClellan, Washington, January 6, 1862 [Monteil wrote 1861], Regimental Papers, box 2992, NY, Fifty-Third–Fifty-Fourth Infantry, Record Group 94, Office of the Adjutant General, NARA I.

17. List of Charges prepared by Lionel J. d'Epineuil, Court Martial Case Files, Viguier de Monteil, NARA I.

18. List of Charges prepared by Lionel J. d'Epineuil; testimony of Franklin W. Willard, Charles Jenkins, George Boulanger, and ruling of the court of inquiry, Lt. Col. Thomas S. Bell, President, Court Martial Case Files, Viguier de Monteil.

19. De Monteil to Morgan, New York, October 5, 1861, box 36, folder 22, Adjutant General Correspondence, NYSA.

20. *Richmond County Gazette*, October 2, 1861, 2, col. 3.

21. McPherson, *For Cause and Comrades*, 46–48.

22. Testimony of Charles Jenkins and Thaddeus C. Ferris, Court Martial Case Files, Viguier de Monteil.

23. *General Regulations for the Military Forces of the State of New York* (Albany, NY: Weed, Parsons, 1858), 1.

24. Testimony of Charles Dustan, Henry Cocheu, and Ernest Fiston, Court Martial Case Files, Viguier de Monteil.

25. Testimony of John George Gundlack, Court Martial Case Files, Viguier de Monteil.

26. Monteil to McClellan, Washington, January 6, 1862, Regimental Papers, box 2992, NARA I; Frederick Cocheu, Charges and Specifications against Lionel J. d'Epineuil, Civil War (Union) Compiled Military Service Records, Fifty-Third NY Infantry (1st Org.), box 25436, jacket 287 (Lionel D'Epineuil), Record Group 94, Adjutant General's Office, NARA I.

27. The three Bliss quotations come, respectively, from Bliss to Hillhouse, New York, November 4, 1861, box 33, folder 17, Bliss to Hillhouse, New York, November 14, 1861, box 33, folder 18, and Bliss to Hillhouse, New York, November 15, 1861, box 33, folder 18, Adjutant General Correspondence, NYSA.

28. De Monteil to Morgan, New York, November 14, 1861, box 34, folder 24, Adjutant General Correspondence, NYSA.

29. Francis M. Rotch to Gov. Morgan, Morris [NY], November 14, 1861, box 34, folder 17, Adjutant General's Correspondence, NYSA.

30. "Military Movements in New York," *New York Herald*, November 18, 1861, 1, col. 6.

31. "Academy of Music," *New York Daily Tribune*, November 1, 1861, 2, col. 1; "Presentation of a Sword to Quartermaster John C. Merriam, of the Fifty-Third Regiment, New York Volunteers," *New York Herald*, October 24, 1861, 4, col. 6; "The D'Epineuil Zouaves," *New York Herald*, November 16, 1861, 8, col. 1; "Sword Presentation," *Richmond County Gazette*, October 30, 1861, 2, col. 3; "Presentation," November 13, 1861, *Richmond County Gazette*, 2, col. 5.

32. "Presentation of Colors to the D'Epineuil Zouaves, Fifty-Third Regiment, NYSV," *New York Herald*, November 13, 1861, 8, col. 3; "National and Regimental Standards," *Frank Leslie's Illustrated Newspaper*, February 15, 1862, 208; "The D'Epineuil Zouaves—Fifty-Third Regiment N.Y.S.V.," *New York Daily Tribune*, November 15, 1861.

33. Bliss to Hillhouse, New York, November 11, 1861, box 33, folder 18, New York Adjutant General's Correspondence, NYSA.

34. "Presentation of Colors to the D'Epineuil Zouaves," *New York Herald*, November 13, 1861.

35. Ambrose E. Burnside, "The Burnside Expedition," paper presented at the Soldiers' and Sailors' Historical Society of Rhode Island, July 7, 1880, http://thomaslegion.net/the_burnside_expedition_by_general_burnside.html.

36. "Local Military Matters," *New York Tribune*, November 18, 1861, 8, col. 2.

37. "Military and Naval Movements," *New York Sun*, November 18, 1861, 2, col. 6; "Local Military Matters," *New York Tribune*, November 18, 1861; Francis S. Pittman, "Civil War Journal, 1861–1863," transcribed by Marilynn Graves Wright, who owns Pittman's diary.

38. "Musical," *New York Herald*, January 5, 1862, 7, col. 3; "Artists' Reception at the Dodworth Studio," *New York Daily Tribune*, February 14, 1862, 4, col. 6; "The Christmas Toast: 'The Union Forever,'" *New York Illustrated News*, January 4, 1862, 138, col. 2, illustration 136.

39. "The New-York Fifty-Third Regiment at Annapolis," *New York Herald Tribune*, November 20, 1861, 8, col. 6; Report, December 3, 1861, roll 17, number 346, Medical Committee archives, Historical Bureau records, United States Sanitary Commission records, New York, NY archives, Manuscript and Archives Division, the New York Public Library, Astor, Lenox and Tilden Foundations (hereafter U.S. Sanitary Commission).

40. "The New-York Allotments," *New York Times*, January 4, 1862, 1, col. 1; "From Washington. The Allotment System," *New York Tribune*, February 26, 1862, 5, col. 4.

41. "D'Epineuil Zouaves," *New York Daily Tribune*, December 4, 1861, 1, col. 2; Bliss to Hillhouse, New York, November 19, 1861 and Bliss to Hillhouse, New York, November 24, 1861, box 33, folder 19, Adjutant General's Correspondence, NYSA; Henry S. Olcott, "The War's Carnival of Fraud," in *The Annals of the War* (Philadelphia: Times Publishing Company, 1879), 708.

42. Bliss to Hillhouse, New York, December 4, 1861, box 33, folder 19, Adjutant General's Correspondence, NYSA.

43. "D'Epineuil Zouaves," *New York Daily Tribune*, December 4, 1861.

44. Lionel J. d'Epineuil to General Ambrose Burnside, Annapolis, December 9, 1861, container 1, folder August–December 1861, Record Group 94, Adjutant General's Office, Civil War, Generals' Papers, Ambrose E. Burnside, NARA I.

45. Bliss to Adj. Gen., New York, December 18, 1861 (no box or folder number), Adjutant General's Correspondence, NYSA.

46. Pittman, "Civil War Journal"; testimony of J. B. Cantel, Court Martial Case Files, Viguier de Monteil, NARA I.

47. "Trouble in the D'Epineuils," *Utica Morning Herald*, January 9, 1862, 2, col. 5. The Protestant soldier probably was Charles Cram (aka Crum), a private in the Fifty-Third NY Infantry who died on December 26, from intoxication according to his compiled service record, although "disease" is the cause of death listed in *Annual Report of the Adjutant-General for the State of New York. For the Year 1900*. See Compiled Military Service Records, Fifty-Third NY Infantry (First Org.), box 25436, jacket 246 (Charles Crum).

48. Compiled Military Service Records, Fifty-Third NY Infantry (First Org.), box 25440, jacket 1033 (Aristide Sieran [Pierard]).

49. Testimony of J. B. Cantel, Court Martial Case Files, Viguier de Monteil, NARA I.

50. Charles W. Dustan to his mother [Phoebe Dustan], Annapolis, November 29, 1861, Charles William Dustan Letters, #3458-z, Southern Historical Collection, Wilson Library, University of North Carolina at Chapel Hill.

51. E. W. Chester to Gov. Morgan, New York, November 27, 1861, box 34, folder 17, Adjutant General Correspondence, NYSA.

52. Geo. F. Chester to Hon. Francis M. Rotch, Camp Richmond, near Annapolis, December 21, 1861, box 37, folder 20, Adjutant General Correspondence, NYSA.

53. Frederick Cocheu, Charges and Specifications against Lionel J. d'Epineuil, NARA I. Other officers, including (and perhaps only) Henry Cocheu and George Chester, wrote the charges, although Captain Frederick Cocheu was the sole individual who signed them. A transcription of Henry Cocheu's diary is in Ralph Whitehead, "The Demise of the D'Epineuil Zouaves," *Civil War Times Illustrated* 36, no. 5 (October 1997). Photocopied pages from the original Cocheu diary (miscataloged as the diary of Charles Dustan) are in box 7, the Harrisburg Civil War Round Table Collection, Army Heritage and Education Center, U.S. Army Military History Institute, Carlisle Barracks, PA.

54. Monteil to McClellan, Washington, January 6, 1862, Regimental Papers, box 2992, NARA I.

55. Testimony of Franklin Willard, Henry Cocheu, and Victor Vifquain, Court Martial Case Files, Viguier de Monteil, NARA I.

56. Monteil to McClellan, Washington, January 6, 1862, Regimental Papers, box 2992, NARA I.

57. Court Martial Case Files, Viguier de Monteil, NARA I.

58. Testimony of William S. Clark, Barry Fox, James H. Sperling, Ferdinand Leytag, and Charles J. Welch, Court Martial Case Files, Viguier de Monteil.

59. Testimony of James H. Sperling, Court Martial Case Files, Viguier de Monteil.

60. Charges and Specifications against Viguier de Monteil, prepared by Lionel J. d'Epineuil, Court Martial Case Files, Viguier de Monteil.

61. Testimony of Henry Scott and Henry John Phillips, Court Martial Case Files, Viguier de Monteil.

62. Charges and Specifications against Lionel J. d'Epineuil, NARA I.

63. Testimony of Victor Thus and Augustus Morse, Court Martial Case Files, Viguier de Monteil, NARA I.

64. Bell to Dr. [William Goodell] & Cass [Caroline Goodell], Camp Union near Annapolis, December 19, 1861, folder 8, L4264, Lt. Col. Thomas S. Bell papers, 1861–1862, Ms. Coll. 173, Chester County Historical Society Library, West Chester, PA.

65. Col. d'Epineuil to the Court of Inquiry, Camp Richmond, December 21, 1861, Court Martial Case Files, Viguier de Monteil, NARA I.

66. Pittman, "Civil War Journal"; George W. Pittman, "Experiences Among the D'Epinuel [sic] Zouaves," *Brooklyn Daily Times*, December 31, 1861, 2, col. 4. The preacher, an eighteen-year-old farmer from Utica named George Cook, may well have been the special correspondent to the *Utica Morning Herald* mentioned above.

67. Fifty-Third New York Infantry, Descriptive Book, Companies D, F, and G, Record Group 94, Records of the Adjutant General's Office, NARA I.

68. Sgt. [Charles] Price to [Adjutant] General [Hillhouse], Annapolis, [December] 30, 1861, box 37, folder 10, Adjutant General Correspondence, NYSA.

69. Lt. Augustus Hatch, Post Guard Report of the Fifty-Third Regt. of NY Vols. at Camp Richmond, December 31, 1861, in the Cole and Taylor Family Papers #163, Southern Historical Collection, Wilson Library, University of North Carolina at Chapel Hill.

70. Monteil to McClellan, Washington, January 6, 1862, Special Order 224 (copy), Headquarters Coast Division, January 2, 1862, and Special Order 3 (copy), Headquarters Third Brigade, Coast Division, January 2, 1862, Regimental Papers, box 2992, NARA I; Cocheu in Whitehead, "The Demise of the D'Epineuil Zouaves."

71. McPherson, *For Cause and Comrades*, 87.

Chapter 5

1. Burnside, "The Burnside Expedition"; Cocheu in Whitehead, "The Demise of the D'Epineuil Zouaves"; for the Cocheu family, see 1850 Census of the United States, Brooklyn, Kings Co., NY, roll 522, 468B, lines 36–42, and 1860 Census of the United States, Newport, Campbell Co., KY, roll 360, 51, line 28; Lionel J. d'Epineuil to John P. Hatch, Annapolis, February 11, 1862, in United States, War Department, *The War of the Rebellion: A Compilation of the Official Records of the Union and Confederate Forces* (Washington, 1883), Series I, vol. 9, 361–62; "The 'John Trucks' and the D'Epineuil Zouaves," *Philadelphia Inquirer*, February 24, 1862, 6, col. 2.

2. Cocheu in Whitehead, "The Demise of the D'Epineuil Zouaves"; Dubreuil to Vanderpool, New York, November 24, 1861, Dubreuil to Morgan, Annapolis,

January 5, 1862, and Dubreuil to Morgan, New York, February 5, 1862, box 3, folder 1, Office of the Surgeon General Correspondence, NYSA. Dubreuil sent the same letter on the same date, January 5, 1862, to Secretary of War Simon Cameron. See box 152, D'Epineuil Zouaves/53d NY Volunteers, VS file W379-VS-1862, Entry 496, Volunteer Service Division Files, 1861–1889, Letters Received, RG 94, NARA I.

3. Pittman, "Civil War Journal."

4. Cocheu in Whitehead, "The Demise of the D'Epineuil Zouaves"; Pittman, "Civil War Journal."

5. Monteil to McClellan, Washington, January 6, 1862 and order of Gen. McClellan, Headquarters of the Army, Adjutant General's Office, Washington, January 9, 1862, Regimental Papers, box 2992, NARA I; Cocheu in Whitehead, "The Demise of the D'Epineuil Zouaves"; S. M. Gladwin to Major Sibley, New York City, August 26, 1862, box 496, D'Epineuil folder, Record Group 92, Records of the Office of the Quartermaster General, Consolidated Correspondence, File 1794-1915, NARA I.

6. Cocheu in Whitehead, "The Demise of the D'Epineuil Zouaves"; Pittman, "Civil War Journal"; Burnside, "The Burnside Expedition"; d'Epineuil to Hatch, Annapolis, February 11, 1862, *The War of the Rebellion*, 361–62; "Our Army Correspondence," *Cleveland Plain Dealer*, February 24, 1862.

7. "The Burnside Expedition," *New York Herald*, February 2, 1862, 1, col. 5; "Aged War Veteran Visits at St. Remy," *Kingston (New York) Daily Freeman*, July 27, 1936, 1, col. 1; Cocheu in Whitehead, "The Demise of the D'Epineuil Zouaves."

8. Volume of Special Orders, 218, box 85, John E. Wool Papers, New York State Library.

9. Cocheu in Whitehead, "The Demise of the D'Epineuil Zouaves"; Styple, *Our Noble Blood*, xxii–xxvi, 28.

10. Cocheu in Whitehead, "The Demise of the D'Epineuil Zouaves"; Charges and Specifications against Lionel J. d'Epineuil, NARA I.

11. Pittman, "Civil War Journal"; Cocheu in Whitehead, "The Demise of the D'Epineuil Zouaves."

12. Lloyd v. Lloyd and Jobert, Divorce Case File L53.

13. Frederick Cocheu, Charges and Specifications against Lionel J. d'Epineuil, NARA I.

14. Bell to Dr. & Cass, Camp Union near Annapolis, December 19, 1861, folder 8, L4264, Lt. Col. Thomas S. Bell papers.

15. "Military Movements in New York," *New York Herald*, September 1, 1861, 1, col. 5.

16. Cocheu in Whitehead, "The Demise of the D'Epineuil Zouaves."

17. "The D'Epineuil Zouaves. Address of the Colonel and Response of his Men," *The National Republican*, March 22, 1862, 2, col. 4.

18. D'Epineuil to Hatch, February 11, 1862, in *The War of the Rebellion*; the nearly identical letter to Thomas is in D'Epineuil Zouaves, Volunteer Service Division Files.

158 / Notes to Chapter 5

19. A. Lincoln to Gen. McClellan [Washington], February 14, 1862, Abraham Lincoln Collection, mssHM 25150, Huntington Library. This letter also is transcribed in Roy P. Basler, ed., *The Collected Works of Abraham Lincoln*, vol. 5 (New Brunswick, NJ: Rutgers University Press, 1953), 132.

20. James C. Slaght, Capt. Asst. Q. M., to General Burnside, Annapolis, February 13, 1862, container 1, folder Letters Received February 1862, Record Group 94, Adjutant General's Office, Civil War, Generals' Papers, Ambrose E. Burnside, NARA I.

21. Record Group 153, Court Martial Case Files, 1809–1894, box 331, folder KK39, John Gillard, Jean B. Billet, Achille Desvouton, NARA I.

22. Pittman, "Civil War Journal."

23. N. H. Davis to Gen. S. Williams, Washington, DC, February 19, 1862, D'Epineuil Zouaves, Volunteer Service Division Files.

24. Cocheu in Whitehead, "The Demise of the D'Epineuil Zouaves."

25. Charles W. Dustan to his mother, Fort Madison, MD, February 19, 1862, Charles William Dustan Letters, University of North Carolina at Chapel Hill.

26. Special Order 42, February 26, 1862, Regimental Papers, box 2992, NARA I.

27. Pittman, "Civil War Journal"; d'Epineuil to General Hatch, Fort Madison, February 28, 1862, Compiled Military Service Records, Fifty-Third NY Infantry (1st Org.), box 25437, jacket 405 (Ernest Fiston); James C. Slaght, Capt. Asst. Q. M., to General Burnside, Annapolis, February 28, 1862, folder Letters Received February 1862, Civil War, Generals' Papers, Ambrose E. Burnside.

28. Pittman, "Civil War Journal"; Charles W. Dustan to his mother, Camp [Hatch, Fort Madison, MD], March 3, 1862, Charles William Dustan Letters; Henry Phillips to Vanderpool, Annapolis, March 3, 1862, box 3, folder 1, Office of the Surgeon General Correspondence, NYSA.

29. Report, December 3, 1861, U.S. Sanitary Commission; Report, March 8, 1862, roll 22, no. 904, U.S. Sanitary Commission.

30. Pittman, "Civil War Journal"; Court Martial Case Files, 1809–1894, John Gillard.

31. *Annual Report of the Adjutant-General . . . For the Year 1900*, 525–652; the quotation comes from "The D'Epineuil Zouaves," *National Republican* (Washington, DC), March 17, 1862, 3, col. 3.

32. "The D'Epineuil Zouaves. Address of the Colonel and Response of his Men," *National Republican*, March 22, 1862.

33. "The D'Epineuil Zouaves. Address of the Colonel and Response of his Men," *National Republican*, March 22, 1862; "The d'Epineuil Zouaves," *Evening Star* (Washington, DC), March 14, 1862, 3, col. 1.

34. Special Order 66, March 8, 1862, Regimental Papers, box 2992, NARA I; "Our Washington Letter," *Troy (New York) Daily Times*, January 29, 1864, 2,

col. 3; Special Order 72, March 13, 1862, and George F. Chester to Silas Casey, Washington, March 13, 1862, D'Epineuil Zouaves, Volunteer Service Division Files; *Annual Report of the Adjutant-General . . . For the Year 1900*, 525–652.

35. James Moor, MD, *History of the Cooper Shop Volunteer Refreshment Saloon* (Philadelphia: James B. Rodgers, 1866), 149; Laurence M. Hauptman, *Seven Generations of Iroquois Leadership: The Six Nations since 1800* (Syracuse, NY: Syracuse University Press, 2008), 102, 107–8, 243, 245. Hauptman identifies by name five Tuscarora men, including Cornelius Cusick, from (the second organization of) the 53d NY who joined the 132d NY. Hauptman, in an earlier work, *The Iroquois in the Civil War: From Battlefield to Reservation* (Syracuse, NY: Syracuse University Press, 1993), 19, repeated the error of describing the Tuscarora soldiers as d'Epineuil Zouaves recruits—a mistake initiated by Frederick Phisterer, *New York in the War of the Rebellion*, vol. 3, 3d ed. (Albany, NY: J. B. Lyon Company, 1912), 2436.

36. "Arrival of the Remains of Lieut.-Colonel De Monteuil [sic]," *New York Tribune*, March 14, 1862, 3, col. 4; "Funeral of Lieut.-Col De Monteil," *New York Times*, March 16, 1862, 5, col. 4; Drew Gilpin Faust, *This Republic of Suffering: Death and the American Civil War* (New York: Alfred A. Knopf, 2008), 76–77.

37. Thomas Bell to Dr. & Cass, Camp Jordan, Roanoke Island, February 20, 1862, folder 10, L4286, Lt. Col. Thomas S. Bell papers.

38. "Burnside's Expedition," *National Tribune* (Washington, DC), April 12, 1883, 1, col. 3.

39. E. W. Chester to Thomas Hillhouse, New York, February 14, 1862 and Ern[est] Fiston, et al. to Gov. Morgan, [Fort Madison, undated], box 37, folder 20, New York Adjutant General's Correspondence; NYSA; Cocheu in Whitehead, "Demise of the d'Epineuil Zouaves."

40. Cocheu in Whitehead, "The Demise of the D'Epineuil Zouaves"; "The Burnside Expedition," *New York World*, Semi-Weekly Edition, February 21, 1862, 8, col. 1; "Obsequies of Departed Heroes," *New York Daily Tribune*, March 17, 1862, 8, col. 1; State of New York, *Fifth Annual Report of the Chief of the Bureau of Military Statistics*, Albany, 1868, 48.

41. D'Epineuil to General Hatch, Camp Hatch Fort Madison [undated], Compiled Military Service Records, Fifty-Third NY Infantry (1st Org.), box 25436, jacket 287 (Lionel D'Epineuil).

42. Marie J. Viguier de Monteil to General Burnside, New York City, March 3, 1862, folder Communications Received March 1862, Civil War, Generals' Papers, Ambrose E. Burnside.

43. "Obsequies of Departed Heroes," *New York Daily Tribune*, March 17, 1862. Today only the word "Roanoke" can be discerned on the column standing next to a relatively recent marker that identifies Monteil's grave in Green-Wood Cemetery.

44. Gerald E. Wheeler and A. Stuart Pitt, "The 53rd New York: A Zoo-Zoo Tale," *New York History* 37, no. 4 (October 1956): 431.

Chapter 6

1. Lionel d'Epineuil to Hillhouse, Washington, March 28, 1862, box 35, folder 2, Adjutant General's Correspondence, NYSA.

2. Clayton R. Newall and Charles R. Shrader, *Of Duty Well and Faithfully Done: A History of the Regular Army in the Civil War* (Lincoln: University of Nebraska Press, 2011), 55.

3. Ward to Stanton, Washington, April 12, 1862, D'Epineuil Zouaves, Volunteer Service Division Files.

4. Vifquain, *The 1862 Plot to Kidnap Jefferson Davis*, xviii–xx, 7, 167. The editors of Vifquain's memoir refer to Dufloo as Armond Duclos, although official and other sources during and after the Civil War, including Colonel d'Epineuil, called him Dufloo and Dufloo himself signed his name that way. See, for example, Compiled Military Service Records, Fifty-Third NY Infantry (1st Org.), box 25436, jacket 332 (Arman C. Dufloo), and Dufloo's signed oath of allegiance dated January 14, 1862, D'Epineuil Zouaves, Volunteer Service Division Files; "Company A, D'Epineuil Zouaves," *New York Tribune*, April 30, 1862, 8, col. 5; "The Three French Officers," *New York Herald*, May 30, 1862, 8, col. 2; "Letter from Colonel D'Epineuil," *New York Herald*, June 23, 1862, 5, col. 3.

5. "Letter from Colonel D'Epineuil," *New York Herald*, June 23, 1862.

6. Ward to Stanton, Washington, April 12, 1862 and C. P. B., Brigadier General and Assistant Adjutant General, to Elijah Ward, Washington, June 26, 1862, D'Epineuil Zouaves, Volunteer Service Division Files.

7. Brig. Genl. James Cooper to A. Lincoln, Baltimore, March 12, 1862, Record Group 59, Records of the Department of State, Letters of Application & Recommendation during the Administrations of Abraham Lincoln and Andrew Johnson, 1861–1869, M650, cabinet 28, box 9, National Archives, College Park, MD (hereafter NARA II); Charles W. Dustan to his mother, Washington, March 17, 1862, Charles W. Dustan Papers.

8. D'Epineuil to Lincoln, undated [Washington, August 1862], D'Epineuil Zouaves, Volunteer Service Division Files. The letter contains d'Epineuil's transcription of Burnside's letter, with underscoring for emphasis no doubt added by d'Epineuil.

9. Lionel J. d'Epineuil to J. J. Crittenden, National Hotel, Washington, DC, undated [probably August 1862], John Jordan Crittenden Papers, vols. 27–28, reel 14, Manuscript Division, Library of Congress. D'Epineuil transcribed the Burnside and Lincoln letters within his letter to Crittenden. Lincoln's letter also appears transcribed in Roy P. Basler, ed., *The Collected Works of Abraham Lincoln, Supplement 1832–1865* (Springfield, IL: Greenwood Press, 1974), 146.

10. Lionel J. d'Epineuil to J. J. Crittenden, National Hotel, Washington, DC, undated, John Jordan Crittenden Papers.

11. Unsigned statement, August 22, 1862, Washington, DC, D'Epineuil Zouaves, Volunteer Service Division Files.

12. S. M. Gladwin to Major Sibley, New York City, August 26, 1862, box 496, D'Epineuil folder, Records of the Office of the Quartermaster General.

13. Case Papers, Trial #662, Records of District Courts of the United States.

14. Lloyd v. Lloyd and Jobert, Divorce Case File L53; "Passengers Sailed," *New York Daily Tribune*, October 13, 1862, 3, col. 4.

15. Return of Sergeant John R. Cronin, seventh precinct, November 11, 1862, Daily Returns of Precincts, vol. November & December 1862, Record Group 351, Records of the Government of the District of Columbia, Records of the Metropolitan Police, NARA I; "Colonel of the Chasseurs D'Afrique Charged with Swindling," *New York Evening Express*, November 15, 1862, back page, col. 2. The newspaper article referred to the plaintiff as John D'Castor instead of Decatur.

16. D'Epineuil to Stanton, Washington, March 13, 1863, and P. H. Watson, Assistant Secretary of War, to d'Epineuil, Washington, March 14, 1863, D'Epineuil Zouaves, Volunteer Service Division Files.

17. R. Stanley Thomson, "The Diplomacy of Imperialism: France and Spain in Cochin China, 1858–63," *Journal of Modern History* 12, no. 3 (September 1940): 345, https://www.jstor.org/stable/1874762; Benjamin Franklin Gilbert, "French Warships on the Mexican West Coast, 1861–1866," *Pacific Historical Review* 24, no. 1 (February 1955): 26, 28, https://www.jstor.org/stable/3635229.

18. Dossier of Lionel Jobert, MV CC7 Alpha no. 1243, Service historique de la défense, Vincennes, France. The correspondence related to Jobert's request for the auxiliary ensign position is all that is contained in his Service historique de la défense file, reflecting his lack of Crimean War service.

19. Matricules de Gens de Mer, quartier de Rouen, Capitaines au long cours, Jobert, ADSM.

20. Dossier of Lionel Jobert, Service historique de la défense.

21. Pension record of James M. Letts, app. 263104, cert. 163293, Record Group 94, Pension Records, NARA I; United States Patent Office, Letters Patent no. 38,568 of May 19, 1863, Improvement in Iron Street-Crossings. The patent is referenced in a relatively recent patent for a road spillway. See patent no. 5,839,852 of November 24, 1998 at http://patft.uspto.gov; "Office Wanted," *Evening Star* (Washington, DC), February 18, 1863, 3, col. 4; "The New Street Crossings," *Daily National Intelligencer* (Washington, DC), July 20, 1863, 3, col. 4; "To the Editors," *Daily National Intelligencer*, July 22, 1863, 3, col. 3; Benjamin Brown French, *Witness to the Young Republic: A Yankee's Journal, 1828–1870*, Donald B. Cole and John J. McDonough, eds. (Hanover, NH: University Press of New England, 1989), 3, 7–11, 374.

22. Lloyd v. Lloyd and Jobert, Divorce Case File L53; Case Papers, Trial #662, Records of District Courts of the United States. Brooks Brothers asked for pecuniary damages above and beyond the cost of d'Epineuil's bill with the store, but the case record provides no formal document, only a small strip of paper, referencing damages. Still, without even considering the interest or damages, the $551.65 d'Epineuil owed

Brooks Brothers in 1863 amounts to a real price value of $11,600 in 2019 dollars, as calculated using https://www.measuringworth.com/calculators/uscompare/.

23. U.S. House of Representatives, *Executive Documents*, 38th Congress, 1st Session (1863–64), vol. 13 (Washington, DC: Government Printing Office, 1864), Doc. No. 62, 15; "Local Matters," *Daily National Intelligencer*, September 11, 1863, 3, col. 4 and December 16, 1863, 3, col. 4.

24. Lloyd v. Lloyd and Jobert, Divorce Case File L53.

25. U.S. House of Representatives, *Executive Documents*, 38th Congress, 2d Session (1864–65), vol. 13 (Washington, DC: Government Printing Office, 1865), Doc. No. 63, 23–24.

26. Lionel J. d'Epineuil to Major General George McClellan, [probably Washington, DC], March 5, 1864, accompanying George B. McClellan to [William C.] Prime, ca. March 8, 1864, container 14, reel 49, George B. McClellan Sr. Papers, Library of Congress. A transcription of McClellan's letter appears in Stephen W. Sears, ed., *The Civil War Papers of George B. McClellan: Selected Correspondence 1860–1865* (Cambridge, MA: De Capo Press, 1992), 567.

27. Lionel J. d'Epineuil to W. H. Seward, Washington, July 27, 1864, and d'Epineuil [to State Dept.], August 13, 1864, Record Group 59, Records of the Department of State, Letters of Application & Recommendation during the Administrations of Abraham Lincoln and Andrew Johnson, cabinet 28, box 14, NARA II; d'Epineuil to McClellan, Washington, DC, August 26, 1864, Manton Marble Papers, General Correspondence, box 8, Manuscript Division, Library of Congress.

28. Campbell Gibson, *Population of the 100 Largest Cities and Other Urban Places in the United States: 1790 to 1990* (Washington, DC: U.S. Bureau of the Census, 1998), tables 9 and 10, 35–36.

29. *Philadelphia Inquirer*, January 25, 1865, 5, col. 4 and February 6, 1865, 5, col. 5; Lionel J. d'Epineuil to Adjutant General of West Virginia [Francis P. Peirpoint], Philadelphia, May 12, 1865, West Virginia Adjutant General's Papers, Union Regiments, 1861–1865, Miscellaneous Correspondence, 1861–1865, Ar382, box 31, West Virginia State Archives.

30. Mark R. Grandstaff, "De Trobriand, Regis" in David S. Heidler and Jeanne T. Heidler, eds., *Encyclopedia of the American Civil War: A Political Social and Military History* (New York: W. W. Norton Company, 2002), 578; Pension Record, Jean B. Cantel, app. 670449, cert. 472421, NARA I; memo of C. A. Dana, Assistant Secretary of War, Washington, February 9, 1865, Cantel folder and J. B. Cantel to Rufus Ingalls, Quartermaster General, Washington, DC, February 14, 1876, Cantel 1876 folder, box 270, Records of the Office of the Quartermaster General; Cantel naturalization in box 14, Oct. Term 1862–Term 1868, folder Terms for 1864 #3 of 3, and Law Minutes, Supreme Court, DC, vol. 1, 501–2, Record Group 21, Records of District Courts of the United States, US Supreme Court for DC Naturalization Recs., Declarations of Intention, with Supporting Papers,

1802–1903, NARA I; J. B. Cantel to Abraham Lincoln, Washington, November 17, 1864 and Thomas H. Hicks to William H. Seward, Washington, DC, December 9, 1864, Record Group 59, Records of the Department of State, Letters of Application & Recommendation during the Administrations of Abraham Lincoln and Andrew Johnson, cabinet 28, box 9, NARA II. Among the books authored by Cantel while at the Patapsco Institute is J. B. Cantel, *Pronunciation of French Made Easy: A New Method of Learning to Pronounce French Correctly* (Baltimore, MD: John W. Woods, 1860).

31. Pension Record, James M. Letts, app. 263104, cert. 163293; Thomas Corwin to Wm. H. Seward, Washington, DC, December 9, 1864 and F. W. Kellogg to Wm. H. Seward, Washington, DC, December 13, 1864, Record Group 59, Records of the Department of State, Letters of Application & Recommendation during the Administrations of Abraham Lincoln and Andrew Johnson, cabinet 28, box 29, NARA II; James Letts to F. W. Seward, Washington, DC, January 4, 1865, Record Group 59, Records of Foreign Service Posts of the Department of State, Despatches from U.S. consuls in St. Marc, Haiti, 1861–1891, T486, cabinet 41, box 1, NARA II; service data for Chester, Cocheu, and Ferris may be accessed through the Division of Military and Naval Affairs page of the New York State website at http://dmna.ny.gov/historic/reghist/civil/civil_index.htm; Ferris's interment may be found using http://www.green-wood.com/burial_search/; Massachusetts, Town and Vital Records, 1620–1988, ancestry.com.

32. *Philadelphia Inquirer*, June 28, 1865, 5, col. 1.

33. *McElroy's Philadelphia City Directory for 1867*, 1096; two of the many advertisements are "Heller's Shutter Bolt," *Illustrated New Age* (Philadelphia), August 22, 1865, 3, col. 7, and "To Inventors and Patentees," *Evening Star* (Washington, DC), October 7, 1865, 2, col. 2; "Valuable American Patent" and "For Sale. Barque 'John Trucks,'" *Philadelphia Inquirer*, March 1, 1866, 7, col. 2; d'Epineuil and Evans to the Commissioner of Patents of the British Provinces of Canada, Philadelphia, June 20, 1866, RG 17, vol. 11, file nos. 791–810, Library and Archives Canada (Ottawa).

34. United States Patent Office, Letters Patent no. 62,686 of March 5, 1867, Improved Broom and Brush Head; "Projectiles Used During the Crimean War," *Scientific American*, Apr. 14, 1866, 244, col. 3; *Public Ledger* (Philadelphia), May 3, 1867, 2, col. 2; *McElroy's Philadelphia City Directory for 1867*, 748; *Scientific Journal* (Philadelphia), May 15, 1867, 32, col. 2 and 24, col. 1; James Mussell, *The Nineteenth-Century Press in the Digital Age* (London: UK: Palgrave Macmillan, 2012), 88, 90; "Wants," *Philadelphia Inquirer*, May 19, 1868, 6, col. 1.

35. Births in the Parish of Eastwood, County of Renfrew, Scotland, 1868, 94, record no. 281, keyword *Epineuil*, accessed at www.scotlandspeople.gov.uk.

36. 1871 Scotland Census, Burgh of Pollokshaws, 33; for business locations in Philadelphia, see the business directory section in *McElroy's Philadelphia City Directory for 1867*, 1007; recruiting card for Col. D'Epineuil's Zouave-Regiment,

Library Company of Philadelphia; *Gopsill's Philadelphia City and Business Directory for 1868–9* (Philadelphia: James Gopsill, 1868), 465; *Scientific Journal*, May 29, 1867, 56, col. 3; "The Scientific Journal's Patent Offices," *Philadelphia Inquirer*, April 4, 1868, 6, col. 2; see appendix for a list of patents handled by d'Epineuil's firm.

37. For examples of translations of French and German articles in *Scientific Journal*, see "On the Technical Analysis of Soap," March 5, 1870, 148, col. 3 and "Spontaneous Combustion of Tracing Paper," March 19, 1870, 183, col. 2; *Public Ledger*, August 24, 1870, 2, col. 3; Thirteenth Census of the United States: 1870, Darby, Delaware County, PA, roll 1336, 236B, lines 25–29.

38. "The Fire at Our Office," *Scientific Journal*, January 8, 1870, 24, col. 1. The editors meant to publish the article in the January 1, 1870 issue, thus explaining the opening statement "on Sunday last."

39. *Daily Evening Bulletin* (Philadelphia), December 27, 1869, 4, col. 3 and 6, col. 3.

40. *American Newspaper Directory*, New York: Geo. P. Rowell, 1870, 455; "New Publications," *Scientific Journal*, June 18, 1870, 393, col. 3.

41. Scott Sandage, *Born Losers: A History of Failure in America* (Cambridge, MA: Harvard University Press, 2005), 78–79.

42. "To Our Subscribers and the Public," *Scientific Journal*, January 1, 1870, 8, col. 1.

43. "Amateur Performance," *Daily Evening Telegraph* (Philadelphia), May 17, 1869, 5; "Spectacle du jeudi 20 octobre 1853," *L'Intérêt Public*, October 19, 1853, 3, col. 3; Victor Massé, *The Marriage of Jeanette. A Comic Opera in One Act*, Chas. E. Locke [trans.]. New York: Charles D. Koppol, 1886, 19–50.

44. Lionel J. d'Epineuil to Mr. Tirel, Secretary of the French Benevolent Society of Philadelphia, Philadelphia, January 4, 1868, Historical Society of Pennsylvania, MSS 141, Sub Series A-Series "K," Box 12; "Philadelphia Fountain Society," *Philadelphia Inquirer*, March 18, 1870, 5, col. 1; "The Relapsing Fever and the Fountain Society," *Scientific Journal*, July 16, 1870, 41, col. 3.

45. "A New Amateur Drawing Room Wanted," *Scientific Journal*, March 12, 1870, 168, col. 1.

46. "The New Amateur Drawing Room," *Scientific Journal*, March 26, 1870, 201, col. 1.

47. John W. Forney v. Lionel J. d'Epineuil, Appearance Docket, District Court, June 1867 term, Archibald McElroy v. Lionel J. d'Epineuil, Appearance Docket, District Court, September 1868 term, and Archibald McElroy v. Lionel J. d'Epineuil, Appearance Docket, District Court, June 1869 term, Philadelphia, City Archives of Philadelphia. Damages assessed in the 1867 case amounted to $578.22, and in 1868 $228.82, with the 2019 equivalent real price value calculated using https://www.measuringworth.com/calculators/uscompare/.

48. "A Famous Belle," *The Times* (Philadelphia), January 10, 1886, 3, col. 3. Emilie Schaumburg went unnamed as d'Epineuil's defender in a much earlier article; see "The Story of an Adventurer," *Paterson Daily Guardian*, November 22, 1872, 2, col. 3.

49. Note recording J. W. Schaumburg [to Adjutant General], Philadelphia, October 10, 1868, d'Epineuil to Adjutant General, Philadelphia, October 24, 1868, and d'Epineuil to Adjutant General, Philadelphia, May 22, 1869, D'Epineuil Zouaves, Volunteer Service Division Files; Frederick A. Virkus, ed., *The Abridged Compendium of American Genealogy* (Chicago, IL: A. N. Marquis, 1925), 393.

50. "Gottschalk," *New York Times*, May 18, 1870, 5, col. 5; "The Memory of Gottschalk," *New York Times*, May 22, 1870, 4, col. 7; "Miss Carlotta Patti," *New York Times*, May 23, 1870, 4, col. 7; "Amusements," *New York Times*, October 28, 1861, 7, col. 5; T. Allston Brown, *A History of the New York Stage: From the First Performance in 1732 to 1901*, vol. II (New York: Dodd, Mead, 1903), 44.

51. "Amateur Opera at the Union League Theatre, New York, for the Benefit of the Gottschalk Memorial Fund," *Daily Evening Bulletin* (Philadelphia), June 6, 1870, 6, col. 1.

52. "The Memory of Gottschalk," *New York Times*, May 22, 1870.

53. Lionel J. d'Epineuil to Oliver Ames, Philadelphia, June 1, 1869, box 1, 1869, incoming correspondence, Union Pacific Railroad Company, Manuscript Collections, Nebraska State Historical Society.

54. "French Examination at the Patapsco Institute, MD," *Scientific Journal*, July 2, 1870, 7, col. 3.

55. "The War in Europe," *Philadelphia Inquirer*, July 23, 1870, 4, col. 6; "Financial," *Scientific Journal*, July 23, 1870 (article dated July 13, 1870), 59, col. 2, August 13, 1870, 107, col. 1, and August 20, 1870, 121, col. 3.

56. D'Epineuil to Secretary of War, Philadelphia, September 18, 1870, and Assistant Adjutant General to d'Epineuil, [Washington], September 27, 1870, D'Epineuil Zouaves, Volunteer Service Division Files.

57. S. W. Burley v. Lionel J. d'Espineuel [*sic*], Appearance Docket, June 1870 term, Common Pleas, Louis Schuman v. Louise [*sic*] J. d'Epineuil, Appearance Docket, District Court, September term 1870, and James S. McCalla and J. T. Stavely v. d'Epineuil & Dimpfel, Appearance Docket, District Court, March term 1871, City Archives of Philadelphia; "Messrs. McCalla & Stavely and the Scientific Journal," *Scientific Journal*, April 23, 1870, 264, col. 1.

Chapter 7

1. Sir H. H. Wraxall, bart., "The Naked Truth," in *Wit and Wear* (London: A. Lynes and Son, 1871), 9–20.

2. Census of England, 1871, civil parish of Battersea, County of Surrey, Wandsworth, 97(b); Henry Horace [sic] Wraxall, entry 30,011, Merchant Navy Seamen Records, BT 114/22, National Archives, Kew, United Kingdom; "A Young Pawnbroker Baronet," *New York World*, April 25, 1882, 7, col. 2.

3. *Annuaire Diplomatique et Consulaire de la République Française Pour 1881*, tome II (Paris: Berger-Levrault et Cie., Èditeurs, 1881), 143–44; England and Wales, National Probate Calendar, Administrations, 1870, 306, accessed at ancestry.com.

4. "Personal Intelligence," *New York Herald*, October 5, 1870, 6, col. 6; *New York Herald*, October 18, 1870, 10, col. 6; *Anglo American Times* (London), October 22, 1870, 20, col. 3.

5. England and Wales, National Probate Calendar, Administrations, 1870, 305–6; "New Projects," *Railway News and Joint Stock Journal* (London), December 31, 1870, 789.

6. Census of England, 1871, civil parish of Paddington, ward 4, 66; *Daily News* (London), March 14, 1871, 5, col. 3; "A New American Songstress," *Penny Illustrated Paper* (London), April 15, 1871, 234; George Clement Boase and William Prideaux Courtney, *Bibliotheca Cornubiensis: A Catalogue of the Writings, Both Manuscript and Printed, of Cornishmen, and of Works Relating to the County of Cornwall*, vol. II (London: Longmans, Green, Reader, and Dyer, 1878), 487.

7. "A New American Songstress," *Penny Illustrated Paper*, April 15, 1871.

8. "The Levée," *London Times*, May 15, 1871, 8, col. 1; "The Chevalier De Kontski's Matinee," *The Standard* (London), July 3, 1871, 3, col. 5; *London City Press*, October 28, 1871, 5, col. 4; *Morning Post* (London), November 6, 1871, 5, col. 3.

9. David Hancock, *Citizens of the World: London Merchants and the Integration of the British Atlantic Community, 1735–1785* (New York: Cambridge University Press, 1997), 280–81, 284.

10. "Death of Colonel H. C. C. Somerset," *The Capricornian* (Rockhampton, Queensland, Australia), April 1, 1905, 34, col. 3; "Death of Countess D'Epineuil," *Essex Chronicle*, February 5, 1926, 2, col. 5; *The United Service Journal and Naval and Military Magazine*, part I (London: Henry Colburn, 1841), 430; Census of England, 1881, civil parish of Ashford, 23.

11. David Verey, ed. *The Diary of a Victorian Squire: Extracts from the Diaries and Letters of Dearman & Emily Birchall* (Gloucester, England: Alan Sutton, 1983), ix, 29, 31–32, 35.

12. Marriage Register for St. Clement Danes, Vol. 48, 1869–1875, record no. 205, 103, City of Westminster Archives. Some newspaper announcements of the marriage incorrectly rendered some relevant names and misidentified the marriage date as January 3 as seen in "Marriages," *Morning Post*, January 11, 1872, 8, col. 6; *London Gazette*, February 27, 1872, 803, col. 1. For Georgiana Somerset's relationship to Adeline Bryant, see *Debrett's Illustrated Peerage*, http://nzetc.victoria.ac.nz/etexts/Stout84/Stout84P007004.gif and the Bryant family tree at http://www.mytrees.com/ancestry/Other/Born-1786/Br/Bryant-family/Jeremiah-Bryant-me001831-9267.html;

also baptism certificate of Adeline Montagu Bryant, transcription from baptismal register, Chanter family collection. On Tromp, see "Obituary," *The Electrician* (London), October 6, 1899, 847, col. 1.

13. Post Office London Directory, 1872 (London: Kelley); Marriage Register for St. Clement Danes, vol. 48, record no. 205; "Chevalier De Kontski's Opera Comique," *The Standard* (London), March 12, 1872, 6, col. 2; *London Gazette*, February 27, 1872, 803 and May 14, 1872, 2356; "Miss Elizabeth Philp's Concert," *The Era* (London), May 19, 1872, 14, col. 3; *The Morning Post* (London), June 12, 1872, 1, col. 4.

14. *Funérailles de Napoléon III: Procés-Verbal Rédigé par le Duc de Cambacérès, Grand Maitre de Cérémonies* (Paris: Librairie Générale, 1873), 33–34, 50; "The European Imbroglio," *Scientific Journal*, August 6, 1870, 88, col. 1; *The Athenæum: Journal of Literature, Science, the Fine Arts, Music, and the Drama*, April 5, 1873, 448, col. 3.

15. Letter from the Treasurer of the United States. Receipts and Expenditures for the Fiscal Year Ending June 30, 1873, in *Executive Documents Printed by Order of the House of Representatives, 1874–'75* (Washington, DC: Government Printing Office, 1875), 87; *Chronological and Descriptive Index of Patents Applied for and Patents Granted* (London: Office of the Commissioner of Patents, 1873), 178.

16. Peter Mansfield, *A History of the Middle East* (New York: Viking, 1991), 88; the quotation is from "Trial Trip of the Charkieh," *The Engineer* (London), September 26, 1873, 198, col. 1.

17. "The Mails," *Hampshire Telegraph and Sussex Chronicle*, November 29, 1873, 6, col. 3; *London Gazette*, January 27, 1874, 385, col. 1.

18. *Hampshire Advertiser* (Southampton), December 6, 1873; "List of Passengers," *Pall Mall Budget*, January 9, 1874, 37, col. 2.

19. Ian Pearce, "In Town Tonight: Some of the Interesting People in Cairo and Alexandria in the 1870s—Part One," *Astene Bulletin* (United Kingdom), 60 (Summer 2014): 13–14.

20. Parish of Ashford Electoral Registers, 1879, accessed through "England, London Electoral Registers, 1847–1913" on familysearch.org; Inscription maritime, quartier de Paris, Matricule des Capitaines de la Marine Marchande, no. 15, 7P4/206, ADSM.

21. Romances from Real Life," *New York Times*, November 10, 1879, 2, col. 1.

22. Jean-Yves Tréhin, "Arnoux Hippolyte," in François Pouillon, ed., *Dictionnaire des orientalistes de langue française* (Paris: Éditions Karthala, 2012), 29.

23. *The British Mail* (hereafter cited as BM), 1, no. 1 (January 30, 1875), 24, col. 4; BM, 1, no. 2 (February 27, 1875), 56, col. 4; BM, 1, no. 3 (March 31, 1875), 63, col. 1.

24. BM, 7, no. 46 (October 1, 1878), 849, col. 1; "Lack v. d'Expineuil" [sic], *The Morning Post*, June 2, 1881, 7, col. 4 (the article incorrectly calls the firm "Whatley and Co." instead of Whiteley); "Slandering a Builder—Lack v. d'Epineuil," *The Building News and Engineering Journal* (London), June 3, 1881, 660, col. 2.

25. BM, 10, no. 72 (December 1, 1880), 919.

26. *Annuaire Diplomatique et Consulaire de la République Française Pour 1881*, 143–44; "Attempt to Assassinate the French Consul," *San Francisco Bulletin*, June 4, 1872, 3, col. 3; James Grant Wilson, ed., *The Memorial History of the City of New York: From Its First Settlement to the Year 1892*, vol. IV (New York: New-York History Company, 1893), 213; "Banquet to M. Breuil," *New York Herald*, April 27, 1881, 7, col. 6.

27. Parish of Ashford Electoral Registers, 1879, 1880, 1881, accessed through "England, London Electoral Registers, 1847–1913" on familysearch.org; Folio 139, Lodge no. 1616, in "England, United Grand Lodge of England Freemason Membership Registers, 1751–1921," on ancestry.com; Census of England, 1881, civil parish of Ashford, 23; "Marriage of Capt. R. A. Montgomery and Miss Gosling," *Belfast News-Letter*, January 14, 1881, 5, col. 4; "Boyle's System of Ventilation. Experiments at the London Custom House," BM, February 1, 1881, 136, col. 3.

28. "Lack v. d'Expineuil" [sic], *Morning Post*, June 2, 1881; "Slandering a Builder Lack v. d'Epineuil," *Building News and Engineering Journal* (London), June 3, 1881.

29. "Middlesex," *Morning Post*, September 28, 1881, 2, col. 3.

30. *The Law Reports. Supreme Court of Judicature. Cases Determined in the Chancery Division and in Bankruptcy and Lunacy, and on Appeal Therefrom in the Court of Appeal*, vol. XX (London: William Clowes and Sons, 1882), 758–59.

31. Death certificate of Count Lionel D'Epineuil, Registration District of Staines, Sub-district of Sunbury in the County of Middlesex, no. 418, October 10, 1881 in Ashford, General Register Office, England; Burials in the Parish of Ashford in the County of Middlesex in the Years 1881–2, Church of England Parish Records, 1813–1906, 88, no. 698, London Metropolitan Archives, accessed through "London, England, Deaths and Burials, 1813–1980" on ancestry.com; Parish of Ashford Electoral Registers, 1882, on familysearch.org.

32. *The Times* (London), August 18, 1875, 11, col. 1.

33. Trial of Sir William Henry Wraxall, Bart., October 1878, www.oldbaileyonline.org, keyword Wraxall.

34. Cited in "Barren Baronets," *Newtown Register* (New York), August 24, 1882, 4, col. 3.

35. *The Law Reports. Supreme Court of Judicature*, 758–59.

36. "Nécrologie," *Le Moniteur du Calvados*, June 7, 1861, 2, col. 3. St. Edme Jobert's speech is found in *L'Ordre et la Liberté* (Caen), February 21, 1861, 3, col. 1.

37. E. Michel, nee Ernestine Jobert, to Général Février, Paris, November 18, 1893, and accompanying note signed by her siblings D'Eon Jobert and Henriette Jobert, in Louis Edme Jobert's Legion of Honor file, Archives Nationales de France online, http://www.culture.gouv.fr/public/mistral/leonore_fr?ACTION=NOUVEAU&USRNAME=nobody& USRPWD=4%24%2534P, search Louis Edme Jobert, file number LH/1367/74.

38. This is the only reference to Lionel Jobert as the "7th" Count d'Epineuil. Why seventh instead of sixth is a bit of a mystery, as his great-grandfather Pierre Jobert was first Count d'Epineuil, his sons Pierre and Balthazar the second and third, Pierre's sons Louis and Charles the fourth and fifth, and Louis's sons Lionel and Pierre the sixth and seventh. Charles had no sons, so unless Balthazar—whose descendants, if any, I have not been able to trace—had a son, then Lionel's courtesy title should have been the sixth Count d'Epineuil.

39. In Richard Anderson, *The Lightning Rod* (London: Marshall Brothers, Sanderson, 1882), 40.

40. "Tribunal Correctionnel de Nantes," *Journal de Rouen*, October 21, 1879, 2, col. 5.

41. "Romances from Real Life," *New York Times*, November 10, 1879, 2, col. 1.

42. "M. Le Comte D'Epineul [sic]," *The Times* (Philadelphia), November 11, 1879, 2, col. 4.

43. *The Times* (Philadelphia), November 18, 1879, 2, col. 4.

44. "A Famous Belle," *The Times* (Philadelphia), January 10, 1886, 3, col. 3.

45. W. W. Crane, "American Patronymics," *Appleton's Journal of Science, Literature, and Art* 5, no. 109 (April 29, 1871), 500, col. 2.

46. "The D'Epinueil [sic] Zouaves," *Saturday Globe* (Utica, NY), July 18, 1896, 2, col. 5.

47. "The 53d N.Y.," *National Tribune* (Washington, DC), July 29, 1909, 3, col. 7. Stone's name appears in the 1910 U.S. Census on 10 Sargent Avenue, age 66, with the Civil War survivor box checked and filled in with "UA" for Union Army. 1910 US Census, done April 15, 1910, fourth ward, Somerville, Middlesex Co., MA, roll 604, 257B, line 80.

48. Francis Trevelyan Miller, ed., *The Photographic History of The Civil War* (New York: Review of Reviews, 1912), vol. 8, 80.

49. Application 874985, certificate 679150, John C. Merriam, application 670449, certificate 472421, Jean B. Cantel, application 556925, certificate 349812, Frederick Cochen [sic], and application 1287224, certificate 1093226, William Bosworth, Record Group 94, Pension Records, NARA I; Los Angeles, California County Clerk, Death Certificate #6761, February 28, 1922; Post, *The Life and Memoirs of Comte Régis de Trobriand*, 463, 519; Theodosia Augusta Lloyd, England and Wales National Probate Calendar, ancestry.com.

50. Verey, ed. *The Diary of a Victorian Squire*, 44–45.

51. Chanter family collection.

52. *The Standard* (London), January 19, 1882, 7, col. 1; *The Post Office Directory of the Six Home Counties: Essex, Herts, Middlesex, Kent, Surrey and Sussex* (London: Kelly, 1882), 792.

53. *Debrett's Illustrated Peerage*, http://nzetc.victoria.ac.nz/etexts/Stout84/Stout84P007004.gif.

170 / Notes to Chapter 7

54. "Exciting Trip of a British Pleasure Steamer," Philadelphia Inquirer, December 6, 1884, 1, col. 1.

55. "Jottings from 'Truth,'" *Yorkshire Gazette*, March 19, 1885, 3, col. 6. The *Tyburnia*'s captain's name likely was Kennedy, not Kennerly. See "Alleged Assault on the Tyburnia," *London Daily News*, October 13, 1884, 6, col. 3.

56. Census of England, 1891, Essex County, civil parish of Springfield, 44; "Sudden Death of Mrs. Showers," *Essex Newsman*, December 10, 1892, 1, col. 6 (she died December 5, 1892); "For Australia," *New York Evening Post*, August 19, 1885, 3, col. 7; Georgiana Somerville against Arthur Somerville, Findings of Fact and Conclusions of Law, Special Term of the Supreme Court of the State of New York, Brooklyn, August 21, 1894, Chanter Family Collection.

57. W. L. Bond to Capt. Showers, New York, February 14, 1894, and the quotation is from Showers to Bond, [England] March 2, 1894, Chanter Family Collection.

58. The two quotations, respectively, are from Bond to Showers, New York, March 12, 1894, and Bond to Showers, New York, April 9, 1894, Chanter Family Collection.

59. Bond to Showers, New York, May 2, 1894, and the quotation comes from Showers to Bond, London, May 20 [1894], Chanter Family Collection.

60. Bond to Mrs. Georgiana Somerville [i.e., Somerset], New York, June 1, 1894, Chanter Family Collection.

61. Georgiana Somerville against Arthur Somerville, Findings of Fact and Conclusions of Law, August 21, 1894 and Georgiana Somerville against Arthur Somerville, Decree Divorce Absolute, August 21, 1894, Chanter Family Collection. Pansy's birth year on her gravestone in St. Clement's churchyard, Powderham, Devon, England, reads September 16, 1885, instead of 1886. Given the deliberate obscuring of her birth, both dates are possible.

62. "Marriage of Capt. Showers and Countess d'Epineuil," *Chelmsford Chronicle*, August 17, 1894, 7, col. 2; Census of England, 1901, Essex County, civil parish of Springfield, 24; Marriage record of Clarence Preston Gunter and Pansy E. M. Somerville, July 23, 1919, St. Matthew's Church, West Kensington, accessed at ancestry.com.

63. Births in the Parish of Eastwood, 1868, 94; 1871 Scotland Census, Civil Parish of Eastwood, Burgh of Pollokshaws, 33, keyword "Epinenil" and 1881 Scotland Census, Civil Parish of Govan, Police Burgh of Govan, 41, keyword "De Penniel," accessed at www.scotlandspeople.gov.uk; *Twelfth Census of the United States*, 1900, Philadelphia, Philadelphia County, PA, roll 1480, enumeration district 1012, 260A, line 4; *Thirteenth Census of the United States*, 1910, Ontario, San Bernardino County, CA, roll 94, enumeration district 224, 74B, line 100; Los Angeles, California County Clerk, Death Certificate #9959, June 2, 1960.

Conclusion

1. Régis de Trobriand to Lina, Camp near Fredericksburg, VA, December 21, 1862, in Styple, *Our Noble Blood*, 85.

Bibliography

Archives

FRANCE

Archives Départmentales de Seine-Maritime, Rouen
    Inscription Maritime
Archives Départmentales du Calvados, Caen
    Inscription Maritime
    Notarie de Caen
    Recensements de Population
    Registres d'État Civil
Archives Départmentales du Val-de-Marne, Saint-Mandé
    Registres d'État Civil
Archives des Affaires Étrangères, La Courneuve
    Haiti, Correspondance Politique
Archives des Ministère des Affaires Étrangères, Nantes
    Correspondance avec les Agents Diplomatiques et Consulaires
    Correspondance avec Ministère de la Marine
Archives Nationales, Paris
    Notarie de Paris
Archives Nationales d'Outre-mer, http://anom.archivesnationales.culture.gouv.fr
    État Civil, St. Pierre, Martinique
Centre Historique des Archives Nationales à Paris, http://en.geneanet.org/archives/registres/
    Registres de Tutelles
Service Historique de la Défense, Cherbourg
    Registre Matricule des Marins provenant du Recrutement de 1846

Service Historique de la Défense, Vincennes
    Dossiers of Joseph Viguier and Lionel Jobert

UNITED KINGDOM

City of Westminster Archives
    Marriage Register for St. Clement Danes, vol. 48, 1869–1875
National Archives, Kew, United Kingdom
    Divorce Case Files
    Merchant Navy Seamen Records
    Records of the General Register Office, Marriages and Deaths of British
        Subjects Abroad

UNITED STATES AND CANADA

City Archives of Philadelphia
    Appearance Docket, Common Pleas, 1870
    Appearance Docket, District Court, 1867–1871
Library and Archives Canada (Ottawa)
    Letters, Commissioner of Patents of the British Provinces of Canada
Library of Congress
    George B. McClellan Sr. Papers
    John Jordan Crittenden Papers
    Manton Marble Papers
National Archives and Records Administration
    Microfilm Publication M221, Letters Received by the Secretary of War,
        Registered Series, 1801–1870
    Microform Publication M492, Letters Received by the Secretary of War,
        Irregular Series, 1861–1866
    Record Group 21, Records of District Courts of the United States
    Record Group 59, Records of the Department of State
    Record Group 92, Records of the Office of the Quartermaster General
    Record Group 94, Records of the Adjutant General's Office
    Record Group 153, Records of the Office of the Judge Advocate General
        (Army)
    Record Group 233, Records of the U.S. House of Representatives
    Record Group 351, Records of the Government of the District of Columbia
New York State Archives
    New York Adjutant General Correspondence
    Office of the Surgeon General Correspondence
West Virginia State Archives
    West Virginia Adjutant General's Papers, Union Regiments, 1861–1865

Government Publications and Records

A Record of the Commissioned Officers, Non-Commissioned Officers and Privates, of the Regiments which Were Organized in the State of New York and Called into Service of the United States to Assist in Suppressing the Rebellion. Albany, NY, 1864.

Annales des Ponts et Chaussées, Mémoires et Documents Relatifs a l'Art des Constructions et au Service de l'Ingénieur; Lois, Ordonnances et Autres Actes Concernant l'Administration des Ponts et Chaussées, 2e série. Paris: Carilian-Goeury et V. Dalmont, 1843.

Annuaire Diplomatique et Consulaire de la République Française Pour 1881. Tome II. Paris: Berger-Levrault, Èditeurs, 1881.

Annual Report of the Adjutant-General for the State of New York. For the Year 1900. Albany, NY, 1901.

Bulletin des Lois de L'Empire Francais, 11th Series. Supplemental vol. XVI. Paris, 1861.

Bulletin des Lois du Royaume de France, IX série, Partie Supplémentaire, tome douzième. Paris: l'Imprimerie Royale, 1838.

Chronological and Descriptive Index of Patents Applied for and Patents Granted. London: Office of the Commissioner of Patents, 1873.

Executive Documents Printed by Order of the House of Representatives during the Third Session of the Fortieth Congress, 1868–'69. Vol. 1. Washington: Government Printing Office, 1869.

Fifth Annual Report of the Chief of the Bureau of Military Statistics. Albany, NY, 1868.

General Register Office. UK. Death certificate of Count Lionel D'Epineuil.

General Regulations for the Military Forces of the State of New York. Albany, NY: Weed, Parsons, 1858.

Gibson, Campbell. *Population of the 100 Largest Cities and Other Urban Places in the United States: 1790 to 1990.* Washington, DC: U.S. Bureau of the Census, 1998.

Journal du Palais, Jurisprudence Administrative. Tome X, 1845–1849. Paris, 1851.

Légion d'Honneur files, http://www.culture.gouv.fr/public/mistral/leonore_fr.

Los Angeles, California County Clerk. Death Certificates.

Mairie de Paris, état civil, http://canadp-archivesenligne.paris.fr/archives_etat_civil/index.php.

Procès-Verbal des Séances de L'Assemblée Provinciale de L'Isle de France, Tenues à Melun, en Novembre & Décembre 1787. [Paris] Chez la Ve. Tarbé & Fils, Impr. De l'Assemblée Provinciale, 1788.

State of New York. *Fifth Annual Report of the Chief of the Bureau of Military Statistics.* Albany, NY, 1868.

Statistique de la France. Paris: Imprimerie Nationale, 1850.

United States. Census of the United States. 1850, 1860, 1870, 1900, 1910.

United States Census Bureau. *The Statistical History of the United States from Colonial Times to the Present.* New York: Basic Books, 1976.

United States House of Representatives.
  Journal of the House of Representatives, 1861.
  Executive Documents, 38th Congress, 1st Session.
  Documents, 40th Congress, 2nd Session.
  Executive Documents Printed by Order of the House of Representatives, 1874–'75.
United States, War Department. *The War of the Rebellion: A Compilation of the Official Records of the Union and Confederate Forces.* Washington, DC, 1883.

Books and Articles

American Newspaper Directory. New York: Geo. P. Rowell, 1870.
Ameur, Farid. *Les Français dans le Guerre de Sécession, 1861–1865.* Rennes, France: Presses Universitaires de Rennes, 2016.
Anderson, Richard. *The Lightning Rod.* London: Marshall Brothers, Sanderson, 1882.
Annuaire des Cinq Départements de L'Ancienne Normandie. Caen, France: l'Association Normande, 1840.
Annuaire Historique du Département de L'Yonne, 1852. Auxerre, France: Perriquet, Imprimeur-Libraire, Éditeur, 1852.
Annuaire Statistique du Département de L'Yonne, Année 1847. Auxerre, France: Ed. Perriquet, Imprimeur-Lithographe, Editeur [1847].
Archives des Découvertes et des Inventions Nouvelles. Paris: Treuttel et Würtz, 1822.
Basler, Roy P., ed. *The Collected Works of Abraham Lincoln.* Vol. 5. New Brunswick, NJ: Rutgers University Press, 1953.
———. *The Collected Works of Abraham Lincoln, Supplement 1832–1865.* Springfield, IL: Greenwood Press, 1974.
Bayles, Richard M., ed. *History of Richmond County (Staten Island) New York: From Its Discovery to the Present Time.* New York: L. E. Preston, 1887.
Boase, George Clement, and William Prideaux Courtney. *Bibliotheca Cornubiensis: A Catalogue of the Writings, Both Manuscript and Printed, of Cornishmen, and of Works Relating to the County of Cornwall.* Vol. II. London: Longmans, Green, Reader, and Dyer, 1878.
Bottin, Séb. *Almanach du Commerce de Paris, de la France et des Pays Étrangers.* Paris: Bureau de L'Almanach du Commerce, 1833.
Brown, T. Allston. *A History of the New York Stage: From the First Performance in 1732 to 1901.* Vol. II. New York: Dodd, Mead, 1903.
Bruce, Susannah Ural. *The Harp and the Eagle: Irish-American Volunteers and the Union Army, 1861–1865.* New York: New York University Press, 2006.
Calendrier Maçonnique du Grand-Orient de France. Paris: 1852.
Calvert, Monte A. *The Mechanical Engineer in America, 1830–1910.* Baltimore, MD: Johns Hopkins Press, 1967.

Canny, Nicholas, and Philip Morgan, eds. *The Oxford Handbook of the Atlantic World, c. 1450–c.1850*. Oxford, UK: Oxford University Press, 2011.

Cantel, J. B. *Pronunciation of French Made Easy: A New Method of Learning to Pronounce French Correctly*. Baltimore, MD: John W. Woods, 1860.

Catalogue des Produits des Arts du Département du Calvados. Caen, France: Société Royale d'Agriculture et de Commerce de Caen, 1834.

Chambers, Mortimer et al. *The Western Experience Since 1600*. 3d ed. New York: Alfred A. Knopf, 1982.

Coffman, D'Maris et al. *The Atlantic World*. London: Routledge, 2015.

Doyle, Don H., ed. *American Civil Wars: The United States, Latin America, Europe, and the Crisis of the 1860s*. Chapel Hill: University of North Carolina Press, 2017.

Faust, Drew Gilpin. *This Republic of Suffering: Death and the American Civil War*. New York: Alfred A. Knopf, 2008.

Figes, Orlando. *The Crimean War: A History*. New York: Picador, 2012.

Forsyth, David P. *The Business Press in America, 1750–1865*. Philadelphia, PA: Chilton Books, 1964.

French, Benjamin Brown. *Witness to the Young Republic: A Yankee's Journal, 1828–1870*. Donald B. Cole and John J. McDonough, eds. Hanover, NH: University Press of New England, 1989.

Funérailles de Napoléon III: Procés-Verbal Rédigé par le Duc de Cambacérès, Grand Maitre de Cérémonies. Paris: Libraire Générale, 1873.

Gilbert, Benjamin Franklin. "French Warships on the Mexican West Coast, 1861–1866," *Pacific Historical Review* 24, no. 1 (February 1955): 25–37. https://www.jstor.org/stable/3635229.

Grandstaff, Mark R. "De Trobriand, Regis." David S. Heidler and Jeanne T. Heidler, eds. *Encyclopedia of the American Civil War: A Political Social and Military History*. New York: W. W. Norton, 2002.

Haines, Michael R. "French Immigration to the United States: 1820 to 1950," *Annales de Démographie Historique* 1 (2000): 77–91.

Hancock, David. *Citizens of the World: London Merchants and the Integration of the British Atlantic Community, 1735–1785*. New York: Cambridge University Press, 1997.

Hauptman, Laurence M. *Seven Generations of Iroquois Leadership: The Six Nations Since 1800*. Syracuse, NY: Syracuse University Press, 2008.

———. *The Iroquois in the Civil War: From Battlefield to Reservation*. Syracuse, NY: Syracuse University Press, 1993.

Henri-Wentz, F. *Opuscules Maçonniques*. Grand Ordre de France, 1864.

Jurien de la Gravière, Edmond. *Voyage de la Corvette La Bayonnaise dans les Mers de Chine*. Troisième édition. Paris: Henri Plon, 1872.

La Librairie Ollendorf, ed. *Victor Hugo: Correspondance*. Vol. IV. Paris: Albin Michel, 1952.

Lamartine, Alphonse de. *Jocelyn: An Episode, Journal Found at the House of a Village Curé.* Frances Henrietta Jobert, trans. Paris: Baudry, 1837.

Law Reports. Supreme Court of Judicature. Cases Determined in the Chancery Division and in Bankruptcy and Lunacy, and on Appeal Therefrom in the Court of Appeal. Vol. XX. London: William Clowes and Sons, 1882.

Léger, J. N. *Haiti: Her History and Her Detractors.* New York: Neale Publishing Company, 1907.

Légitime, F. D. *Une année au ministère de l'agriculture et de l'intérieur.* [Paris?], 1883.

Lincoln, Abraham. *The Collected Works of Abraham Lincoln.* Vol. 5. New Brunswick, NJ: Rutgers University Press, 1953.

Mansfield, Peter. *A History of the Middle East.* New York: Viking, 1991.

Massé, Victor. *The Marriage of Jeanette. A Comic Opera in One Act.* Chas. E. Locke, trans. New York: Charles D. Koppol, 1886.

McPherson, James M. *For Cause and Comrades: Why Men Fought in the Civil War.* New York: Oxford University Press, 1997.

———. *Ordeal by Fire: The Civil War and Reconstruction.* New York: Alfred A. Knopf, 1982.

Mémoires de la Société Royale d'Agriculture et de Commerce de Caen. Tome II. Caen, France, 1827.

Miller, Francis Trevelyan, ed. *The Photographic History of The Civil War.* Vol. 8. New York: Review of Reviews, 1912.

Moor, James, MD. *History of the Cooper Shop Volunteer Refreshment Saloon.* Philadelphia, PA: James B. Rodgers, 1866.

Mussell, James. *The Nineteenth-Century Press in the Digital Age.* London: Palgrave Macmillan, 2012.

Nagler, Jörg, Don H. Doyle, and Marcus Gräser, eds. *The Transnational Significance of the American Civil War.* [London]: Palgrave Macmillan, 2016.

Newall, Clayton R., and Charles R. Shrader. *Of Duty Well and Faithfully Done: A History of the Regular Army in the Civil War.* Lincoln: University of Nebraska Press, 2011.

Olcott, Henry S. "The War's Carnival of Fraud." *The Annals of the War.* Philadelphia, PA: Times Publishing, 1879.

Pearce, Ian. "In Town Tonight: Some of the Interesting People in Cairo and Alexandria in the 1870s—Part One." *Astene Bulletin* (United Kingdom), 60 (Summer 2014): 9–14.

Phisterer, Frederick. *New York in the War of the Rebellion.* 3d ed. Albany, NY: J. B. Lyon, 1912.

Pope, Charles H., comp. *Merriam Genealogy in England and America.* Boston, MA: Charles H. Pope, 1906.

Post, Marie Caroline. *The Life and Memoirs of Comte Régis de Trobriand, Major-General in the Army of the United States.* New York: E. P. Dutton, 1910.

Sand, Maurice. *Six mille lieues à tout vapeur.* Paris: Michel Lévy Frères, 1862.

Sandage, Scott. *Born Losers: A History of Failure in America*. Cambridge, MA: Harvard University Press, 2005.
Sauers, Richard A. *"A Succession of Honorable Victories": The Burnside Expedition in North Carolina*. Dayton, OH: Morningside House, 1996.
Sears, Stephen W., ed. *The Civil War Papers of George B. McClellan: Selected Correspondence 1860–1865*. Cambridge, MA: De Capo Press, 1992.
Styple, William B, ed. *Our Noble Blood: The Civil War Letters of Régis de Trobriand, Major General U.S.V.* Kearny, NJ: Bell Grove, 1997.
Thomson, R. Stanley. "The Diplomacy of Imperialism: France and Spain in Cochin China, 1858–63." *Journal of Modern History* 12, no. 3 (September 1940): 334–56. https://www.jstor.org/stable/1874762.
Tréhin, Jean-Yves. "Arnoux Hippolyte," in François Pouillon, ed. *Dictionnaire des orientalistes de langue français*. Paris: Éditions Karthala, 2012.
United Service Journal and Naval and Military Magazine. Part I. London: Henry Colburn, 1841.
Verey, David, ed. *The Diary of a Victorian Squire: Extracts from the Diaries and Letters of Dearman & Emily Birchall*. Gloucester, UK: Alan Sutton, 1983.
Vifquain, Victor. *The 1862 Plot to Kidnap Jefferson Davis*. Jeffrey H. Smith and Phillip Thomas Tucker, eds. Lincoln: University of Nebraska Press, 2005.
Virkus, Frederick A., ed. *The Abridged Compendium of American Genealogy*. Chicago, IL: A. N. Marquis, 1925.
Wheeler, Gerald E. "D'Epineuil's Zouaves." *Civil War History* 2, no. 4 (December 1956): 93–100.
Wheeler, Gerald E., and A. Stuart Pitt, "The 53rd New York: A Zoo-Zoo Tale." *New York History* 37, no. 4 (October 1956): 414–31.
Whitehead, Ralph. "The Demise of the D'Epineuil Zouaves." *Civil War Times Illustrated* 36, no. 5 (October 1997).
Whitehouse, H. Remsen. *The Life of Lamartine*. Vol. II. Boston, MA: Houghton Mifflin, 1918.
Wilson, James Grant, ed. *The Memorial History of the City of New York: From Its First Settlement to the Year 1892*. Vol. IV. New York: New-York History, 1893.
Wraxall, Sir H. H. bart. "The Naked Truth." *Wit and Wear*. London: A. Lynes and Son [1871], 9–20.

Collections

Army Heritage and Education Center, U.S. Army Military History Institute. Carlisle Barracks, PA. Harrisburg Civil War Round Table Collection
  Diary of Henry Cocheu (photocopy)
Bancroft Library, University of California, Berkeley
  Letters to and from St. Edme Jobert

180 / Bibliography

Chanter Family Collection
Chester County Historical Society Library, West Chester, PA
    Lt. Col. Thomas S. Bell Papers
Gilder Lehrman Institute
    Egbert Viele to Edwin Morgan Letter
Historical Society of Pennsylvania
    Papers of the Philadelphia Fountain Society
Huntington Library
    Abraham Lincoln Collection
Library Company of Philadelphia
    Recruiting ephemera, Colonel d'Epineuil's regiment
Marilynn Graves Wright Collection
    Francis S. Pittman, "Civil War Journal, 1861–1863."
Nebraska State Historical Society
    Manuscript Collections, Union Pacific Railroad Company
New York Public Library
    Eugene Maximilien Haitian Collection, Schomburg Center for Research in Black Culture
    Manuscript and Archives Division, United States Sanitary Commission Records
New York State Library
    John E. Wool Papers
Southern Historical Collection, Wilson Library, University of North Carolina at Chapel Hill
    Charles William Dustan Letters
    Cole and Taylor Family Papers

Websites

Ambrose E. Burnside, "The Burnside Expedition." http://thomaslegion.net/the_burnside_expedition_by_general_burnside.html
Ancestry.com
    Census of England, 1871, 1881, 1891, 1901
    England, Alien Arrivals, 1810–1811, 1826–1869
    England and Wales, National Probate Calendar
    England, United Grand Lodge of England Freemason Membership Registers, 1751–1921
    London, England, Deaths and Burials, 1813–1980
    London, England, Marriages and Banns, 1754–1921
    Mariages de Paris et ses environs, France, 1700 à 1907
    Massachusetts, Town and Vital Records, 1620–1988

New York, Passenger Lists, 1820–1957
Paris, France and Vicinity Births, 1700–1899
FamilySearch, familysearch.org
England Births and Christenings, 1538–1975
England, London Electoral Registers, 1847–1913
New York Passenger Lists, 1820–1891
Green-Wood Cemetery, http://www.green-wood.com/
Kindred Britain. http://kindred.stanford.edu/
John Zephaniah Holwell Family Tree
Measuring Worth, https://www.measuringworth.com/
MyTrees.com, http://www.mytrees.com/
Jeremiah Bryant Family Tree
National Park Service, http://www.itd.nps.gov
Civil War Soldiers and Sailors Database
New York State Military Museum, http://dmna.ny.gov/historic/reghist/civil/civil_index.htm
Proceedings of the Old Bailey, 1674–1913, www.oldbaileyonline.org
ScotlandsPeople, www.scotlandspeople.gov.uk
1871, 1881 Scotland Census
Births in the Parish of Eastwood, County of Renfrew, Scotland, 1868
United States Patent and Trademark Office, http://patft.uspto.gov
Victoria University of Wellington, http://nzetc.victoria.ac.nz
Debrett's Illustrated Peerage
Ville de Paris: Population & Density from 1600. http://www.demographia.com/dm-par90.htm

Newspapers and Periodicals

A Flor do Oceano (Funchal)
Anglo American Times (London)
Appleton's Journal of Science, Literature, and Art (NY)
Army and Navy Gazette (London)
Athenæum (London)
Belfast News-Letter
British Mail (London)
Brooklyn Daily Times (NY)
Buffalo Daily Courier (NY)
Building News and Engineering Journal (London)
Capricornian (Rockhampton, Queensland, Australia)
Chelmsford Chronicle (UK)
Cleveland Plain Dealer (OH)

Daily Advertiser (Portland, ME)
Daily Evening Bulletin (Philadelphia, PA)
Daily Evening Telegraph (Philadelphia, PA)
Daily National Intelligencer (Washington, DC)
Daily News (London)
Daily Saratogian (NY)
Eco del Comercio (Santa Cruz de Tenerife, Spain)
Electrician (London)
Engineer (London)
Era (London)
Essex Chronicle (UK)
Essex Newsman (UK)
Evening Star (Washington, DC)
Feuille de Commerce (Port-au-Prince, Haiti)
Frank Leslie's Illustrated Newspaper (NY)
Fraser's Magazine for Town and Country (London)
Gopsill's Philadelphia City and Business Directory (PA)
Hampshire Advertiser (Southampton, UK)
Hampshire Telegraph and Sussex Chronicle (UK)
Illustrated New Age (Philadelphia, PA)
Innsbruker Nachrichten (Austria)
Journal de Caen (France)
Journal de Gèneve (Switzerland)
Journal de la Société des Américanistes de Paris (Paris)
Journal de Rouen (France)
Journal des Débats Politiques et Littéraires (Paris)
Journal Politique et Annonces Judiciaires du Département du Calvados (Caen, France)
Kingston Daily Freeman (NY)
La Presse (Paris)
La République (Port-au-Prince, Haiti)
Lain's Brooklyn City Directory (NY)
Le Moniteur du Calvados (France)
L'Industrie (Bordeaux, France)
L'Intérêt Public (Caen, France)
Liverpool Mercury (UK)
London City Press
London Daily News
London Gazette
L'Ordre et la Liberté (Caen, France)
Le Pilote du Calvados (Caen, France)
Le Suffrage Universal (Caen, France)
L'Union Bretonne (Nantes, France)

McElroy's Philadelphia City Directory (PA)
Metropolitan Catholic Almanac, and Laity's Directory, for the United States, Canada, and the British Provinces (Baltimore, MD)
Morning Courier and New York Enquirer
Morning Post (London)
National Repulican (Washington, DC)
National Tribune (Washington, DC)
Newtown Register (NY)
New York Daily Tribune
New York Evening Express
New York Evening Post
New York Herald
New York Illustrated News
New York Sun
New York Times
New York World
O Parlamento (Lisbon, Portugal)
Pall Mall Budget (London)
Paterson Daily Guardian (NJ)
Penny Illustrated Paper (London)
Philadelphia Inquirer (PA)
Plattsburg Republican (NY)
Post Office Directory of the Six Home Counties: Essex, Herts, Middlesex, Kent, Surrey and Sussex (UK)
Post Office London Directory
Public Ledger (Philadelphia, PA)
Railway News and Joint Stock Journal (London)
Revue des Races Latines (Paris)
Richmond County Gazette (Staten Island, NY)
St. Thomae Tidende (Virgin Islands)
San Francisco Bulletin (CA)
Saturday Globe (Utica, NY)
Scientific American (NY)
Scientific Journal (Philadelphia, PA)
Standard (London)
Times (London)
Times (Philadelphia, PA)
Troy Daily Times (NY)
Utica Morning Herald (NY)
Yorkshire Gazette (UK)

Index

Ardouin, Alexis B., 19–20, 22–23, 25, 145n. 5
  and comments about Lionel Jobert, 21, 24, 26–28, 30–32
Armitage, David, xi
Armstrong, W. W., 42–43, 66–67, 90
Arnoux, Hippolyte, 120
Atlantic region, xi
  See also Jobert, Lionel, and Atlantic region

La Bayonnaise, 5–7, 94
Bell, Thomas, 78, 85
  and de Monteil's court of inquiry, 66, 69–70, 71
Birch, Frances, 1, 2, 3, 5
Birchall, John Dearman, 115
Bliss Jr., George, 46, 59
  and comments about d'Epineuil, 47, 53, 57–58, 61
Bosworth, William P., ix, *41*, 129
Breard, Jacques, 2
Breuil, Edmond, 7, 98, 112, 122
Brooks Brothers
  and lawsuit against d'Epineuil, 93, 97, 161n. 22
  and uniforms, 41, 43
Burnside, Ambrose, 58, 61, 70, 71, 86
  and Fredericksburg, 93

as reference for d'Epineuil, 92, 98, 101
  and Roanoke expedition, 35, 59, 73, 75–76

Caen, 4, 9
Calvados, 2
Cantel, Jean B., 43–44, 91–92, 99–100
  and comments about de Monteil, 62, 63
  death of, 128
  as major, 57, 59, 81, 82, 85
  and Patapsco Institute, 100, 163n. 30
Chester, E. W., 63, 85
Chester, George F., 48, 64, 84, 100
  and promotion, 58, 63–64, 85–86
Cipriani, Alfred, 52, 90
Cocheu, Frederick, 128
Cocheu, Henry, 56, 65, 71, 86
  and comments about d'Epineuil, 74, 79
  death of, 100
  diary of, 73
Compagnie des Berlines de Caen, 4–5
Crimean War, 10
  See also Jobert, Lionel, and Crimean War

185

Crittenden, John J. *See* Lloyd, Theodosia, and John J. Crittenden

Davis, Nelson, 80–81
de Beaumont, Maurice, 90
de Kontski, Anton, 114, 118
Delva, Damien, 31–32
de Monteil, Joseph A. Viguier, 49, 56, 58
   and conflict with d'Epineuil, 54, 55, 57, 71, 75
   court martial trial of, 66–70, 71
   death and burial of, 85, 86–87
   early career of, 43
   and incident with Franklin Willard, 65–66
d'Epineuil, Count (Edme Pierre), 1–2
   descendants of, 137–38
d'Epineuil, Countess. *See* Somerset, Georgiana
De Pineuil, Frederick J., 102, 133
d'Epineuil, Lionel Jobert. *See* Jobert, Lionel
d'Epineuil Zouaves. *See* Fifty-Third New York Volunteers
de Trobriand, Régis, 49, 76, 135
   background of, 36
   Civil War service of, 47, 76, 79, 99
   death of, 128
Dimpfel, William O'Shea, 103
Dixon, Waynman, 119
Doyle, Don, xi
Dubreuil, Jules, 53–54, 74
Dufloo, Armand, 90, 160n. 4
Duke of Nemours, 3
Dustan, Charles, 56, 58, 71, 81, 92
   and comments about regiment, 63, 82

Evans, Charles, 101, 103

Fargueil, Anaïs, 8
Faulkner, Mary, 102
Ferris, Thaddeus, 40–41, 56, 100
Fifty-Third New York Volunteers
   and allotment system, 60
   at Camp Lesley, 51, 59
   at Camp Richmond, 60, 63, 65, 70
   civilian occupations of, 48
   and desertions, 52, 53, 61, 70, 80
   disbanding of, 81, 83–84
   enlisted men fraternizing with officers, 68
   ethnic tension within, 62–64
   at Fort Madison, 80–81
   at Fort Monroe, 75, 76
   French composition of, 47–48, 151n. 36
   on *John Trucks*, 73, 75–76, 80
   and parade through Manhattan, 59
   public memory of, 127–28
   recruiting of, 48
   second battalion of, 60–61
   second organization of, 84–85
   uniforms of, 41–43, 76, 82
Fiston, Ernest, 47, 57
Forster, John, 23, 24, 26, 147n. 30
Forth-Rouen, Alexandre, 5
Foster, John G., 65, 66, 98
French, Benjamin Brown, 96, 97
French population in United States, 36, 49–50

Galiby, Louis, 12
Geffrard, 18, 19, 22
   crew of, 22, 23, 24, 31
   maiden voyage of, 24–29
   scuttled, 31
Geffrard, Fabré, 15–16, 29, 31
Gladwin, Stephen, 93
Gundlack, John G., 57

Haitian Naval School
   cadets of, 16–17, 19, 20–21, 24, 146n. 12
   creation of, 16

Hamelin, Ferdinand-Alphonse, 19, 22, 23
Hancock, David, 114
Haudry, Alexis, 2
Hillhouse, Thomas, 46, 52, 61, 70
　and d'Epineuil's letter to, 89
Hugo, Victor, 9–10

Jobert, Charles, 2, 5, 8, 9
Jobert, Clémence, 9, 10, 112, 122
　birth of, 3
　marriage of, 7
Jobert, Ernestine, 125
Jobert, Frances. *See* Birch, Frances
Jobert Frères, 2, 4–5, 8
Jobert, Lionel, 8–9, 15, 22, 23
　arrest of, 94
　in Ashford, 122, 129
　and Atlantic region, xii, 95, 112, 124, 133, 135–36
　bankruptcy of, 117–18, 119
　birth of, 1
　and blackout period, 119–20
　and book projects, 98, 99
　and *British Mail*, 121
　in British society, 113–14, 115
　as businessman, 31, 104, 107, 113, 121
　as capitaine au long cours, 11–12
　as captain of *Geffrard*, 21, 24, 26–27, 31
　and charges against as colonel, 64–65, 76–77
　and charges against in Haiti, 29
　childhood of, 4
　and civic betterment, 104–5
　as colonel of d'Epineuil Zouaves, 40, 74
　and correspondence with Crittenden, 93
　and Crimean War, 11, 161n. 18
　death of, 123
　and debt, 12, 36, 106, 116, 123
　and definition of gentleman, 114
　and departure from United States, 109, 112
　and disbanding of regiment, 83, 89, 91, 92
　and Egypt, 118–19
　and estate of his father, 112, 113
　as father, 102
　and flight from Haiti, 30, 32
　and Franco-Prussian War, 108, 118
　as French citizen, 18
　grave marker of, 125–26, 169n. 38
　and Haitian Naval School, 16–17, 19, 33, 95
　on *John Trucks*, 74
　lawsuits against
　　in England, 123
　　in United States, 93, 96–97, 97–98, 106, 109
　marriage of, 116–17
　and masonic lodge membership, 122
　as master mariner, 11, 12
　as mate, 9, 10
　as novice seaman, 5
　and organizing his regiment, 43–45
　as patent broker, 100–101, 103, 139
　patents of, 96, 118
　and pay as colonel, 90
　physical appearance of, 7
　political views of, 91
　and post-colonelcy job search, 92–93, 94–95, 98–99
　public memory of, 125–28
　and recruiting soldiers, 51–52
　and reflections on life, 108
　and representation of his military background, 43
　as ship's boy, 4
　and surname d'Epineuil, 12, 28–29, 35–36, 113
　theatrical performances of
　　in England, 113, 114, 118
　　in United States, 104, 105, 107

Jobert, Lionel *(continued)*
  and Treasury Dept. clerkship, 97, 98
  and Union Volunteer Squadron proposal, 37–40
  and voting, 123
  See also *Scientific Journal*
Jobert, Louis. *See* Jobert, St. Edme
Jobert, Pierre. *See* d'Epineuil, Count (Edme Pierre)
Jobert, Pierre (born 1767), 1, 2, 115
Jobert, Pierre Ambroise, 3, 7, 9
Jobert, St. Edme, 9, 11, 13, 19
  birth of, 2
  as city councilman, 5, 8
  death of, 36
  early occupations of, 2
  as firefighter, 3, 8
  as freemason, 8
  as Legion of Honor member, 3
  marriage to Emilie Mathieu, 10
  marriage to Frances Birch, 2
  memorial for, 125
  as theater manager, 8
John Trucks, 35, 101
  See also Fifty-Third New York Volunteers, on *John Trucks*; Jobert, Lionel, on *John Trucks*
Jurien de la Gravière, Edmond, 5, 6, 7

Kontski, Anton de. *See* de Kontski, Anton

Lamartine, Alphonse, 1, 3, 7
Lamartine, Marianna, 1, 142n. 1
Lesley, James, 43, 44, 46, 51
Letts, James, 96, 100
Lincoln, Abraham, 79–80, 92, 94, 98
Lloyd, Theodosia, 77–79
  death of, 128–29
  and departure from United States, 93
  divorce of, 97–98
  and John J. Crittenden, 92
  and Lionel Jobert, 28–29, 30, 33, 36
Louis Napoleon, Emperor of France, 9, 50, 94, 118
Louis Philippe, King of France, 3, 7

Maggi, Albert C., 66, 85, 100
Mathieu, Emilie, 10, 36
McClellan, George, 75, 80, 81, 84, 98
Méquillet, Sophie, 8, 144n. 20
Mercier, Jacques, 11, 12
Merriam, John C., 40, 58, 128
  and *American Engineer*, 37
Monteil, Joseph A. Viguier de. *See* de Monteil, Joseph A. Viguier
Morgan, Edwin, 44, 45, 46, 58, 74
  and d'Epineuil's second battalion, 60

Nast, Thomas, 60

Olcott, Henry, 61

Parke, John G., 59, 71
Patti, Carlotta, 58, 107, 118
Pattu, Jacques, 3
Phillips, Henry J., 44, 68, 82
  and Dubreuil, 53–54, 152n. 12
Pierard, Aristide, 46, 59, 62
Pittman, Francis, 62, 70, 71, 80, 82
  on *John Trucks*, 74, 77
Plésance, Victorin, 32
Pradine, Auguste, 19

Reed, George T., 101–102
Rotch, Francis M., 58, 64

Sandage, Scott, 104
Schaumburg, Emilie, 104, 105, 106–107, 126
Scientific Journal, 101–102, 103, 109
Showers, Edward MacLean, 131–32

Silvie, Jerréal, 22, 24
Sisyphus myth, xiii, 33, 130
Slaght, James, 80, 82
Somerset, Georgiana, 114, 129–31
  courtship of, 115
  death of, 132–33
  in Egypt, 119
  marriage to Edward MacLean Showers, 132
  marriage to Lionel Jobert, 116–17
  parents of, 115, 116
Somerville, Effie May (Pansy), 131, 132, 170n. 61
Soulouque, Faustin, 15, 31

Thouvenel, Édouard, 23
Trobriand, Régis de. *See* de Trobriand, Régis

Tuscarora, 84–85, 159n. 35
22 Décembre, 18, 31

Vanderkeift, Bernard, 54, 69, 82
Vanderpool, S. Oakley, 44, 54
Venard, Isidore, 12, 15
Viele, Egbert, 44, 45
Vifquain, Victor, 46, 66, 90
Viguier de Monteil, Joseph A. *See* de Monteil, Joseph A. Viguier

Ward, Elijah, 40, 90, 91
  as reference for d'Epineuil, 98, 101
Willard, Franklin W., 48, 56, 57, 65–66, 85
Wool, John E., 76
Wraxall, Horatio H., 111–12, 113, 124–25

www.ingramcontent.com/pod-product-compliance
Lightning Source LLC
Chambersburg PA
CBHW020737230426
43665CB00009B/468